Marketing Your Law Firm

A Solicitors' Manual

Marketing Your Law Firm

A Solicitors' Manual

Lucy Adam

The Law Society

ISBN 1 85328 745 8

Published in 2002 by the Law Society
113 Chancery Lane, London, WC2A 1PL

Typeset by Columns Design Ltd, Reading
Printed by TJ International Ltd, Padstow, Cornwall

Contents

2 Market and client research 153

3 Promotion 223

Tables, questionnaires and other resources

Tables

Checklists

Reports

Questionnaires

Preface and acknowledgements

I started this manual after speaking to a number of small to medium-sized solicitors' firms about their marketing requirements. Repeatedly they told me that although they understood the value of marketing and had a need for it, all too frequently they did not have the in-house structure to carry it out.

It often proves expensive to use an external agency for a broad range of marketing activities, especially as many solicitors' firms do not have the expertise or staff available to ensure that activities are undertaken in a cohesive and co-ordinated way.

The solution appeared to be a manual explaining how a marketing professional would analyse their firm and the services offered, giving enough information for research to be conducted in-house together with a practical guide to putting together different promotional materials.

I was helped throughout by a number of people whose input and encouragement were invaluable. I would particularly like to mention Paul Marsh, senior partner with Carter Bells Solicitors in Kingston upon Thames, who gave up valuable time to discuss and analyse the manual for usability as it was written.

To complement this manual, a web site offering marketing services has been set up at **www.clientlink.co.uk**. The services offered are designed to work alongside the information provided here and give you access to a virtual marketing planning, copywriting, design and production department.

At **www.clientlink.co.uk** the following services are provided:

- Articles of varying lengths personalised for your firm for inclusion in newsletters, together with illustrations and photographs for each article. Clientlink can also put your newsletters together, print them and distribute them.
- Brochures, leaflets, advertisements, direct mail letters and any other promotional information professionally written and produced for you.
- Press releases written and checked by professionals which can then be distributed if you wish. Clientlink can even provide a telephone number and manage your press office for you.
- Questionnaires collated, sent out and analysed on your behalf.

- Action plans assessed, costed and commented on by professionals.
- Production according to any design requirements you may have.
- Client care or promotional letters and materials assessed by professionals who will provide you with a critique and suggestions (if needed).

Because these services are provided via the Internet, overheads are kept to a minimum and you will receive a valuable service at a workable price.

Lucy Adam
September 2001

Introduction

Solicitors' firms are facing increasing competition both from within and outside their profession. This is straining the ability of some firms to maintain a steady and reasonable income from areas that traditionally have been viewed as 'bread and butter' work. This can be seen in commercial litigation where there has been a move towards arbitration by non-lawyers; in matrimonial work, solicitors have seen moves towards mediation and conciliation in family proceedings; conveyancing work is now under pressure because of the advent of licensed conveyancers; and wills and probate work is being threatened by authorised probate practitioners.

Solicitors firms must also face and overcome challenges from within their profession, including issues of quality such as the ISO 9000 standard and Lexcel certification based on the Law Society's Practice Management Standards; computerisation; legal aid franchising and conditional fees; and more recently, e-commerce and the need to offer services via the internet.

Whilst solicitors have been meeting the challenges outlined in the paragraphs above, a further, and in some ways more disquieting, revolution has been taking place: *the public has become increasingly cost sensitive and sophisticated*. Clients are now likely to 'shop around' for their legal services, testing solicitors on price, service, initial impression, brochures, letters, in fact every aspect of a solicitor's service and presentation.

There is a trend for solicitors' firms to merge and pool resources and expertise in order to become more competitive and survive. The need to become more business- and market-oriented is not just about size, however, and has created a dilemma for many solicitors – how to combine the complex and highly individual business of law with a commercial approach, without losing the credibility of that service.

Generally, solicitors need to become more aggressive and proactive in client contact and marketing, so that when the sceptical public seeks legal services, the solicitors they approach can respond with legal services offered to suit the needs of the customer.

Marketing can help solicitors to do this. Each legal service a solicitors firm offers is a distinct product. It has a product profile, meets particular needs and has a target market. A firm that offers clients a broad range of services will benefit from a clear understanding of how those different legal services work as individual products and together as a range of products – their product mix. This understanding will help the firm to offer services in the most efficient, cost-effective and client-oriented manner and will enable targeted efforts to maximise profits and return on hours worked from existing clients, as well as targeting efforts to attract new clients.

This manual has been written to help solicitors' firms analyse their clients, their legal services and consequently target their efforts to build market share, increase profitability and compete effectively in their market.

Divided into three parts, the manual has tables which can be used to build a profile of your firm and the services you offer. The first part concentrates on analysing the different legal services and includes tables that, when completed and the information put into a blueprint, will result in a profile of and the basis of a marketing plan for the firm; the second part discusses client research methods and opportunities, giving example questionnaires that can be used; and the final part outlines the different promotional methods that can be used, how to produce them and when and where it is best to use them.

A brief outline of each of the three parts is set out below.

1. Marketing Planning

This part aims to bring together the information you need about your clients, the services you provide, your competitors and your operating environment. The table exercises create a framework for you to study your firm and the legal services you offer. Much of the information requested here, you will see, is information you use daily to make management decisions. Marketing is a management function and as a discipline is primarily concerned with the analysis and examination of information to enable you to draw conclusions about your clients, firm and market place so that you can formulate plans and strategies to shape the future of your firm.

2. Market and Client Research

Research is the key to understanding your clients – what they want from you, what they think of you and how your firm is performing against those requirements and in the market place.

Research can be extremely complex or fairly straightforward. However, it is fairly simple to undertake basic research exercises in-house. The main focus of this part is on client research through postal questionnaires.

3. Promotion

Methods of promoting your firm will vary according to the result you want to achieve. The main promotional methods are identified and a practical guide outlined of when to use them, how to produce them and how to evaluate their effectiveness.

Using this manual with the CD

Included in the manual are tables, an example marketing report and question-naires. These can help you to collate information, pull together a marketing report and create your own market research questionnaires.

The tables, report, questionnaires and checklists are included on the CD enclosed with this manual in Microsoft Word.

To use them, simply copy the required files onto your computer and amend them to suit your firm. Users with older versions of Word or operating system are advised to open the documents within Word, rather than directly from the file manager, Windows Explorer or Macintosh desktop.

Part 1

Marketing planning

Introduction

Information about your market place, your clients, your services and your competitors will help you to control and move your firm in the direction you wish, effectively and efficiently. Part 1 aims to help you collate this information and to see how your business might be viewed by a marketing consultant, without actually having to employ one.

Table exercises in this section create a framework for you to study your firm and bring together information from within your firm and your market place. In section (f), a script has been written to pull the figures and information you have gathered together into a report which will provide you with a starting point you can use to direct work and investment towards the firm's different legal services, in the short and long term.

Doing the table exercises

The exercises should all be finished fairly quickly and the project should not be left to gather dust whilst waiting for figures to be found or research undertaken. You should complete the tables consecutively, as the information on your firm builds up in a logical order and many tables lead on from others. As you work through the exercises you will see that you already have a lot of the information to hand, especially where financial information about the value of your clients is required, or simply the number of your clients.

However, as you go through you will also see that methods have been suggested to help you quickly arrive at rough figures where information is not available. In addition, you will see that a number of the tables ask you to make assumptions, estimates and 'guesstimates'. These methods should only be used in the short term but have been included because the most important thing about these tables is that you complete them. Time is money, and a function such as marketing planning can all too often be pushed to the bottom of the heap when work piles up. Once you have undertaken this exercise for the first time, you will be able to see where you need to collect, update or verify the information you have only been able to estimate.

Getting going

The first question is 'who should actually undertake the project?' This should be someone who is enthusiastic and understands or is keen to understand more about marketing. Their input and enthusiasm will be vital. The manual has been written so that it does not need to be completed by someone who knows everything. Their main role will be to collect the information required, co-ordinate sending out the tables to the members of the firm and collate their responses.

Second, it is a good idea if someone senior in the firm sponsors the project. Their support and authority will help drive the project forward and raise its importance where requests for information are passed to others in the firm.

Third, because a number of the exercises suggest that the tables are distributed to appropriate members of the firm to obtain their views, it is a good idea to gain their agreement to the project. Everyone in the firm can contribute, and in some instances their contribution will be vital where they are in the front line with regard to a particular legal service.

One of the most important things is that this part is completed. Before starting this project, there are a number of ways to ensure you reach the end:

1. Set a deadline to complete the plan, i.e. one month.
2. Have review meetings every week to ensure that work is progressing at a reasonable pace.
3. When you send out requests for information, ensure that a realistic deadline is given for the work to be returned. Give people as long as possible and send reminders before the deadline to jog their memories.
4. At the beginning of the project, set a meeting to review the results, perhaps even an 'away day'.
5. Keep everyone updated to maintain enthusiasm.

Final point: Don't put other marketing work on hold while undertaking the review.

Section 1(a)

The profile of your firm

Classifying the legal services your firm offers

The legal services your firm is able to offer clients represents the range of products you have to market.

Some legal services will have a similar profile with regard to their target audience or they can be linked together under a heading because of their subject area, and so for the purposes of marketing they have been grouped under a single heading. The groups set out in Table 1 and referred to throughout these exercises tie in with the categories identified in Law Society research so that you can compare your firm with the broader market place.

If the groupings of the legal services do not match the distinct areas of income in your firm as identified in Table 2, or, if you do not agree with them, create groupings or headings that more closely resemble the way that work is undertaken by your firm. Once set, these groupings should be maintained throughout these exercises.

❏ Complete **Table 1** and **Table 2** on pp. 6 and 7.

Table 1 Which legal services does your firm offer?

Area of law	✔ ✗	Groups
Commercial		
Commercial property		Commercial property
Investment and tax advice		Commercial finance
Insolvency and liquidations		
Financial advice		
Litigation – commercial		General commercial
Employment		
Environmental law		Specialist commercial
Charity law		
Liquor licensing/gaming		
Intellectual property		
Insurance		
Private		
Conveyancing – residential		Residential property
Landlord and tenant		
Crime		Crime
Family		Family
Personal Injury		Personal injury/Clinical negligence
Medical negligence		
Consumer problems		General private
Neighbour disputes		
Litigation – general		
Welfare benefits		
Immigration and nationality		Specialist private
Mental health		
Employment		
Wills and probate		Wills and probate
Taxation		
Trusts		

Table 2 Number of clients and income for each legal service offered

Groups	✔ ✗	Number of clients	Income over a 12-month period
Commercial			
Commercial property			
Commercial finance			
General commercial			
Specialist commercial			
Private and legal aid			
Residential property			
Crime			
Family			
Personal injury/ Clinical negligence			
General private			
Specialist private			
Wills and probate			

Understanding your firm's profile

In order to understand the contribution that each legal service makes towards the firm's overall performance, the following exercise aims to identify the number of chargeable hours attributable to each activity, the percentage of annual fees it represents and a quick judgement on its profitability.

> ❏ Now complete **Table 3** on p. 10.

The majority of firms will have this information as part of their accounting system and will be able to find it quickly. However, for those that do not, rough calculations can be made as shown below.

Assessing chargeable hours

Table 3, Column 1: Many firms will have this information readily available as revenue earned per fee earner. However, if you do not have revenue broken down by each legal service, follow the rough calculation shown in the example.

Example

Two solicitors spend approximately 50% of their time on wills. There are five solicitors in the practice, therefore wills take up one-fifth of the practice's chargeable hours, i.e. 2 × 50% = one solicitor ÷ five solicitors = 20% or one-fifth of the practice's total chargeable time.

The above approach is crude but, for the purposes of this exercise, sufficient.

Percentage of fees over a 12-month period

Table 3, Column 2: Take the fees brought in by each legal service over a 12-month period, divide those fees by the total fees the firm earned, and multiply the result by 100. You now have the percentage of fees earned by each legal service.

If you do not have the specific breakdown for each legal service you provide, it might be worked out in the same way as the following example:

Example

There are two solicitors who provide legal advice on employment law within a firm of five. *Solicitor A* bills £40,000 fees per year; 30% of his time is spent on the provision of employment law advice; therefore approximately £12,000 gross fees are raised in the area of employment law by this solicitor.

Solicitor B bills £46,000 fees per year; 50% of his time is spent on the provision of employment law advice; therefore £23,000 fees are earned in employment law by this solicitor.

Overall, £35,000 fees are earned by employment law within the firm. The firm bills £260,000 fees per year. £35,000 ÷ £260,000 × 100 = 13.5%. This is the percentage of fees brought in by employment law.

Your estimation of the profitability of the different legal services you offer

Table 3, Column 3: This exercise asks you to make a judgement of how profitable each legal service is, or if you do not have figures to hand, your *estimate* of how profitable. There are four categories: 'very profitable', 'quite profitable', 'break-even' and 'loss-making'. 'Very profitable' is where the legal service yields a profit margin of 20 per cent or more, 'quite profitable' is where a legal service demonstrates a profit margin between one per cent and 19 per cent. If you already know what your profit margins are, then you can fill in the column immediately. If you don't know them, you can arrive at an estimation of what they probably are.

Take the time spent on each legal service (as previously worked out for Column 1) and then calculate the cost of that time, i.e. *Solicitor A* spends 50 per cent of his time, he is paid £40,000 per annum, therefore 50 per cent of £40,000 (£20,000) is the cost of the solicitor's time on that area of law. In addition you need to add a figure for overheads. One way of doing this is to allocate a percentage of the firm's overall overheads against the area of law according to the percentage of work time it takes up, i.e. 20 per cent of the firm's chargeable hours would translate to 20 per cent of the firm's overheads.

Important note

When looking at the overheads, in order to be as accurate as possible you need to take into account the variable requirements of the different areas. For example, conveyancing will take up a greater percentage of the time of the accounts department, so this should be taken into account as it will not only increase the overheads for conveyancing but will decrease them for other areas.

Below are some of the areas that might commonly use an increased or decreased quantity of a particular firm's resource:

- Conveyancing   will probably use the accounts department to a greater extent than other areas.
- Litigation   will probably make a greater use of the photocopying and stationery overheads.

You will know whether there are areas that use an additional *significant* amount of any resource.

Example

Firm A has seven fee earners and provides legal services in four areas, including residential conveyancing, wills and probate, personal injury and general private work.

To work out the profitability of residential conveyancing, the following approach has been used.

Two fee earners work on residential conveyancing full time. They are paid £50,000 between them. This equals £50,000 as an expense against residential conveyancing income.

The firm has overheads equalling £120,000 each year. The two solicitors equal 28.5% of the firm's overall hours and are therefore allocated 28.5% of the overheads or £34,200.

Total cost of residential conveyancing = £50,000 + £34,200	=	(£84,200)
Gross fees for residential conveyancing	=	£100,000
Profit	=	£15,800

This indicates that residential conveyancing has an annual profit margin of 15.8% (i.e. profit divided by gross fees and then multiplied by 100 (£15,800/ £100,000 × 100 = 15.8%). This means that for this firm, residential conveyancing is 'quite profitable'.

Table 3 Initial evaluation of the legal services your firm offers

| Area of work | Percentages | | Actual/estimate of profitability of each legal service provided by the firm | | | |
| | Column 1 | Column 2 | Column 3 | | | |
	Percentage of firm's chargeable hours %	Percentage of firm's annual gross fees %	Very profitable ✔	Quite profitable ✔	Break-even ✔	Loss-making ✔
Commercial						
Commercial property						
Commercial finance						
General commercial						
Specialist commercial						
Private						
Residential property						
Crime						
Family						
Personal injury						
Wills and probate						
General private						
Specialist private						

Section 1(b)

Analysing your clients

Identifying your clients

Introduction

In order to market your legal services, it is important to understand who your clients are.

It is useful to identify:

- who your clients are;
- how valuable different clients are to your firm;
- what your clients' buying frequency and habits are;
- where your clients are located;
- what your clients expect and want from you as a service provider;
- what your clients think of your firm.

This information will enable you to provide legal services to your clients that are:

- tailored to their needs;
- competitive in your local market place.

Research is the ideal way of obtaining this information. Research includes both information you already hold in-house as well as asking clients questions to identify what they want, expect or need. However, as stated in section 1(a), one of the keys to this manual is that you finish these exercises in a reasonable time, i.e. over a month, rather than waiting for client research to be undertaken or for year-end accounts. Therefore at this stage estimates, perceptions and assumptions might be the only information you have to work with.

Having worked through these exercises you will be in a good position to determine what it is you need to know about your clients, services, firm and market place. If or when you do carry out any research, you will then be able to target the most useful and appropriate areas.

Grouping your clients

To enable you to identify common factors, values and requirements among your clients, it is useful to divide them into groups that display identifiable common characteristics.

A good starting point is to divide your clients between private and commercial. Having done this, you can then go into further detail and sub-divide private clients between self-funded private clients and legally aided private clients. You can also split your business clients into smaller groups according to the size of their organisation.

The amount of detail you will be able to go into will depend on the way you hold your client details. If you do not hold much information, this section will provide you with a starting point and guide to the information you might like to gather on your existing clients or find out from any new clients in the future. You should make educated 'guesstimates' about the groups of clients who purchase legal services from you, based on your experience and that of other fee earners.

Suggested categories are set out below:

1. **Private clients:** clients who are self-funded or with whom you are working on a 'no win, no fee' basis. They will mainly be purchasing legal services for private purposes such as residential conveyancing, wills and probate, family law, personal injury and employment law.
2. **Legal aid clients:** clients who depend upon legal aid funding to pay for the legal services they require. Again, they will mainly be purchasing legal services for private purposes such as crime, personal injury, employment, housing law, welfare benefits and family law. If a client is partially funded they should fall within this group.
3. **Commercial and business clients:** these clients can be classified according to the type of trading organisations and their size. Suggested categories are:
   - sole traders;
   - partnerships (e.g. 2 partners, 3–6 partners, 7–10 partners, 11+ partners);
   - limited companies: (e.g. up to £250,000 turnover, £250,000–1 million turnover, £1–5 million turnover, £5 million+ turnover).
4. **'Connector clients':** these are organisations or individuals in allied fields who pass clients to you, such as accountants, estate agents and banks. These organisations have been treated separately to the other clients as they are once removed from your firm and provide income indirectly. If they do use your services themselves, they should be slotted into one of the first three client groups whose characteristics they share.

Analysing the activity levels of the client groups

In the following pages, approaches to analysing these client groups have been set out. Private, legal aid and commercial clients have been grouped together in tables whilst 'connector clients' have been given a separate section. This is because the first three groups are clients who you deal with directly, whereas connector clients are those referring clients to you.

What is a client?

Prior to embarking on an exercise to determine numbers of clients, it is important to identify what qualifies a client as such. In the following table, lifespan/activity levels of clients have been set out. According to their level of activity, your clients might fall within the 'active', 'passive' or 'single transaction' (ST) client type. An outline of these parameters has been set out in Box 1.

Box 1 Lifespan/activity levels of clients

Type of client	Level of activity qualifying individuals within these groups as clients
Passive	Your firm has acted for them more than once in the last three years but not in the last 12 months. Your firm is their recognised legal service provider.
Single transaction clients (ST clients)	Your firm has acted for them in the last 12 months. Your firm is unlikely to be called upon to act for them again.
Active	Your firm has undertaken more than one transaction for them in the last 12 months.

Why identify the activity levels of the different clients you have?

By identifying the activity levels of clients for the different legal services, you will be able to see whether they have different buying patterns. For example conveyancing will probably demonstrate a very high level of ST clients, whereas other more specialist legal services will have a greater number of passive clients. Viewing your clients in this way allows you to formulate a realistic picture of your client base and the short-term or long-term value of different clients.

An understanding of your clients' buying patterns helps you identify the best time to promote and increase your income by selling other services to them – cross-selling. This is an extremely important part of any organisation's marketing plan: maintaining existing clients and selling across the product range to them. Part 3 on promotion gives further details of how to cross sell to clients.

You might set your own criteria as to what qualifies as a client; the important thing is to have a set of parameters to work to.

When tables require numbers of clients, it is 'active' and 'ST' clients who should be counted. In addition, because each legal service is a separate product, clients who use your firm for different services should be counted once for each service they use.

Using a benchmark

When identifying activity levels of your clients, you are asked to use the past 12 months as a benchmark. This time period should also be used when collating other figures such as income and hours required. The previous 12 months, as opposed to your financial year or a calendar year, allows you to update the figures on a regular basis, as a rolling 12 months, to identify any trends for different legal services. Once you have the figures for a calendar year, seasonal trends will show themselves such as an uplift in conveyancing in the spring, or an increase in insolvencies or bankruptcies around the first quarter of each year when tax is due, etc.

> ☐ Collate the figures for the number of types of client you have in **Table 4** below.

Table 4 Activity levels of clients for each legal service

Legal service purchased	Level of activity qualifying individuals within these groups as clients			
	Passive	Single transaction clients (ST)	Active	Total ST and active clients
Commercial property				
Commercial finance				
General commercial				
Specialist commercial				
Residential property				
Crime				
Family				
Personal injury				
General private				
Specialist private				
Wills and probate				

Note: See Box 1 on p. 13 for a definition of lifespan/activity levels of clients.

Estimating the value of your clients

Introduction

This section asks you to identify your clients, how they contribute to the income of the firm and most importantly, what you think they want (information that can later be confirmed through client research). It also asks you to evaluate how your firm approaches your clients.

The way in which the tables ask you to view your clients and collate the information requires you to take a 'marketing' approach to your clients for the different legal services you offer. This section will help you identify the differences inherent in supplying the different legal services by asking you to:

1. Focus on the importance of your different clients.
2. Establish an average value and time cost of your clients.
3. View your legal services as individual products with each transaction representing a single sale.
4. Focus on your clients' needs and your firm's performance in providing for those needs.

This information is important to help you formulate a strategy or marketing plan for the future of the firm. It will enable you to forecast the capacity the firm will need and the income that might be brought in by clients gained in promotions. In addition, it will ensure you promote in a way that is likely to attract the most valuable clients to your firm.

Number of clients and client groups

Table 5 simply asks you to list the number of clients in each of the client groups who purchase legal services from you.

If your accounts do not identify numbers in the different client groups who purchase the different legal services, then it is a good idea to circulate this table to the fee earners in these services and to ask them to fill in the table according to their workload. If you choose to do this, it will be necessary to distribute Table 4 showing who qualifies as a client. Remember: you are only counting active and ST clients over the last 12 months.

> ❑ Complete **Table 5** on p. 16. Simply add up the number of active and ST clients for each legal service within each client group.

Table 5 Number of clients you are providing legal services to, broken down by client type and legal service provided

Legal service provided	Numbers of active and ST clients who fall in the different client groups			
	Private clients	Legal aid clients	Commercial and business clients	Total
Commercial property				
Commercial finance				
General commercial				
Specialist commercial				
Residential property				
Crime				
Family				
Personal injury				
General private				
Specialist private				
Wills and probate				
TOTAL				

Note on multi-user clients: Where you have clients who purchase a number of legal services from you, please count them once for each legal service you provide. In addition, if a client purchases legal services for both private and business reasons, please count them once for each client group.

Value of different client groups

Having identified how many clients you have worked with over the last 12 months, this exercise looks at the average value of those clients.

You may have the information needed to fill in Table 6 to hand. If not, then it can be done roughly in the following way: divide the revenue (income over the last 12 months minus disbursements such as searches, but not overheads) from each legal service, by the number of active or ST clients who have purchased each legal service during the same period. Again, where clients use the firm for a number of legal services, count them as one client for each legal service.

Large clients: Before you begin this exercise, if you have any large clients for a single legal service, you need to take them and the revenue they generate out of the client base. This will help make the figures for smaller individual clients as accurate as possible. A client qualifies as a large client if they are responsible for paying fees that make up 25 per cent or more of the revenue (not including disbursements) generated by a particular legal service over the 12-month period.

Example

If the firm has a fee income of £120,000 over a 12-month period from commercial property (minus disbursements) and there are 18 active or ST clients in this area, then (after removing any particularly large clients and their income) each of the 18 clients brings in an average of £6,666.66 per year.

❏ Complete **Table 6** below.

Table 6 Overall average fee generated from each client

Legal service provided	Amount of fees for the last 12 months (minus disbursements)	Firm's fees minus the revenue from any large clients	Total number of large clients	Total number of clients minus large clients	Fee income divided by number of clients to give average fees per client
Commercial property					
Commercial finance					
General commercial					
Specialist commercial					
Residential property					
Crime					
Family					
Personal injury					
General private					
Specialist private					
Wills and probate					
TOTAL					

Income from the different client groups

In Table 6, the fees are set out as an average per client when looking at active or ST clients for a legal service. However, this average, though a useful benchmark, now needs to be refined to look at the average figure each client within each client group brings in for each legal service.

There are two different methods you can use to work out the average income from each client group, depending how much information you have available.

Method 1 can be used where you have information on the fees brought in from the different client groups in each area of law. **Method 2** can be used where you have very little information but can make an educated 'guesstimate'.

METHOD 1

This method can be used where you have a clear idea of the income from the different client groups broken down by the different legal services you offer.

> ❏ In **Table 7** below, simply list the fee income for the different client groups for each area of law.

Table 7 Fees brought in by different client groups in each area of law

Legal service provided	Fees for private clients £	Fees for legal aid clients £	Fees for commercial and business clients £	TOTAL £
Commercial property				
Commercial finance				
General commercial				
Specialist commercial				
Residential property				
Crime				
Family				
Personal injury				
General private				
Specialist private				
Wills and probate				

❏ Simply fill in **Tables 8–10** as outlined below:

Column 1: Fill in the amount of fee income over 12 months (minus disbursements) from this client group in each area of law as set out in **Table 5** on p. 16.

Column 2: Fill in the number of active or ST clients of this client group who are clients in each legal service.

Column 3: Divide Column 1 by Column 2 to give the average fee income from each client in this client group for each legal service.

*Now go to **Table 14** on p. 27, and transfer the figures from Column 3.*

Table 8 *Private clients*: average fee income

Legal service provided	Fees from private clients minus the revenue from any large clients £	Number of private clients	Average income from each private client £
Residential property			
Crime			
Family			
Personal injury			
General private			
Specialist private			
Wills and probate			

Table 9 *Legal aid clients*: average fee income

Legal service provided	Fees from legal aid clients minus the revenue from any large clients £	Number of legal aid clients	Average income from each legal aid client £
Crime			
Family			
Personal injury			
General private			
Specialist private			

Table 10 *Commercial or business clients*: average fee income

Legal service provided	Fees from commercial or business clients minus the revenue from any large clients £	Number of commercial or business clients	Average income from each commercial or business client £
Commercial property			
Commercial finance			
General commercial			
Specialist commercial			

METHOD 2

This method can be used where you have very little information about the fee income from the different client groups for each area of law.

Because the division is between private clients and legal aid clients, this exercise concentrates on two client groups. The approach has been broken down into steps: simply go through the steps for each area of law.

Step 1

Visualise the hypothetical figure of £100 in fees. If there were 10 legal aid clients and 10 private clients whose fees all added up to £100, calculate the percentage that have been brought in by the private clients and the percentage of that £100 by the legal aid clients. Those percentages should then be used in Table 11 on p. 21.

As you will see, commercial and business clients are the only ones who utilise the firm's commercial legal services, hence they score 100 per cent.

❏ Fill in **Table 11** below.

Table 11 Percentage of fees brought in by each client group

Legal service provided	Percentage share of fees for private clients %	Percentage share of fees for legal aid clients %	Percentage share of fees for commercial and business clients %	TOTAL %
Commercial property			100	100
Commercial finance			100	100
General commercial			100	100
Specialist commercial			100	100
Residential property	100			100
Crime				100
Family				100
Personal injury				100
General private				100
Specialist private				100
Wills and probate				100

Step 2

Having established any differences between different client groups with regard to the income from each, those percentages need to be converted into average monetary income for each legal service.

The following formulae will enable you to determine the average fee income per client group in each area of law. An example has been worked through to demonstrate them.

Example

70% of fee income in an area of law, e.g. personal injury, is generated by private clients and 30% by legal aid clients and the total fee income is £30,000.

Private clients	=	a	=	10 clients bringing in 70% of fee income
Legal aid clients	=	b	=	20 clients bringing in 30% of fee income
Total fee income	=	c	=	£30,000 (100%)

Divide percentage fee income for private clients by fee income for legal aid clients for ratio of $a:b$ = 70/30 = 2.3:1.

$a \times 2.3$ = 10 × 2.3 = 23 fee units
$b \times 1$ = 20 × 1 = 20 fee units

Total fee units = 43

These now need to be converted into percentages. Therefore:

23/43 × 100 = 53%
20/43 × 100 = 47%

Total = 100%

To find the fee income from 10 private clients (a) who bring in 70% compared to 20 legal aid clients (b) who bring in 30%, simply multiply the total fee income (c) by each of the percentages.

$c \times 53\%$ → £30,000 × 53% = £15,900
$c \times 47\%$ → £30,000 × 47% = £14,100

Total = £30,000

Hence if a, which is equal to 10, is the total number of private clients for this area of law, then the average income per private client is £15,900/10 = £1,590; and the average income per legal aid client is £14,100/20 = £705 per client.

To check this, simply multiply the average with the number of clients, add the two totals together and this should equal the total fee income.

❑ After working this out for each client type and for each legal service put the totals into **Table 12** on p. 24, then fill in **Table 13** on p. 25. You should print out or photocopy Table 12 according to the number of different legal services you are assessing prior to completing it.

Box 2 Example Table 12 – Average fee income from each client in each client group for specific legal services

Legal service: <u>Personal injury</u>

	Private clients	Legal aid clients	TOTAL
Number of clients	10	20	30
Percentage share of fees (also known as fee units)	70% (70 fee units)	30% (30 fee units)	100% (100 fee units)
Total fee income			£30,000
Ratio of private clients' fee units to legal aid clients' fee units (divide the highest percentage by the lowest)	2.3	1	
Number of clients multiplied by applicable fee units	2.3 (×10) 23	1 (×20) 20	
Total fee units			43
Fee units as percentages (divide clients' fee units by total fee units and multiply by 100)	53%	47%	100%
Fee income from each client type (multiply total fee income by percentages in row above)	£15,900	£14,100	
Total fee income			£30,000
Average fee income from each client in the different client groups (divide fee income from each client group by the total number in that client group)	(£15,900/10) £1,590	(£14,100/20) £705	

Table 12 Average fee income from clients in each client group for specific legal services

Legal service: _____

	Private clients	Legal aid clients	TOTAL
Number of clients			
Percentage share of fees (also know as fee units)			100% (100 fee units)
Total fee income			
Ratio of private clients' fee units to legal aid clients' fee units (divide the highest percentage by the lowest)			
Number of clients multiplied by applicable fee units			
Total fee units			
Fee units as percentages (divide clients' fee units by total fee units and multiply by 100)			100%
Fee income from each client type (multiply total fee income by income by percentages in row above)			
Total fee income			
Average fee income from clients in each client group (divide fee income from each client group by the total number in that client group)			

❑ Please print this table from the disk for each legal service your firm offers.

Table 13 Average fee income from clients in each client group for each area of law

Legal service provided	Average fee income per private client £	Average fee income per legal aid client £	Average fee income per commercial and business client £
Commercial property			
Commercial finance			
General commercial			
Specialist commercial			
Residential property			
Crime			
Family			
Personal injury			
General private			
Specialist private			
Wills and probate			

Average time taken for each transaction

Having looked at the average value in fees of each client to the firm, the next step is to identify how much time each client transaction takes.

As solicitors tend to work out their fees based on time spent, the majority will have this information to hand. In this case, simply fill in the third column in Table 14.

However, for those who do not have the information easily accessible, a rough estimation can be made as in the example on p. 26. As a base for the number of chargeable hours, each fee earner might contribute 1,840 hours per annum. This is equivalent to a 40 chargeable hour week with 4 weeks' holiday and bank holidays taken out.

Example

If the firm has three fee earners, each is capable of contributing 1,840 chargeable hours per year. If commercial property takes up 30% of the firm's chargeable work hours, then the following equation would apply:

$1,840 \times 3 = 5,520$ $5,520 \times 30\% = 1,656$ chargeable hours

1,656 divided by number of active or ST clients during a 12-month period = number of hours per client

Therefore, if we use the 18 clients from the previous example, each client needs 92 hours per year and brings in an average of £6,666 per year, so the average charge per hour is £72.45.

Large clients: Prior to this exercise, if you have any particularly large clients in any area, you need to take the hours they use out of the client base. This will help make the figures for smaller individual clients as accurate as possible. A client qualifies as a large client if they are responsible for paying fees which make up either 10 per cent of the firm's overall revenue over 12 months, or if they pay fees that make up 25 per cent or more of the revenue brought in from a particular service over a 12-month period.

❏ Fill in **Table 14** on p. 27.

Table 14 Average time taken by each client

Legal service provided	Number of firm's chargeable hours over a 12-month period	Total number of active or ST clients over a 12-month period	Average hours per client (chargeable hours divided by total number of clients)
Commercial property			
Commercial finance			
General commercial			
Specialist commercial			
Residential property			
Crime			
Family			
Personal injury			
General private			
Specialist private			
Wills and probate			
TOTAL			

Average hours taken per transaction by client type

In Table 14, the number of hours per client is set out as an average when looking at active and ST clients for a legal service. However, this average, though a useful benchmark, now needs to be refined to look at the average number of hours that each client within each client group requires for each legal service. This takes into account whether different clients require different amounts of time – including non-chargeable hours.

There are two different methods you can use to work out the average hours for each client group, depending how much information you have available.

Method 1 can be used where you have information on the hours spent on the different client groups in each area of law. **Method 2** can be used where you have very little information but can make an educated 'guesstimate'.

METHOD 1

This method should be used where you have a clear idea of the time required by the different client types broken down by the different legal services you offer.

❑ In **Table 15** below, list the total hours used for the different clients for each area of law.

Table 15 Total hours required over a 12-month period for each legal service by each client group

Legal service provided	Hours required for private clients	Hours required for legal aid clients	Hours required for commercial and business clients	Total hours
Commercial property				
Commercial finance				
General commercial				
Specialist commercial				
Residential property				
Crime				
Family				
Personal injury				
General private				
Specialist private				
Wills and probate				

❑ Complete **Tables 16–18** as outlined below:

Column 1: Fill in the number of hours required by this client group over a 12-month period in this area of law.

Column 2: Fill in the number of active and ST clients of this client group who are clients for each legal service.

Column 3: Divide Column 1 by Column 2 to give the average hours required by each client in this client group for each legal service.

Now go to Table 22 on p. 36, and transfer the figures from Column 3.

Table 16 Average time required by *private clients* for each legal service

Legal service provided	Hours required for active and ST private clients (minus the time taken by any large clients) over a 12-month period	Number of active or ST private clients	Average hours required for each private client
Residential property			
Crime			
Family			
Personal injury			
General private			
Specialist private			
Wills and probate			

Table 17 Average time required by *legal aid clients* for each legal service

Legal service provided	Hours required for active and ST legal aid clients (minus the time taken by any large clients) over a 12-month period	Number of active and ST legal aid clients	Average hours required for each legal aid client
Crime			
Family			
Personal injury			
General private			
Specialist private			

Table 18 Average time required by *commercial/business clients* for each legal service

Legal service provided	Hours required by active and ST commercial/ business clients (minus the time taken by any large clients) over a 12-month period	Number of active and ST commercial/ business clients	Average hours required for each commercial or business client
Commercial property			
Commercial finance			
General commercial			
Specialist commercial			

METHOD 2

This method can be used where you have limited information about the time required by the different client groups in the different areas of law.

Because the main division is between private clients and legal aid clients, this exercise concentrates on these two client groups. The approach has been broken down into steps; simply go through the steps for each area of law.

Step 1

Visualise the hypothetical figure of 100 hours. If there were 10 legal aid clients and 10 private clients whose time added up to 100 hours, calculate the percentage of hours spent on the private clients and the percentage of those 100 hours spent on the legal aid clients. Those percentages should then be used in Table 19 on p. 31.

As you will see, commercial and business clients are the only ones who utilise the firm's commercial legal services, hence they score 100 per cent.

❑ Fill in **Table 19** on p. 31.

Table 19 Percentage of time in hours required by each client group

Legal service provided	Percentage share of hours for private clients %	Percentage share of hours for legal aid clients %	Percentage share of hours for commercial and business clients %	TOTAL %
Commercial property			100	100
Commercial finance			100	100
General commercial			100	100
Specialist commercial			100	100
Residential property	100			100
Crime				100
Family				100
Personal injury				100
General private				100
Specialist private				100
Wills and probate				100

Step 2

Having established any differences between different client types with regard to the hours used by each, those percentages need to be converted into average hours per client for each appropriate legal service.

The following formulae enable you to determine the average hours used per client group in each area of law. To explain, an example has been worked through.

Example

In the example, 70% of the 100 hours in an area of law, i.e. personal injury, are used by private clients and 30% by legal aid clients, and the total hours are 3,680 hours.

Private clients   = a =   10 clients using 70% of the hours

Legal aid clients   = b =   20 clients who use 30% of the hours

Total fee income   = c =   3,680 (100%)

Divide 70 by 30 = 2.3, therefore $a{:}b = 2.3{:}1$

$a \times 2.3$ = $10 \times 2.3 = 23$ hour units
$b \times 1$ = $20 \times 1 = 20$ hour units

Total hour units =   43

These now need to be converted into percentages. Therefore:

$23/43 \times 100$ =   53%
$20/43 \times 100$ =   47%

Total   =   100%

To find the hours used by 10 private clients (a) who use 70% compared to 20 legal aid clients (b) who use 30%, simply multiply the total hours (c) by each of the percentages.

$c \times 53\%$ ->   3,680 hours $\times$ 53%   =   1,950 hours
$c \times 47\%$ ->   3,680 hours $\times$ 47%   =   1,730 hours

Total   =   3,680 hours

Hence if a, which is equal to 10, is the total number of private clients for this area of law, then the average hours required per private client is 1,950/10 = 195 hours; and the average hours required per legal aid client is 1,730/20 = 86.5 hours.

To check this simply multiply the average with the number of clients, add the two totals together and this should equal the total hours used.

☐ After working this out for each client type and for each legal service, put the totals into **Table 20** on p. 34. You should print out or photocopy Table 20 according to the number of different legal services you are assessing prior to filling it in. Then fill in **Table 21** on p. 35.

Box 3 Example Table 20 – Average hours required by clients in each client group for each area of practice

Legal service: <u>Personal injury</u>

	Private clients	**Legal aid clients**	**TOTAL**
Number of clients	10	20	30
Percentage share of hours (also known as hour units)	70% (70 hour units)	30% (30 hour units)	100% (100 hour units)
Total hours			£30,000
Ratio of private clients' hour units to legal aid clients' hour units (divide the highest percentage by the lowest)	2.3	1	
Number of clients multiplied by applicable hour units	2.3 (×10) 23	1 (×20) 20	
Total hours			43
Hour units as percentages (divide clients' hour units by total hour units and multiply by 100)	53%	47%	100%
Hours required by each client group (multiply total hours by percentages in row above)	1,950	1,730	
Total hours			3,680
Average hours required by each client in each client group (divide total hours for each client group by the number of clients in that group)	(1,950/10) 195	(1,730/20) 86.5	

❏ Please print this table from the disk for each legal service.

Table 20 Average hours required by clients in each client group for different legal services

Legal service: _____

	Private clients	Legal aid clients	TOTAL
Number of clients			
Percentage share of hours (also known as hour units)			100%
Total hours			
Ratio of private clients' hour units to legal aid clients' hour units (divide the highest percentage by the lowest)			
Number of clients multiplied by applicable hour units			
Total hours			
Hour units as percentages (divide clients' hour units by total hour units and multiply by 100)			100%
Hours required by each client group (multiply total hours by percentages in row above)			
Total hours			
Average hours required by each client in each client group (divide total hours for each client group by the number of clients in that group)			

❏ Please print this table from the disk for each legal service.

Comparison of average fees per client and average hours required by a client

After working out what the average income from each client group is and the average hours required by the different clients in the different client groups per transaction (Tables 20 and 21), you can put them together in Table 22, so the average charge per hour for each client group can be worked out.

Table 21 Average hours required by clients in each client group for each area of practice

Legal service provided	Average hours required per private client	Average hours required per legal aid client	Average hours required per commercial and business client
Commercial property			
Commercial finance			
General commercial			
Specialist commercial			
Residential property			
Crime			
Family			
Personal injury			
General private			
Specialist private			
Wills and probate			

In Table 22 you can fill in the following columns:

Fees: take the average fees charged per hour for each client group.

Hours: input the average hours taken per transaction.

Hourly charge: divide the average income from each client by the average hours required to find the average fees charged per hour.

The average hourly charges give you a benchmarking figure for new work and this allows you to see which are the most valuable transactions. This table can be used as a way of telling whether your firm's work is directed towards the most profitable areas in terms of return on hours. Furthermore, it enables you to see where you might want to reduce the time spent on a client group in an area of law, for example by systemising the work or handing work to non-fee earners to free up fee-earning time in more profitable areas.

❑ Fill in **Table 22** on p. 36.

Table 22 Chargeable hours taken for each legal service, by client group

Legal service provided	Private clients			Legal aid clients			Commercial and business clients		
	Fees	Hours	Hourly charge	Fees	Hours	Hourly charge	Fees	Hours	Hourly charge
Commercial property									
Commercial finance									
General commercial									
Specialist commercial									
Residential property									
Crime									
Family									
Personal injury									
General private									
Specialist private									
Wills and probate									

Client profiles

In the previous pages you have investigated the different groups of clients to establish the average fees they pay and hours they use. You have been looking for differences between groups of clients and have concentrated only on your active clients or ST clients.

In the following exercises you are now asked to look at all of your clients (active, ST and passive) to see whether there are any similarities, common characteristics or values.

The tables have been split by legal service and then clients within that legal service identified as active, ST or passive.

Note: To complete the following exercises, you will need to make educated assumptions in the absence of the information being readily to hand. Ideally, this exercise needs to be approached through client research or database verification projects. However, in the first instance, assumption is an exact enough method.

Reminder of client types and their lifespan/activity levels

Type of client	Level of activity qualifying individuals within these groups as clients
Passive	Your firm has acted for them more than once in the last three years but not in the last 12 months. Your firm is their recognised legal service provider.
Single transaction clients (ST clients)	Your firm has acted for them in the last 12 months. Your firm is unlikely to be called upon to act for them again.
Active	Your firm has undertaken more than one transaction for them in the last 12 months.

> ❑ You have already identified the numbers of different client types for each legal service. See Table 5 for those numbers and then transpose them onto **Tables 23–6** on pp. 41–6.
>
> It is suggested that you print out or photocopy these tables for each legal service and client group before filling them in.

Client characteristics

Your clients will, in all probability, cover the spectrum of society and have their own requirements and expectations. The purpose of this exercise is to place them in bandings so that when you target new clients, you will have some general guidance as to where and how you should be promoting your firm.

The bandings have been split between the different main groups and those used for this exercise are listed overleaf.

Non-commercial clients

These fall under legal aid and private clients.

1. **Gender.** Obviously, this is a split between male and female.
2. **Age.** There are five age bands commonly referred to:
   - 18–24
   - 25–34
   - 35–44
   - 45–64
   - 65+
3. **Social groups.** There are four main categories people are commonly divided into:
   - AB – professional, senior and middle management
   - C1 – junior managerial and all other non-manual workers
   - C2 – skilled manual workers
   - DE – semi-skilled and unskilled manual workers, people dependent on state benefits and those with no regular income.
4. **Locality.** How far away are your clients based in relation to your firm? There are three bands:
   - 0–5 miles
   - 5–10 miles
   - 10+ miles

Commercial clients

These are those that fall under the general commercial and business groups.

1. **Sole traders.** This is obviously a single group.
2. **Partnerships.** They can be sub-divided by size.
   - 2 partners
   - 3–6 partners
   - 7–10 partners
   - 11+ partners
3. **Limited companies.** Again, these fall within sub-divisions according to size measured by level of turnover.
   - Up to £250k
   - £250k – £1million
   - £1million – £5million
   - £5+ million turnover
4. **Locality.** How far away are your clients in relation to your firm? There are three bands:
   - 0–5 miles
   - 5–10 miles
   - 10+ miles

Why sub-divide client groups?

There are two main reasons why purchasers, in this instance buyers of legal services, are profiled and sub-divided. These are:

1. **Targeting.** To expand its client base, a firm should promote itself. By understanding who your clients are, you will be able to target those promotions more closely at the most likely potential clients. This might involve direct mailshots to a purchased list or it might involve holding workshops or seminars for specific-sized businesses. Whatever the activity employed to gain new clients, if you know the profile of your existing clients you will have an indication as to which new clients might find your firm most attractive.

2. **Image and positioning of your firm.** If you understand the profile of your clients and you update this on an annual basis, you will be able to see how your firm is viewed by present and potential clients according to which clients your firm is attracting at present. This can then be fed back into how you might wish to position your firm and what you would like its image to be.

Profiling your client groups

Tables 23–6 are to be filled in with the numbers and percentages of clients who match each profile.

You might have fairly extensive profile information about your clients available through research, or you may hold profile information on your database, but if not it will be sufficient to 'guesstimate' until you are in a position to undertake verification work. The method outlined below indicates how you might do this.

In addition, you will see that Tables 23–6 can be filled in for each client type, i.e. active, ST and passive clients. This is to establish whether there are any differences in the profiles of these clients.

METHOD

If you do not have the information of the profiles of your clients to hand, you could do a quick check in the following way.

Ask the fee earners to pull together a list of the names of recent clients for each legal service – perhaps 25 (more if the information is available) – identify whether they are active, ST or passive, and give the gender, age, social status and location of each of them. Add this up and you will have an indication of the profile of clients who purchase this legal service from you. Use this to work out the percentage split of your client groups this represents and put the information into Tables 23–6.

Box 4 Example first row of Table 23

(Active)/ST/Passive

		Gender		Age					Social group				Locality – distance in miles		
		M	F	18–24	25–34	35–44	45–64	65+	AB	C1	C2	DE	0–5	5–10	10+
Residential property	No.	15	15	2	8	10	20		20	10			15	15	
	%	50	50	6.5	26.5	33.5	66.5		66.5	33.5			50	50	
		100%		100%					100%				100%		

In the example in Box 4, it can be seen that active residential property clients are 50 per cent male and 50 per cent female, the majority are 45–64 year olds (66.5 per cent) and the majority are AB (66.5 per cent), they are located 50 per cent 0–5 miles and 50 per cent 5–10 miles away.

❏ Complete **Tables 23–6** on pp. 41–6. A good place to start is by bringing the figures from Table 4 on p. 14 into the first column.

Table 23 *Private clients*: client profiles for each legal service offered

Active/ST/Passive																
Legal service	**T O T A L**	**Gender**		**Age**					**Social group**				**Locality – distance in miles**		
		M	**F**	**18–24**	**25–34**	**35–44**	**45–64**	**65+**	**AB**	**C1**	**C2**	**DE**	**0–5**	**5–10**	**10+**
Residential property No.															
%	100%														
Crime No.															
%	100%														
Family No.															
%	100%														
Personal injury No.															
%	100%														
General private No.															
%	100%														
Specialist private No.															
%	100%														
Wills and probate No.															
%	100%														
TOTAL No															
%	100%	100%		100%					100%				100%		

Table 24 *Legal aid clients*: client profiles for each legal service offered

Active/ST/Passive																
Legal service		T O T A L	Gender		Age					Social group				Locality – distance in miles		
			M	F	18–24	25–34	35–44	45–64	65+	AB	C1	C2	DE	0–5	5–10	10+
Residential property	No.															
	%	100%														
Crime	No.															
	%	100%														
Family	No.															
	%	100%														
Personal injury	No.															
	%	100%														
General private	No.															
	%	100%														
Specialist private	No.															
	%	100%														
Wills and probate	No.															
	%	100%														
TOTAL	No.															
	%	100%	100%		100%					100%				100%		

Table 25 *Commercial clients*: client profiles for each legal service offered

Active/ST/Passive															
Legal service	**T O T A L**	**Sole Trader**	Partnership by number of partners					Limited companies – by turnover				Locality – distance in miles		
			2	**3– 6**	**7– 10**	**11+**	**0– 250k**	**£250k– £1m**	**£1m– £5m**	**£5m+**	**0– 5**	**5– 10**	**10+**	
Commercial property — No.														
%	100%													
Commercial finance — No.														
%	100%													
General commercial — No.														
%	100%													
Specialist commercial — No.														
%	100%													
TOTAL — No.														
%	100%	100%	100%				100%				100%		

Client's priorities and estimations of value

After looking in detail at the breakdown of your client base with regard to numbers, revenue and profiles, it is time to see whether they have any common values and/or requirements from a solicitors' firm when purchasing legal services.

Establishing this information about your clients is something that is best approached through client research. However, because it is important to maintain momentum in finishing these exercises, it is suggested that a useful starting point, until you have done any research, is the knowledge and impression of those within the firm who are in contact with clients. To collect the information together for each legal service, it is a good idea to photocopy Tables 28–30 and distribute them to those 'in the front line' providing each legal service.

The value factors have been divided into three sections:

(a) **What clients are looking for in a solicitors' firm.** This concentrates on your firm as a whole.

(b) **What clients are looking for from the solicitors they choose or work with.** This concentrates on the qualities clients are looking for in individual solicitors or fee earners in a department.

(c) **What clients are looking for in the service they receive.** This concentrates on what client care initiatives clients are looking for and what they want from a service.

Comparing the priorities of different lifespan/activity client types and different client groups

Table 26 asks you (or the fee earners in your firm) to assess how your clients value different aspects of the work of a solicitors' firm according to whether they are passive, ST or active clients. Where do you (or your colleagues) think their priorities lie? Are there any differences in what they want or expect from your legal services?

Table 27 asks you (or the fee earners in your firm) to make a judgement of how your clients value different aspects of the work a solicitors' firm does according to whether they are private, legal aid or business and commercial clients. Again, where do you (or your colleagues) think their priorities lie? Are there any differences in what they want or expect from your legal services?

The three value factor sections have been included together in Tables 26 and 27 – work down the columns within sections, i.e. in section (a) order the value factors 1–7 (the number of value factors in that section, with '7' being the highest rating), in section (b) order the value factors 1–5 and in section (c) order the value factors 1–6. If you add more factors in any section, increase the highest rating proportionately.

Key to the different values/requirements

If the answer is 'yes' to the questions in the key, this means that it is rated highly (put the highest number) and if 'no' then it is lower. Give each factor a different number.

(a) WHAT CLIENTS ARE LOOKING FOR IN A SOLICITORS' FIRM (SCALE OF 1–7)

Convenience of offices: Is this important to these clients?

Large firm: Do the clients for this legal service prefer a large firm?

Small firm: Do the clients for this legal service prefer a small firm?

Smart offices: Is this important to the clients of this legal service?

Local knowledge: Is this a deciding factor when these clients are choosing a solicitors' firm?

Reputation of firm: Is a good reputation important to these clients when selecting a solicitor in this area of practice?

Recommendation: On the whole, do these clients require a recommendation before employing a solicitor?

(b) WHAT CLIENTS ARE LOOKING FOR FROM THE SOLICITORS THEY CHOOSE OR WORK WITH (SCALE OF 1–5)

Approachability of solicitor: Is this an area of practice where these clients need to feel their solicitor is approachable and easy to talk to?

Specialist knowledge: Do these clients need to identify specialist knowledge before choosing a solicitor for this service?

Demonstrable experience: Do these clients look at a solicitor's track record in this area to prove ability before selecting him or her?

Reputation of solicitor: Is a solicitor's good reputation important to these clients when selecting a solicitor in this area of practice?

Ease of contact: Is it important to these clients that they can quickly and easily get in contact with their solicitor?

(c) WHAT CLIENTS ARE LOOKING FOR IN THE SERVICE THEY RECEIVE (SCALE OF 1–6)

Quotations: Do these clients think it important to receive accurate quotations prior to work beginning?

Frequent updates: Do these clients think it important to receive frequent updates on their case?

Price: Are these clients sensitive to price and is this a major deciding factor when they purchase this legal service?

Value for money: Do these clients look positively into whether your service offers them value for money (high grade)? Or do they simply assume that the service costs what it costs (low grade)?

Clearly explained information: Do these clients expect and demand a clear explanation of their case?

Speed: Is it important to the clients for this service?

> ❏ Fill in **Tables 26** and **27** on pp. 46 and 47. Remember to use each rating number only once within each section. The overall rank is indicated in the final column ('1' is the top rank or most important factor – see p. 48 for a similar example).

Table 26 Identifying different priorities, expectations and needs among clients with different lifespans/activity levels

Value factors	Passive clients (no. of clients: _____)	Single transaction clients (no. of clients: _____)	Active clients (no. of clients: _____)	Total divided by 3 (average)	Overall rank
(a) What clients are looking for in a solicitors' firm (1–7)					
Convenience of offices					
Large firm					
Small firm					
Smart offices					
Local knowledge					
Reputation of firm					
Recommendation					
Other					
(b) What clients are looking for from the solicitor they choose or work with (1–5)					
Approachability					
Specialist knowledge					
Demonstrable experience					
Reputation					
Ease of contact					
Other					
(c) What clients are looking for in the service they receive (1–6)					
Quotations					
Frequent updates					
Price					
Value for money					
Clear explanations					
Speed					
Other					

Note: Number the value factors down each column in (a) '1–7', in (b) '1–5', and in (c) '1–6' with '1' being the least important, unless you add other factors to each category, in which case increase the scale accordingly. Use each number only once per column/section, so the order of importance is clear.

Table 27 Identifying different priorities, expectations and needs among different client types

Value factors	Private clients	Legal aid clients	Business/ commercial clients	Total divided by 3 (average)	Overall rank
(a) What clients are looking for in a solicitors' firm (1–7)					
Convenience of offices					
Large firm					
Small firm					
Smart offices					
Local knowledge					
Reputation of firm					
Recommendation					
Other					
(b) What clients are looking for from the solicitor they choose or work with (1–5)					
Approachability					
Specialist knowledge					
Demonstrable experience					
Reputation					
Ease of contact					
Other					
(c) What clients are looking for in the service they receive (1–6)					
Quotations					
Frequent updates					
Price					
Value for money					
Clear explanations					
Speed					
Other					

Note: Number the value factors down each column in (a) '1–7', in (b) '1–5', and in (c) '1–6' with '1' being the least important, unless you add other factors to each category, in which case increase the scale accordingly. Use each number only once per column/section, so the order of importance is clear.

Identifying whether clients with different characteristics have different expectations and priorities

This exercise aims to increase your understanding of your clients. You will benefit from establishing whether clients with different characteristics purchasing different legal services have different needs and priorities.

Do older clients have different needs or expectations than younger clients? Do those from different social groups have different priorities? You should ask these questions for each of your legal services.

Tables 28–30 require you to estimate how clients having the characteristics indicated would rank the different factors. There are 18 different factors listed in three different tables. Please order the value factors in section (a) 1–7, the value factors in section (b) 1–5 and the value factors in section (c) 1–6. Add them together across the table for each factor and divide them by the number of profile sub-groups, i.e. 12. Then put the totals in the penultimate column of the tables and in the final column, give the rank they achieve from top ('1') to bottom. It is important that you number all of the values in each section for each of the different client sub-groups.

For each of the value factors, please refer to the key on p. 45.

Box 5 Example of Table 28(a), rows 1 and 2, showing Client Profile Value Assumptions Clients of Conveyancing (private and legal aid clients)

Sub-division	Age					Social Status				Locality – distance in miles			Total divided by 12 (average)	Overall rank
	18–24	25–34	35–44	45–64	65+	AB	C1	C2	DE	0–5	5–10	10+		
What clients are looking for in a solicitors' firm:														
Convenience of offices	7	7	7	5	7	5	5	7	7	7	2	1	67/12 = 5.58	1
Large firm	4	4	2	3	3	6	3	2	5	1	5	4	42/12 = 3.5	2
Small firm	2	2	5	4	6	2	2	5	3	2	3	3	39/12 = 3.25	3

In the example in Box 5, 'convenience of offices' was perceived to be the most important aspect for conveyancing clients aged 18–24, 25–34 and 35–44 and those over 65, in the social groups of C2 and DE, and those living between 0–5 miles away. It was perceived less important by 45–64 year olds and AB and C1 status clients, however. The average total of 'convenience of offices' was 5.58.

Tip

Look at the client characteristic, e.g. age group 18–24, then look down the list of factors and pick out the most important first, followed by second most important down to least important. Remember, where no research is available, use your experience and that of your colleagues as to what these clients ask and expect from you in order to assess which factors are most important to them.

> ❏ This exercise is quite detailed and **Tables 28–31** on pp. 49–56 should be printed for each legal service. Fill in **Tables 28(a)–(c) and 30(a)–(c)**. Collate the results on **Tables 29 and 31**.

Table 28(a) What clients are looking for *in a solicitors' firm*: client profile value assumptions for each legal service (private and legal aid clients)

Legal service: _____   Total no. of clients: _____

Sub-division	Age					Social group				Locality – distance in miles			Total divided by 12 (average)	Overall rank
	18–24	25–34	35–44	45–64	65+	AB	C1	C2	DE	0–5	5–10	10+		
(a) What clients are looking for in a solicitors' firm (1–7)														
Convenience of offices														
Large firm														
Small firm														
Smart offices														
Local knowledge														
Reputation of firm														
Recommendation														
Other:														

Note: Number the value factors down each column '1–7' where '1' is the least important, unless you add other factors, in which case increase the scale accordingly. Use each number only once per column, so the order of importance is clear.

> ❏ Print out this table from the disk for each legal service.

Table 28(b) What clients are looking for *from the solicitor they work with*: client profile value assumptions for each legal service (private and legal aid clients)

Legal service: _____ Total no. of clients: _____

Sub-division	Age					Social group				Locality – distance in miles			Total divided by 12 (average)	Overall rank
	18–24	25–34	35–44	45–64	65+	AB	C1	C2	DE	0–5	5–10	10+		
(b) What clients are looking for from the solicitor they choose or work with (1–5)														
Approachability														
Specialist knowledge														
Demonstrable experience														
Reputation														
Ease of contact														
Other:														

Note: Number the value factors down each column '1–5' where '1' is the least important, unless you add other factors, in which case increase the scale accordingly. Use each number only once per column, so the order of importance is clear.

❑ Print out this table from the disk for each legal service.

Table 28(c) What clients are looking for *in the service they receive*: client profile value assumptions for each legal service (private and legal aid clients)

Legal service: _____ Total no. of clients: _____

Sub-division	Age					Social group				Locality – distance in miles			Total divided by 12 (average)	Overall rank
	18–24	25–34	35–44	45–64	65+	AB	C1	C2	DE	0–5	5–10	10+		
(c) What clients are looking for in the service they receive (1–6)														
Quotations														
Frequent updates														
Price														
Value for money														
Clear explanations														
Speed														
Other:														

Note: Number the value factors down each column '1–6' where '1' is the least important, unless you add other factors, in which case increase the scale accordingly. Use each number only once per column, so the order of importance is clear.

❏ Print out this table from the disk for each legal service.

Table 29 Collating the priorities of private and legal aid clients in the different areas of law

Legal service: _____

(a) What clients are looking for in a solicitors' firm		
Average	Rank	Value factor
	1	
	2	
	3	
	4	
	5	
	6	
	7	

(c) What clients are looking for in the service they receive		
Average	Rank	Value factor
	1	
	2	
	3	
	4	
	5	
	6	

(b) What clients are looking for from the solicitor they choose or work with		
Average	Rank	Value factor
	1	
	2	
	3	
	4	
	5	

❏ Print this table from the disk for each legal service. List the most important factors first ('1' is the top ranked priority) down to the least important factor.

Table 30(a) What clients are looking for *in a solicitor's firm*: client profile value assumptions for each legal service (business and commercial clients)

Legal service: _____ Total no. of clients: _____

Sub-division	Sole trader	Partnership size				Limited company turnover £				Locality – distance in miles			Total divided by 12 (average)	Overall rank
		2	3–6	7–10	11+	0–£250k	£250k–£1m	£1m–£5m	£5m+	0–5	5–10	10+		
(a) What business and commercial clients are looking for in a solicitors' firm (1–7)														
Convenience of offices														
Large firm														
Small firm														
Smart offices														
Local knowledge														
Reputation of firm														
Recommen-dation														
Other:														

Note: Number the value factors down each column '1–7' where '1' is the least important, unless you add other factors, in which case increase the scale accordingly. Use each number only once per column, so the order of importance is clear.

☐ Print this table from the disk for each legal service.

Table 30(b) What clients are looking for *from the solicitor they work with*: client profile value assumptions for each legal service (business and commercial clients)

Legal service: _____ Total no. of clients: _____

Sub-division	Sole trader	Partnership size				Limited company turnover £				Locality – distance in miles			Total divided by 12	Overall rank
		2	3–6	7–10	11+	0–£250k	£250k–£1m	£1m–£5m	£5m+	0–5	5–10	10+		
(b) What clients are looking for from the solicitor they choose or work with (1–5)														
Approach-ability														
Specialist knowledge														
Demonstrable experience														
Reputation														
Ease of contact														
Other:														

Note: Number the value factors down each column '1–5' where '1' is the least important, unless you add other factors, in which case increase the scale accordingly. Use each number only once per column, so the order of importance is clear.

❏ Print this table from the disk for each legal service.

Table 30(c) What clients are looking for *in the service they receive*: client profile value assumptions for each legal service (business and commercial clients)

Legal service: _____ Total no of clients: _____

Sub-division	Sole trader	Partnership size				Limited company turnover £				Locality – distance in miles			Total divided by 12 (average)	Overall rank
		2	3–6	7–10	11+	0–£250k	£250k–£1m	£1m–£5m	£5m+	0–5	5–10	10+		
(c) What clients are looking for in the service they receive (1–6)														
Quotations														
Frequent updates														
Price														
Value for money														
Clear explanations														
Speed														
Other:														

Note: Number the value factors down each column '1–6' where '1' is the least important, unless you add other factors, in which case increase the scale accordingly. Use each number only once per column, so the order of importance is clear.

☐ Print this table from the disk for each legal service.

Table 31 Collating the priorities of business and commercial clients in the different areas of law

Legal service: _____   Total no. of clients: _____

(a) What clients are looking for in a solicitors' firm		
Average	Rank	Value factor
	1	
	2	
	3	
	4	
	5	
	6	
	7	

(c) What clients are looking for in the service they receive		
Average	Rank	Value factor
	1	
	2	
	3	
	4	
	5	
	6	

(b) What clients are looking for from the solicitor they choose or work with		
Average	Rank	Value factor
	1	
	2	
	3	
	4	
	5	

Note: List the most important factors first ('1' is the top rank) down to the least important factor.

❑ Print this table from the disk for each legal service.

Meeting your clients' requirements

Clients' value requirements and overall positioning of your firm

Having identified some of the factors about a solicitors' firm that you perceive are important to your clients, it is now time to try to evaluate how your firm presents itself to clients with regard to these factors.

Initially it is suggested that you use your own experience, together with the experience of others in the firm, to make assumptions. Having reached an initial assessment through these exercises, you can, at a later date, compare your assumptions with actual research. Please see Part 2 for further information on how to do this.

Before beginning, please ensure you read the key below, as it explains how you need to look at your firm and assess how your clients might perceive your firm.

To evaluate each value factor you need to award your firm marks out of 10 for each (10 being the highest mark descending to 1 which is very poor). This exercise is asking you to give a score to your firm on the way your firm presents itself with regard to different client values (previously you rated the value factors in order of importance).

It is very important that you are as objective as possible when looking at your firm.

Key to analysing the different values/requirements

A score of 10 out of 10 indicates you are extremely good at this factor, decreasing to 1 which indicates you are very poor at presenting this factor.

(a) ASSESSING HOW YOUR FIRM MEETS CLIENTS' REQUIREMENTS FROM A SOLICITORS' FIRM

Convenience of offices: Are your offices convenient? Do you present them as such?

Large firm: Is your firm large and do you present this to those clients who would prefer such a firm?

Small firm: Is your firm small and do you present this to those clients who would prefer such a firm?

Smart offices: Do your offices present your firm in the best manner possible to clients?

Local knowledge: Do you present this as a plus?

Reputation of firm: Does your firm have a good reputation and do you promote this to best advantage?

Recommendation: Do you obtain a number of your clients through personal recommendation and do you promote this fact?

(b) ASSESSING HOW YOUR FIRM PRESENTS THE SOLICITORS IN THE FIRM TO CLIENTS

Approachability of solicitor: Do you promote the solicitors in the firm as being contactable, approachable and easy to talk to?

Specialist knowledge: Do you present your solicitors as having any particular specialisation in this area?

Demonstrable experience: Do you present information to clients about members of the firm having any demonstrable experience in this area?

Reputation of solicitor: Do the fee earners in your firm have a good reputation and do you promote this to best advantage?

Ease of contact: Do you have systems in place to ensure that clients can get in touch either with their solicitor or someone who will be able to talk to them about their matter quickly and easily?

(c) ASSESSING HOW THE SERVICE YOUR FIRM OFFERS MEETS YOUR CLIENTS' REQUIREMENTS

Quotations: Do you give clients quotations prior to beginning work and then stick to them?

Frequent updates: Do you have systems in place to give clients regular updates about their matter?

Price: Are the services you offer clients keenly and competitively priced and do you communicate that to clients?

Value for money: Do you actively promote the impression to your clients that they are receiving value for money in the service you provide them with?

Clearly explained information: Do you ensure all fee earners clearly and accurately explain matters to clients as a matter of course and do you supply back up printed information for clients?

Speed: Where appropriate do you offer a fast service and do you promote this to clients?

☐ Now fill in **Tables 32(a)–(c)**. You should copy the tables for each area of law before filling them in and summarise the overall average scores in **Tables 33(a)–(c)** on pp. 62–4.

Table 32(a) How the service your firm offers meets clients' requirements from a solicitors' firm with regard to the different client value factors

Legal service: _____

Value factors	Score out of 10 for your firm's approach to this aspect
(a) Assessing how your firm meets clients' requirements for this legal service	
Convenience of offices Are your offices convenient? Do you present them as such?	
Large firm Is your firm large and do you present this to those clients who would prefer such a firm?	
Small firm Is your firm small and do you present this to those clients who would prefer such a firm?	
Smart offices Do your offices present your firm in the best manner possible to clients?	
Local knowledge Do you present this as a plus?	
Reputation of firm Does your firm have a good reputation and do you promote this to best advantage?	
Recommendation Do you obtain a number of your clients through personal recommendation and do you promote this fact?	
Other:	
TOTAL	

❑ Print this table from the disk for each legal service.

Table 32(b) How the service your firm offers presents the solicitors in the firm to clients with regard to the different client value factors

Legal service: _____

Value factors	Score out of 10 for your firm's approach to this aspect
(b) Assessing how your firm presents the solicitors working in this legal service	
Approachability of solicitor Do you promote the solicitors in the firm as being contactable, approachable and easy to talk to?	
Specialist knowledge Do you present your solicitors as having any particular specialisation in this area?	
Demonstrable experience Do you present information to clients about members of the firm having any demonstrable experience in this area?	
Reputation of solicitor Do the fee earners in your firm have a good reputation and do you promote this to best advantage?	
Ease of contact Do you have systems in place to ensure that clients can get in touch either with their solicitor or someone who will be able to talk to them about their matter quickly and easily?	
Other:	
TOTAL	

❏ Print this table from the disk for each legal service.

Table 32(c) How the service your firm offers meets your clients' requirements with regard to the different client value factors

Legal service: _____

Value factors	Score out of 10 for your firm's approach to this aspect
(c) Assessing how this legal service meets your clients' requirements	
Packaging of legal service Where possible, do you package your services in a single item package to make it simpler for clients?	
Quotations Do you give clients quotations prior to beginning work and then stick to them?	
Frequent updates Do you have systems in place to give clients regular updates about their matter?	
Price Are the services you offer clients keenly and competitively priced and do you communicate that to clients?	
Value for money Do you actively promote the impression to your clients that they are receiving value for money in the service you provide them with?	
Clearly explained information Do you ensure all fee earners clearly and accurately explain matters to clients as a matter of course, and do you supply back-up printed information for clients?	
Speed Where appropriate do you offer a fast service and do you promote this to clients?	
Other:	
TOTAL	

❏ Print this table from the disk for each legal service.

Table 33(a) Summary of how your firm meets clients' requirements with regard to the different client value factors

Value factors	Score out of 10 for your firm's approach to this aspect
(a) Assessing how your firm meets clients' requirements from a solicitors' firm	
Convenience of offices Are your offices convenient? Do you present them as such?	
Large firm Is your firm large and do you present this to those clients who would prefer such a firm?	
Small firm Is your firm small and do you present this to those clients who would prefer such a firm?	
Smart offices Do your offices present your firm in the best manner possible to clients?	
Local knowledge Do you present this as a plus?	
Reputation of firm Does your firm have a good reputation and do you promote this to best advantage?	
Recommendation Do you obtain a number of your clients through personal recommendation and do you promote this fact?	
Other:	
TOTAL	

Table 33(b) Summary of how your firm presents the solicitors in the firm to clients

Value factors	Score out of 10 for your firm's approach to this aspect
(b) Assessing how your firm presents the solicitors in the firm to clients	
Approachability of solicitor Do you promote the solicitors in the firm as being contactable, approachable and easy to talk to?	
Specialist knowledge Do you present your solicitors as having any particular specialisation in this area?	
Demonstrable experience Do you present information to clients about members of the firm having any demonstrable experience in this area?	
Reputation of solicitor Do the fee earners in your firm have a good reputation and do you promote this to best advantage?	
Ease of contact Do you have systems in place to ensure that clients can get in touch either with their solicitor or someone who will be able to talk to them about their matter quickly and easily?	
Other:	
TOTAL	

Table 33(c) Summary of how the service approach of your firm meets your clients' requirements

Value factors	Score out of 10 for your firm's approach to this aspect
(c) Assessing how the service your firm offers meets your clients' requirements	
Quotations Do you give clients quotations prior to beginning work and then stick to them?	
Frequent updates Do you have systems in place to give clients regular updates about their matter?	
Price Are the services you offer clients keenly and competitively priced and do you communicate that to clients?	
Value for money Do you actively promote the impression to your clients that they are receiving value for money in the service you provide them with?	
Clearly explained information Do you ensure all fee earners clearly and accurately explain matters to clients as a matter of course, and do you supply back-up printed information for clients?	
Speed Where appropriate do you offer a fast service and do you promote this to clients?	
Other:	
TOTAL	

Comparing your perceptions of your own firm's service with your assumptions of your clients' service requirements

To compare your firm's service with your clients' needs, you need to formulate figures that are in the same scale so that they can be compared. In the previous exercises, you established an average rating (within each section (a)–(c)) for all of the 18 client value factors per legal service and then an average rating across all legal services for each value factor (Table 27). However, when making assumptions about your own firm you employed a different method, and you were asked to give yourself a score out of 10 for each value factor for each legal service (Tables 33(a)–(c)).

In order to compare the two, you need to have both as a score out of 10. To do this, take each of the average totals for your clients (see Table 27), divide them by the number in their section, i.e. 7 in (a), 5 in (b) and 6 in (c), multiply by 100, then simply take that percentage figure as a percentage of 10.

Example

If the average total for 'convenience of offices' is 5.58, then the following calculation applies:

5.58 ÷ 7 (number of factors) = 0.78 × 100 = 78%, 78% of 10 = 7.8

Therefore the comparable number for clients is 7.8.

☐ **Table 34** on p. 66 should be photocopied and used to compare your service and your clients' requirements for each legal service.

Tables 35 and 36 on pp. 67 and 68 have three columns for each client type. The first column is for your perceptions of your clients' requirements, the second column for your perception of how your firm presents itself with regard to those factors, and the final column to show the difference between your clients' values and your firm's presentation.

☐ Fill in a copy of **Table 35** for each legal service and **Table 36** to compare your firm's approach overall. Convert the average total ratings by your clients to a score out of 10 as you did for Table 34.

Table 34 Comparison of your firm's presentation of value (Tables 32(a)–(c)) with your perception of clients' requirements *for each legal service* (Tables 28(a)–(c) and 30(a)–(c))

Legal service: _____

Value factors	Your clients' priorities/ expectations/ requirements	Your firm's approach	Difference between your clients' requirements and your approach +/–
(a) What clients are looking for in a solicitors' firm			
Convenience of offices			
Large firm			
Small firm			
Smart offices			
Local knowledge			
Reputation of firm			
Recommendation			
Other:			
(b) What clients are looking for from the solicitor they choose or work with			
Approachability			
Specialist knowledge			
Demonstrable experience			
Reputation			
Ease of contact			
Other:			
(c) What clients are looking for in the service they receive			
Quotations			
Frequent updates			
Price			
Value for money			
Clear explanations			
Speed			
Other:			

❏ Print this table from the disk for each legal service.

Table 35 Comparison of your firm's overall approach (Tables 33(a)–(c)) with your perceptions of the different lifespan/activity level client types (Table 26)

Value factors	Passive clients			Single transaction clients			Active clients		
	Clients	Your firm	Diff. +/–	Clients	Your firm	Diff. +/–	Clients	Your firm	Diff. +/–
(a) What clients are looking for in a solicitors' firm									
Convenience of offices									
Large firm									
Small firm									
Smart offices									
Local knowledge									
Reputation of firm									
Recommendation									
Other:									
(b) What clients are looking for from the solicitor they choose or work with									
Approachability									
Specialist knowledge									
Demonstrable experience									
Reputation									
Ease of contact									
Other:									
(c) What clients are looking for in the service they receive									
Quotations									
Frequent updates									
Price									
Value for money									
Clear explanations									
Speed									
Other:									

Table 36 Comparison of your firm's overall approach (Tables 33(a)–(c)) with your perceptions of the different client types (Table 27)

Value factors	Private clients			Legal aid clients			Business/ commercial clients		
	Clients	Your firm	Diff. +/–	Clients	Your firm	Diff. +/–	Clients	Your firm	Diff. +/–
(a) What clients are looking for in a solicitors' firm									
Convenience of offices									
Large firm									
Small firm									
Smart offices									
Local knowledge									
Reputation of firm									
Recommendation									
Other:									
(b) What clients are looking for from the solicitor they choose or work with									
Approachability									
Specialist knowledge									
Demonstrable experience									
Reputation									
Ease of contact									
Other:									
(c) What clients are looking for in the service they receive									
Quotations									
Frequent updates									
Price									
Value for money									
Clear explanations									
Speed									
Other:									

Analysing presentation and aligning your services more closely to perceived client requirements

So far you have made assumptions about how important the different value factors are to your clients and how your firm presents itself, and compared these two. Having a comparison, however, informative as it is, is not enough. It is now time to analyse what actions you might take to move your firm closer to your perception of your clients' requirements.

Strengths and weaknesses

In Table 34, you set out how your perceptions of your firm's presentation compares to the assumptions you made about your clients' requirements, for each legal service. The difference between these two figures is a useful starting point when determining whether your firm is strong or weak with regard to a particular aspect of a legal service you offer.

If you have done the previous exercises from perception, assumption and experience (as you are asked to do in the absence of client research), this exercise should help you identify priority areas that you do need to research to understand and confirm your perceptions and assumptions. Part 2 of this manual outlines how you can conduct client research to establish whether your assumptions are correct.

HOW TO IDENTIFY A STRENGTH OR WEAKNESS

If the difference in client requirements and in your firm's presentation (as set out in Table 34) is greater than two points, either positively or negatively, your firm is weak in this area. The weakness arises from a mismatch between the service you offer, or the way you offer it, and the needs of your clients. A perfect match or a differential of less than two points indicates that in this factor you are meeting your clients' needs and it can be deemed a strength.

❏ Please use **Table 37** on p. 70 to identify the strengths and weaknesses for each legal service you offer, as identified in Table 34, copying it as many times as appropriate.

Table 37 Strengths and weaknesses

Legal service: _____

Strengths			Weaknesses		
Difference +/–	Rank	Value factor across (a), (b) and (c)	Difference +/–	Rank	Value factor across (a), (b) and (c)
	1 (greatest)			1 (greatest)	
	2			2	
	3			3	
	4			4	
	5			5	
	6			6	
	7			7	
	8			8	
	9			9	
	10			10	
	11			11	
	12			12	
	13			13	
	14			14	
	15			15	
	16			16	
	17			17	
	18			18	
	19 (least)			19 (least)	

Note: Remember, a strength is where the difference in client requirements and in your firm's presentation is less than two points, either positively or negatively, and a weakness is where it is greater than two points positively or negatively.

When identifying your strengths and weaknesses, list them from 1 to 19 (or as many as there are), showing the greatest weakness (largest differential) or strength (smallest differential) to the least weakness (smallest differential over 2) or strength (greatest differential between –2 and +2).

❑ Print this table from the disk for each legal service.

Identifying the actions that might be undertaken to tailor your legal services to more closely meet your clients' requirements

To align your legal services more closely with clients' requirements you need to identify the different actions that might help you do this. These actions might indicate an adjustment to a legal service, the way you present a legal service or the way in which you communicate with your clients.

The aim is to identify actions or communication opportunities which will:

- build on an area you are good at, i.e. a strength;
- reduce a problem area, i.e a weakness.

To identify whether there are any actions that need be taken for each value factor, either strength or weakness, you can ask yourself the following questions about each factor.

Factors that represent strengths

'What actions can we take with regards *xxxx* (value factor), in order to build on and take best advantage of our firm's strength in this area, which would at the same time maintain this strength or move it towards our clients' perceived requirements?'

Factors that represent weaknesses

'What actions can we take with regards *xxxx* (value factor) in order to help make us more competitive and profitable in this area, and which would at the same time move it towards our clients' perceived requirements?'

A list of possible actions has been collated on pp. 72–9 to help you identify options that might be available to you for each value factor.

Scoring the actions identified

After identifying what actions might help, you need to make a judgement about how achievable each action identified is and how effective each one is likely to be (whilst at the same time maintaining or improving profitability). A score of 10 indicates an effective action which is quickly achievable, whereas 1 represents an action that might not be very effective and is difficult to implement, i.e. non-achievable at present.

Note: This exercise is directed towards the value factors previously identified. Section 1(c) is aimed at analysing resource and market factors and their effect on your firm.

> ❑ Study the list below, and fill in **Table 38** for each legal service you offer using the suggested action codes in the list.

Checklist 1 Possible actions or communication initiatives to be considered under each of the different value factors for each legal service offered

Listed below are a number of different actions or communication opportunities that might apply to each value factor. They have been set out to help you arrive at a list of actions for Table 38. Written in italics is the suggested reason for under-taking those actions, i.e. the objectives of those actions. Please copy and use this list for each area of law. Tick boxes have been put next to each action to allow you to indicate those you wish to use.

Each action has a code against it; this is for use when setting objectives.

Key: IA **Internal action.** This is where the action involves internal re-organisation or action.

CA **Communication action.** This is where the message should be communicated to clients, through the way the service is offered, individually by word of mouth or as a part of the message/benefits presented in promotional materials.

PA **Promotional action.** This is where a specific promotional activity is indicated. An outline of different promotional activities and when they can be used is set out in Part 3 of this manual.

A. Approaches to improving your firm's ability to meet client requirements

Convenience of offices

Remove any barriers that location may create and make the firm more accessible to clients.

Provide clients with a map of your office location .... ❑ CA

Provide clients with transport links and car parking .... ❑ CA

Large firm

Remove any barriers to clients preferring to use a small firm or large firm.

If you are a large firm, outline how this can benefit them.

Point out to clients breadth of expertise available .... ❑ CA

Explain how one-stop shop can help overall understanding
of a client's position and ensure the optimum approach
in all areas .... ☐ CA

Provide clients with information about the number and diversity
of other clients to encourage them to trust your firm .... ☐ CA

If you are a small firm, outline how this can benefit them.

Outline the personal service you are able to offer .... ☐ CA

Link with other firms for areas you do not cover .... ☐ IA/CA

Link your firm with the attributes a large firm offers .... ☐ CA

Small firm

Remove any barriers to clients preferring to use a small firm or large firm.

If you are a large firm, outline how you can offer the same benefits as a small firm.

Point out the personal service you offer .... ☐ CA

Explain how one-stop shop can help overall understanding
of a client's position and ensure the optimum approach
in all areas .... ☐ CA

Provide clients with information about the number of small
clients you work with.. ☐ CA

Reassure them about costs not being any higher....................................... ☐ CA

Link your firm with the attributes a large firm offers .... ☐ CA

If you are a small firm, outline how this can benefit them.

Outline the personal service you are able to offer .... ☐ CA

Link with other firms for areas you don't cover .... ☐ IA/CA

Smart offices

Ensure that the impression of the firm created by your offices is a positive one.

Provide resources to make your reception area clean and welcoming .... ☐ IA

Provide resources to make the offices look good from the outside as
well as inside .... ☐ IA

Provide your telephone receptionist with the appropriate training and
emphasise the importance of a pleasant telephone manner .... ☐ IA

Draw up guidelines about how long visitors can be kept waiting .... ☐ IA

Local knowledge

Build clients' trust and the firm's accessibility by presenting the firm as their 'local solicitor'.

If local:

Provide clients with an explanation of why knowledge of the area is important .... ❏ CA

Advertise with a focus on the firm's local knowledge .... ❏ PA

If not local:

Advertise with a focus on the firm's local knowledge .... ❏ PA

Provide clients with information about work for clients in their area .... ❏ CA

Provide clients with transport links and car parking .... ❏ CA

Reputation of firm or solicitor

Increase clients' trust by emphasising the reputation of the firm.

Provide clients with an outline of the reputation of the firm or solicitor .... ❏ CA

Provide clients with an outline of the work your firm undertakes .... ❏ CA

Provide clients with information on how the firm has developed since being established .... ❏ CA

Provide clients with list of clients who are well known .... ❏ CA

Send or show clients copies of information where success achieved media coverage .... ❏ CA

Send out press releases about any changes in law to local newspapers to try to establish the firm as a contact in an area and therefore establish you as 'the' experts .... ❏ PA/CA

Send out press releases with news of growth, new people, new offices .... ❏ PA/CA

Send out press releases about any initiatives being undertaken such as seminars, surgeries, etc. .... ❏ PA/CA

Encourage and help fee earners take part in radio call-ins and other radio opportunities .... ❏ IA/CA

Encourage and help fee earners make presentations to local groups and organisations .... ❏ IA/CA

Undertake relevant charitable work .... ❏ PA

Recommendation

Encourage existing clients to recommend the firm.

Provide clients with testimonials from other clients .... ☐ CA

Encourage clients to recommend your firm by offering them a reward
for any new clients their actions might bring to the firm .... ☐ PA

Provide clients with information about the numbers of those clients
your firm has been able to help .... ☐ CA

B. Actions you can take to better present the solicitors in your firm to clients

Approachability of solicitor

Encourage clients to trust and enjoy working with those in the firm by promoting them as being approachable, friendly and receptive.

Include pictures of fee earners (smiling) in as many materials as
possible .... ☐ PA

Encourage individuals to attend public events .... ☐ IA

Provide clients with outline of individual's experience .... ☐ CA

Encourage individuals to smile as they speak on the telephone –
maybe send them on a training course .... ☐ IA

Provide an outline of the personnel involved .... ☐ CA

Provide contact numbers and names of assistants and secretaries .... ☐ CA

Hold surgeries for clients and potential clients to come in and
'have a chat' .... ☐ PA

Specialist knowledge

Increase clients' trust by raising the profile of the firm as having specialist skills in this area.

Provide clients with outline of benefits of specialist knowledge .... ☐ CA

Provide clients with information to validate specialist credibility .... ☐ CA

Advertise that specialist ability .... ☐ PA

Hold seminars focusing on specific areas to establish the firm's
expertise .... ☐ PA

Hold surgeries for those who might require specialist services .... ☐ PA

Demonstrable experience

Build clients' trust by making them aware of the firm's experience in this area.

Provide clients with a clear outline of experience .... ❑ CA

Provide clients with an explanation of why experience is important .... ❑ CA

Advertise with a focus on an individual's experience in a certain area .... ❑ PA

Have individuals run seminars focusing on specific areas to
establish their expertise .... ❑ PA

Provide clients with background and testimonials to validate
experience .... ❑ CA

Reputation of solicitor

Increase clients' trust by building the reputation of the firm.

Provide clients with an outline of the reputation of the solicitor .... ❑ CA

Provide clients with an outline of the work each solicitor undertakes .... ❑ CA

Provide clients with information on how the solicitor has developed
since being qualified .... ❑ CA

Provide clients with testimonials from clients a solicitor has worked with .... ❑ CA

Send or show clients copies of information where a success has
achieved media coverage .... ❑ CA

Send out press releases about any changes in the law to local
newspapers under individual solicitors' names to try to establish them as
contact in an area and therefore establish them as 'the' experts .... ❑ PA

Send out press releases with news of growth, new people .... ❑ PA

Send out press releases about any initiatives being undertaken such as
seminars, surgeries and details of solicitors who will be present .... ❑ PA

Encourage and help fee earners to take part in radio call-ins and
other radio opportunities .... ❑ PA

Encourage and help fee earners to make presentations to local
groups and organisations .... ❑ IA

Encourage fee earners to undertake relevant charity work .... ❑ PA

Ease of contact

Improve client contact opportunities to encourage client loyalty and satisfaction.

Provide an outline of the personnel involved .... ❑ CA

Provide contact numbers .... ❑ CA

Draw up guidelines for adequate and appropriate sick cover .... ❑ IA

Meet to discuss arrangements on a regular basis with fee earners
and staff .... ☐ IA

Provide staff with the appropriate training .... ☐ IA

Provide all staff with guidelines on telephone etiquette .... ☐ IA

Draw up guidelines about how long callers should be kept waiting on
the line or for a returned call .... ☐ IA

C. Approaches to improving the service your firm offers to better meet client requirements

Quotations

Build client loyalty by providing good client care.

Provide clients with quotations .... ☐ CA

Provide an outline of all the likely costs .... ☐ CA

Provide clients with an indication of how they will be updated and
how frequently .... ☐ CA

Provide clients with ongoing updates .... ☐ CA

Provide guidelines so that quotations are neat, tidy and uniform
in layout .... ☐ IA

Frequent updates

Build client loyalty by providing good client care.

Provide clients with a clear outline of the steps/stages of the work
being undertaken .... ☐ CA

Provide clients with ongoing updates .... ☐ CA

Provide an outline of the time-frame for the work they require
to be done .... ☐ CA

Provide contact numbers .... ☐ CA

Provide clients with an explanation of the legal processes involved .... ☐ CA

Provide guidelines so that letters are neat, tidy and uniform in
layout .... ☐ IA

Price

> *Work towards reducing price as an issue with clients.*

Increase or decrease the price .... ☐ IA

Provide clients with quotations .... ☐ CA

Provide clients with ongoing updates .... ☐ CA

Offer clients the option of instalment payments of large bills .... ☐ PA

Reward clients with discounts for quick payment of bills .... ☐ PA

Value for money

> *Work to improve clients' perception that they are receiving a value-for-money service.*

Provide clients with ongoing updates .... ☐ CA

Provide clients with an outline of what the price covers,
    i.e. six letters, five phone calls, etc. .... ☐ CA

Provide clients with a clear outline of the processes being
    undertaken . ... ☐ CA

Provide clients with clear explanations of work involved .... ☐ CA

Clearly explained information

> *Build client loyalty by providing good client care.*

Provide clients with a clear outline of the steps/stages of the work
    being undertaken .... ☐ CA

Provide clients with quotations .... ☐ CA

Provide clients with ongoing updates .... ☐ CA

Provide an outline of all the likely costs .... ☐ CA

Provide an outline of the time-frame for the work they require to be
    done .... ☐ CA

Provide an outline of the personnel involved .... ☐ CA

Provide contact numbers .... ☐ CA

Provide clients with an explanation of the legal process involved .... ☐ CA

Provide guidelines so that letters are neat, tidy and uniform in
    layout .... ☐ IA

Speed

Build client loyalty by providing good client care.

Provide clients with ongoing updates .... ❏ CA

Provide an outline of the time-frame for the work they require to be
done .... ❏ CA

Provide an outline of the personnel involved .... ❏ CA

Provide contact numbers .... ❏ CA

Provide clients with an explanation of the legal process involved .... ❏ CA

Table 38 Actions you deem appropriate to move your firm's legal services closer to clients' requirements

Legal service: _____

Value factor	Actions to be undertaken	Action code PA/IA/CA	Achievability score out of 10

❏ Print this table from the disk for each legal service.

Connector clients

In the previous exercises of section 1(b), you looked in some detail at the profile, value and revenue brought in from clients with whom you deal directly. This group of tables will help you to collate information about organisations that act as intermediaries and pass on clients to you.

These organisations, though not strictly clients themselves (although they may also be), are a valuable source of clients. Some may be commercial organisations, some non-commercial; whatever they are, by referring their clients to you they are endorsing your firm. Therefore, it will help if your firm is able to demonstrate qualities that have some resonance with their approach to their clients. Some of the organisations that might refer clients to you are given below.

Commercial organisations may include:

- estate agents;
- banks;
- accountants;
- management consultants;
- other solicitors.

Non commercial organisations may include:

- chambers of commerce;
- hospitals;
- doctors;
- local government;
- the police;
- charities;
- Citizens' Advice Bureaux;
- other information centres;
- the Rotary Club;
- other clubs.

All of these organisations can be extremely valuable to any firm as a key source of business.

A clear understanding of the way in which they approach their clients will help you offer legal services to their clients in a way that will complement their approach and ensure that they feel comfortable and confident.

This information is valuable in helping you cultivate and stave off competition for existing connector clients, and will enable you to approach potential new connector clients with a strong rationale as to why they should refer clients to your firm.

❑ In **Table 39** below begin by identifying existing and potential connector clients

Table 39 Existing and potential connector clients who may refer clients to you for each legal service

Legal service: _____

Name of connector client	Existing (E) or potential (P) connector client	Type of organisation i.e. estate agent, bank, etc.	If existing – approximate number of referrals over a 12-month period

❑ Print this table from the disk for each legal service.

Pigeonhole your connector clients

Having identified your connector clients, Table 40 simply asks you to summarise in one descriptive sentence your connector clients and in another descriptive sentence their clients. The purpose of this exercise is, as far as possible, to pigeonhole them.

The descriptive phrases that first spring to your mind to describe your connector clients and their clients are usually the most useful phrases and are the ones your colleagues are likely to think of as well, mainly because they will be obvious.

Example

XQZ connector client: 'an aggressive, large and successful organisation, with a strong emphasis on customer service and competitive pricing'.

XQZ clients: 'young, well-off private clients who look for a high level of service and expertise'.

❏ Fill in **Table 40** below, copying the table for each legal service. To ensure you have the correct view you may wish to hand these forms to your colleagues to see whether their perceptions differ.

Table 40 Pigeonholing your connector clients

Legal service: _____

Name of connector client		Descriptive sentence
	Describing them	
	Describing their clients	
	Describing them	
	Describing their clients	
	Describing them	
	Describing their clients	
	Describing them	
	Describing their clients	
	Describing them	
	Describing their clients	

❏ Print this table from the disk for each legal service.

Connector clients' values

The suggested list of connector organisations with which you might have a relationship includes a variety of types of organisation. Their relationship with clients will vary as will their expectations from you as a service provider for their clients. This exercise focuses on how your different connector clients present themselves to their clients so that you can make assumptions about what they might value in your firm, your staff, and the service you offer, or could offer, their clients.

To complete this exercise it is suggested that you undertake some initial research as well as use your own experience and the experience of others in the firm to make assumptions.

Remember – the most important thing is to work through and finish these exercises.

How do your connector clients' approach their clients?

A good starting point is to obtain a copy of each connector client's brochure or leaflets, visit their web site, or look at any advertising they undertake or client information brochures and leaflets they produce.

In some instances the organisations might not have brochures or sales leaflets, i.e. doctors, hospitals, the police, etc. However these organisations will frequently have charters outlining their levels of service and approach to clients. These can normally be obtained by simply asking for them.

The information that connector clients use to sell themselves or explain their services to their clients will help you gain some understanding and insight into how they approach their clients.

This exercise asks you to use the information you gather on connector clients to identify and rate the importance of different aspects of their service to their clients.

Note: It is probably easiest to collect together connector organisations that are similar and analyse them on the same table (three per table), i.e. analyse three different estate agents on the same table. This means that you can then look across the columns and compare their approaches. However, you should ensure that your opinion of one organisation's approach does not influence your thoughts on another, so it is a good idea to complete the analyses on each one in turn.

❑ Fill in **Table 41**. Start by identifying whether an aspect is present in each connector client's approach along the whole column, then rate its importance according to the weight that factor is given in the information you have.

Table 41 Identifying the way in which existing and potential connector clients present and promote their services to clients

Aspect of the service they present to their clients	Name: _____ Legal service: _____		Name: _____ Legal service: _____		Name: _____ Legal service: _____	
	Is this aspect identified in their client information? ✔ ✗	How important is this aspect to their approach?	Is this aspect identified in their client information? ✔ ✗	How important is this aspect to their approach?	Is this aspect identified in their client information? ✔ ✗	How important is this aspect to their approach?
Do they promote the convenience of their offices or ease of reaching their offices?						
Do they promote the benefits of being a large organisation?						
Do they promote the benefits of being a small organisation?						
Is the way in which they present themselves high quality?						
Do they present their local knowledge as a benefit?						
Do they promote their reputation?						
Do they use testimonials to recommend themselves?						
Do they promote the friendliness and approachability of their staff?						
Do they promote the fact they have specialist knowledge?						
Do they promote their organisation's experience? For example, 'established for over x years'?						
Do they promote their staff's experience?						
Ease of contact – do they promote 24-hour contact, open seven days a week, web site for service, etc.?						
Do they package their service as a one-price item?						

Table 41 *Continued*

Aspect of the service they present to their clients	Name: _____ Legal service: _____		Name: _____ Legal service: _____		Name: _____ Legal service: _____	
	Is this aspect identified in their client information? ✔ ✗	How important is this aspect to their approach?	Is this aspect identified in their client information? ✔ ✗	How important is this aspect to their approach?	Is this aspect identified in their client information? ✔ ✗	How important is this aspect to their approach?
Do they promote a quotation or estimating service?						
Do they promote or identify how clients will be kept up to date with the service?						
Do they promote the way in which they price their service?						
Do they promote the fact their service is value for money?						
Do they offer any guarantees or warranties?						
Do they clearly explain the service they offer?						
Do they promote speed as an aspect of their service?						
Other:						

Note: Number all aspects of their organisation, staff or service according to the number of aspects identified, i.e. '1–8' if eight aspects are identified, with '1' the least important. Use each number only once to show the order of importance.

Identifying your approach to both existing and potential connector clients

Having analysed your connector clients' approach to their clients and the qualities they highlight to their clients, you need to identify how you can match their approach. In Table 41 you were asked to rate aspects according to their importance in connector organisations' approach to their clients. Using those ratings, list the top four aspects for each connector client in Table 42 and next to each one identify how your firm can reflect that approach. Then list the four secondary aspects and do the same with them.

❑ Fill in **Table 42** below

Table 42 Identifying ways your firm can reflect the client approach of your connector clients

Name of connector client: _____

Legal service(s) that could be sold to their clients: _____

_____

Top ranked four aspects of connector clients' services	Description of how your firm can match this aspect in offering a legal service to their clients
1	
2	
3	
4	
Secondary aspects (those ranked below the top four)	Description of how your firm can match this aspect in offering a legal service to their clients
5	
6	
7	
8	

Section 1(c)

Analysing your operating environment

Introduction

In sections 1(a) and 1(b) you analysed your firm and the legal services you offer and collated a great deal of information about your firm's income and clients. The aim of this section is to take a wider look at each of your legal services and examine the effect on them of external factors and internal resource factors.

The purpose is to try to identify whether certain internal and external factors have affected your firm's ability to offer legal services in a client-oriented, competitive and cost-efficient manner in the past, i.e. whether your firm is strong or weak. Could those internal and external factors have an effect on your firm's ability to offer legal services in a client-oriented, competitive and cost-efficient manner in the future – do they represent opportunities or threats?

Factors identified are split into two main sections: external factors and internal factors. In any of the sections, if a factor does not seem relevant to a legal service, there is no need to examine it; there may also be factors you feel are affecting your business that are not mentioned, in which case these should be included in the analysis.

Analysing external factors. When you look at the external factors that might affect each legal service you are asked to make broad policy statements about how you might combat identified negative effects or take advantage of potential opportunities.

Analysing internal factors. When looking at the internal factors and how they might affect each legal service, you are asked to identify actions that you need take to improve your firm's resources or approach to using those resources.

These actions then feed into creating an action plan at the end of Part 1.

To draw the maximum information possible from these exercises, it is suggested that not only do you make a judgement yourself on the different aspects, but you also ask your colleagues to do so. This will ensure you capture all of the relevant information for each legal service as your colleagues might have different assessments from yourself.

Identifying factors external to the firm

Understanding the factors external to your firm that affect your ability to offer legal services in a client-oriented, competitive and cost-efficient manner enables you to identify and set objectives and actions to combat any negative effects (threats) or take advantage of any positive effects (opportunities) that these factors create for your firm.

This exercise is split into two phases:

1. You are asked to identify the effect of external factors on this legal service *in general*.
2. You are asked to identify the effect of external factors on *your firm* in particular.

A list of external factors that might affect the different legal services have been identified in the following pages. Using these lists, examine each legal service you offer to which the list applies with regard to the effect you think the different factors on the list will have. Tables 43–5 have been drawn up to lead you through examining each external factor.

Remember – to ensure you collect the maximum and best information it is a good idea to ask your colleagues their views and ask them to fill in these forms.

Checklist 2 Suggested external factors

Commercial

Property

- ☐ The economic climate
- ☐ Interest rates
- ☐ Stamp duty
- ☐ Town planning considerations
- ☐ Competition from other solicitors
- ☐ Licensed conveyancers
- ☐ Changing economic nature of area
- ☐ New office developments
- ☐ Transport – local
- ☐ Transport – national

Other: _____

Other: _____

Finance

- ❑ In-house solicitors
- ❑ The national economy
- ❑ Interest rates
- ❑ Government policy, new legislation
- ❑ Competition from accountants and other advisors
- ❑ Competition from other solicitors
- ❑ Geographic factors
- ❑ Local economic factors

Other: _____

Other: _____

General commercial

- ❑ In-house solicitors
- ❑ The national economy
- ❑ Government policy, new legislation
- ❑ Competition from other agencies such as trade unions and specialist advisors
- ❑ Competition from other solicitors
- ❑ Geographic factors
- ❑ Local economic factors

Other: _____

Other: _____

Specialist commercial

- ❑ Employed solicitors
- ❑ The national economy
- ❑ Government policy, new legislation
- ❑ Competition from other agencies such as environmental auditors and other specialist advisors
- ❑ Competition from other solicitors

- ❏ Geographic factors
- ❏ Local economic factors

Other: _____

Other: _____

Private/legal aid

Residential conveyancing

- ❏ Licensed conveyancers
- ❏ Interest rates
- ❏ Stamp duty
- ❏ Public perceptions
- ❏ Competition from other solicitors
- ❏ Solicitors selling property
- ❏ Estate agents with in-house conveyancing
- ❏ Changing economic nature of area
- ❏ New housing developments
- ❏ Transport – local
- ❏ Transport – national

Other: _____

Other: _____

Crime

- ❏ Competition from other solicitors
- ❏ Changing economic nature of area
- ❏ Government funding of legal aid
- ❏ Competing specialist solicitors

Other: _____

Other: _____

Family

- ❏ Competition from other solicitors
- ❏ Development of ADR
- ❏ Government funding of legal aid
- ❏ Competing specialist solicitors
- ❏ Changes in civil litigation system
- ❏ DIY divorces, separation agreements

Other: _____

Other: _____

Personal injury

- ❏ Government funding of legal aid
- ❏ Introduction of conditional fees
- ❏ Competition from other solicitors
- ❏ PI panel and medical negligence panel
- ❏ Competing specialist solicitors
- ❏ Raised public awareness of opportunities to sue
- ❏ Legal insurance

Other: _____

Other: _____

General private

- ❏ Government funding of legal aid
- ❏ Introduction of conditional fees
- ❏ Competition from other solicitors
- ❏ Competing specialist solicitors
- ❏ Raised public awareness of their rights
- ❏ Increased tendency to sue
- ❏ Legal insurance

Other: _____

Other: _____

Specialist private

- ❑ Government funding of legal aid
- ❑ Government policies
- ❑ Competition from other solicitors
- ❑ Litigation
- ❑ Competition from specialist advisors
- ❑ Competing specialist solicitors
- ❑ National economy

Other: _____

Other: _____

Wills and probate

- ❑ Professional will-writers
- ❑ DIY packs
- ❑ The Internet
- ❑ Banks and other corporate executors
- ❑ Economics of area
- ❑ Litigation
- ❑ Competition from other general solicitors
- ❑ Competing specialist solicitors
- ❑ Public perception
- ❑ Government tax policy

Other: _____

Other: _____

Guidelines for completing Table 43

Column 1: External factors

> From the list of suggestions and your experience, identify which external factors you think have had an impact on this legal service and outline the elements of the factor that have caused an effect.

Column 2: Probable specific effects on market for this service

> In this column you need identify what you think are the probable specific effects from this factor on the market place for this legal service.

Column 3: Opportunity or threat

> In this column you need to decide whether this factor poses an opportunity for solicitors' firms or a threat, when looking at the existing structure of the majority of solicitors' firms.

Column 4: Score

> In this column you need to decide how great a threat or opportunity the factor represents to the majority of solicitors. To measure this you need to give each factor a score out of 10 for whether it represents a neglible threat (1), a great threat (10), an opportunity that is realistic and achievable (10) or an opportunity that is not achievable (1).

Column 5: Action solicitors can take to capitalise on opportunity or negate threat

> This column asks you to make some sort of judgement on what actions solicitors as a whole can take to negate this factor as a threat or capitalise on the opportunity this factor represents.

❑ Fill in **Table 43** on p. 94, copying the table for each legal service you offer.

Table 43 Effects *in general* of external factors on the different legal services your firm offers

Legal service: _____

Column 1	Column 2	Column 3	Column 4	Column 5
External factors	**Probable specific effects on market for this service**	**Opportunity (O) or threat (T)**	**Score out of 10**	**Action solicitors can take to capitalise on opportunity or negate threat**

❏ Please print this table from the disk for each legal service.

Effects of external factors on your firm

Having identified and looked into the effects of different factors on solicitors' firms in general, the next exercise asks you to narrow down that analysis and look into the specific effects those factors will have on *your firm* over the next two years. However, you should also take into account your firm's present standing with regard to those factors.

Table 44 has been set out on p. 98 to help you undertake this analysis. An explanation of the process and corresponding columns is set out below.

How to conduct this analysis

To begin to understand the extent of the effect of this external factor on your firm, you need to look at your firm from two different angles. First of all you need to look back over the previous two years and understand how your firm has acted with regard to this factor (Part A). Next, you need to project forwards and make a judgement about what position your firm will be in as a consequence of the specific effects on the market place you have identified this factor as having over the next two years (Part B).

PART A: LOOKING BACK OVER THE PAST TWO YEARS

Column 1. Outline the factor being examined.

Column 2. To identify the effects over the past two years, ask yourself the following question:

> Q. 'How has this factor impacted on the firm's ability to offer this legal service in a profitable and competitive way?'

> A. Negatively/Positively

If the answer is negatively, your firm is not in a good position with regard to this factor. If the answer is positively, then your firm is in a good position.

Column 3. Now refine this further by pinpointing the specific reason that this factor has impacted on your firm's ability to offer this legal service in either a negative or positive way.

> Q. 'What is the main reason why this factor has impacted upon the firm's ability to offer this legal service over the last two years?'

The answer to this question might be any one of a number of things, such as the way your firm has presented itself in the market place, your resources, the locality, or any other element that has affected the way your firm has offered this legal service over the past two years.

Column 4. You now need to make a judgement as to how your firm has progressed with regard to this factor and whether your firm's performance is at present improving or deteriorating as a consequence of the effect of this factor.

Q. 'How has our ability to offer this legal service changed so as to combat/take advantage of the effects of this factor?

A. Our ability has: Improved/Deteriorated

Column 5. You now need to pinpoint what action(s) or lack of action(s) taken by your firm have caused this improvement or deterioration.

Q. 'Which action(s) or lack of action(s) have contributed to this improvement or deterioration?'

PART B: LOOKING FORWARD TWO YEARS

Column 6. You have already established how you think this factor is likely to affect the local market place. Now you need to make a judgement about how the factor will specifically affect your firm's ability to offer this legal service in a profitable and competitive way over the next two years. You obviously need to take into account your firm's capabilities with regard to its structure and resources.

Q. 'How will this factor specifically affect the firm's ability to offer this legal service over the next two years?'

Your answer may be the same as the overall market effect. Make sure you answer this question in light of your firm's capabilities.

Column 7. You now need look at whether this effect constitutes an opportunity for your firm or poses a threat to your firm.

Q. 'Is this effect likely to threaten our ability to offer this legal service or does it represent opportunities which we will be able to take advantage of?'

Column 8. Having established this, you need to understand how great a threat it poses or how achievable an opportunity it represents. You can do this by giving this factor a score out of 10. A score of 1 is a negligible threat or non-achievable opportunity and 10 is a serious threat or very achievable opportunity.

Column 9. The final question is to establish what your firm's approach, with regards this factor, might be in the future.

Q. 'What approach can we take to combat any negative effects from this factor, or take advantage and build upon any positive effects?'

Actions you might take to negate a threat or take advantage of an opportunity

To help you identify approaches you might take, some suggestions are given below. The level of your approach will depend upon the seriousness of the threat or opportunity presented by the external factor.

The approaches identified are broad policy statements of approaches you might take. You may identify a number of different approaches for each legal service and factor, i.e. that you invest in promoting and streamline the way in which you offer this service.

As you go through it is helpful to rank each factor according to the seriousness of the threat or opportunity, i.e. the highest scoring threat or opportunity should be ranked first (whichever scores higher).

Actions to combat negative effects or threats

- Invest in promoting this legal service to build the client base.
- Reduce prices and work to increase the number of clients.
- Focus investment towards another legal service with good prospects of growth and away from this area.
- Streamline the way in which you offer this service.
- Re-package this legal service in line with market trends.

Actions to take advantage of positive effects or opportunities

- Invest in promoting this legal service.
- Invest in positioning the firm as an authority in this area.
- Promote against competitors.
- Package the legal service to take advantage of strong aspects.
- Bring in greater manpower to expand firm's capacity.

> ❏ Fill in **Tables 44 and 45** on pp. 98 and 99 printing the forms for each legal service. In Table 45 include the approaches you might take in descending order of importance.

Table 44 *Specific* effects felt by your firm from a particular external factor

Legal service: _____

Column 1	Column 2	Column 3	Column 4	Column 5	Column 6	Column 7	Column 8	Column 9
Factor	Impact of this factor on firm over past two years (positive/ negative)	Specific reason why factor has impacted in this way	Has firm improved or deteriorated in response to effect?	Action(s) or lack of action taken by your firm contributing to improvement or deterioration	How will factor specifically affect firm's ability to offer service over the next two years?	Opportunity or threat? What are these?	Score	Actions to combat negative effects of take advantage of positive effects

☐ Print this table from the disk for each legal service.

Table 45 Approaches you might take to combat negative effects or take advantage of positive effects from external factors

Legal service: _____

Description of approaches you might take (Table 44, Column 9)	Score taken from Table 44, Column 8 showing whether serious threat or opportunity

□ Print this table from the disk for each legal service.

Identifying factors internal to your firm

Having taken a look at your firm and its standing with regard to different factors active in the market place, the following exercise takes you further into the analysis process by looking at the strengths, weaknesses, opportunities and threats of factors internal to your firm which have an impact on the different legal services you provide.

As with external factors, the object of this exercise is to establish how the different internal factors affect your ability to offer legal services in a client-oriented, competitive and cost-effective way.

An internal factor, for the purpose of this exercise, is a resource over which you have some control, such as technology, staff or skills.

When analysing the different internal factors, a time-frame needs to be imposed. To see whether a factor represents a strength or weakness in the firm, look at the past two years building to the present; when looking at the opportunity or threat a factor might pose, look at the present and then project that forward two years.

To draw the maximum information possible from this exercise, it is suggested that not only do you make a judgement yourself on the different aspects, but you also ask your colleagues to do so. This will make sure sure you capture all of the relevant information for each legal service as your colleagues might have different experiences to yourself.

A list of internal factors you might like to examine with regard to the legal services your firm offers has been sent out on pp. 100–102.

Checklist 3 Suggested internal factors

Technology

This refers to the technological resources available to solicitors' firms which might be utilised in the supply of this legal service either as an internal system or as a client facing system.

- ❏ Word-processing software
- ❏ Specific precedents software
- ❏ Computers
- ❏ Time-recording systems
- ❏ Client database system
- ❏ Client contact system
- ❏ The Internet
- ❏ Information sharing/management

Other: _____

Other: _____

Fee earners' skills

This refers to the skills mix required by fee earners working within each legal service your firm offers.

- ❏ Management skills
- ❏ Client care skills
- ❏ Administrative skills

❏ Planning skills

❏ Market knowledge

❏ Computer literacy

❏ Sales ability

❏ Marketing ability

Other: _____

Other: _____

Management time and systems

This refers to the management time available to undertake planning and analysis and look at the broader aspect of each service to ensure proper control is being imposed upon the supply to clients of each legal service. It also includes areas such as reporting methods.

❏ Planning time

❏ Analysis time

❏ People management time

❏ Training time

❏ Marketing implementation time

Other: _____

Other: _____

Administration staff skills

This refers to the capabilities of administration staff and their ability to contribute to the servicing of clients and processing of administrative matters.

❏ Computer literacy

❏ Familiarity with the firm's systems

❏ Ability to work under own direction

❏ Understanding of work being done

❏ Ability to take repetitive tasks away from fee earners

❏ Ability to relate to clients over the telephone

❏ Ability to work with all fee earners in the firm

Other: _____

Other: _____

keting systems

This refers to the client information systems and client communication systems in place to encourage business growth such as cross-selling, newsletters, promotional activities.

- ❏ Systems to exploit cross-selling opportunities
- ❏ Targeted client newsletters
- ❏ Targeted promotions to gain new clients
- ❏ Targeted promotions to expand business from existing clients
- ❏ Targeted promotions to encourage referral business
- ❏ Promotions targeted at connector organisations
- ❏ Public relations exercises
- ❏ Promotions aimed at passers-by to encourage them to drop in
- ❏ Promotions targeted at raising the firm's profile
- ❏ Promotions aimed at encouraging client loyalty and maintaining contact with clients
- ❏ Investment in marketing activities

Other: _____

Other: _____

Client care systems

This refers to the systems required or the approach needed to enable and ensure a consistent level of client care such as standardised letters, quotations, updates and information dissemination.

- ❏ Telephone manner
- ❏ Quotations
- ❏ Update letters
- ❏ Electronic communications
- ❏ Prompt service targets
- ❏ Specific updates on changes in the law that might affect specific clients, i.e. a change in death duties being explained in a letter to all those whose wills you have written or hold
- ❏ Information telephone lines
- ❏ Client friendly complaints systems
- ❏ Research into clients' needs

Other: _____

Other: _____

Strengths and weaknesses

Using the relevant internal factors from this list you now need to identify whether your firm is currently in a position of strength or weakness with regard to these factors.

Before beginning this exercise it is important to identify exactly how to decide whether your firm is in a position of strength or weakness.

When evaluating whether your firm is strong or weak you need look back over the past two years to the present.

The 'ideal solicitors firm'

One way to achieve an understanding of whether your firm is strong or weak with regard to a factor, is to measure your firm's performance against the performance of an 'ideal solicitors' firm'.

The 'ideal solicitors' firm' is a solicitors' firm offering the same legal services as your firm, of the same size and location as your firm and running at full capacity with regard to income, that has unlimited resources and the most up-to-date approach to the market place and the internal factor in question. It is the way your firm would offer a legal service in an 'ideal' world.

How might this internal factor impact on the 'ideal solicitors' firm'?

There are a number of questions you need to ask yourself about each internal factor. First, it is necessary to understand how this factor has affected solicitors' abilities generally, i.e. the 'ideal solicitors' firm', with regard to offering this legal service. Next, it is a good idea to establish how your firm has reacted or acted over the past two years to the present with regard to this factor when offering legal services to clients.

Guidelines for completing Table 46

Column 2. Ask yourself the question below to understand how the 'ideal solicitors' firm' might have utilised this internal factor:

'How has this factor impacted upon this legal service and the way in which the 'ideal solicitors' firm' is able to offer the service in a client-oriented, competitive and cost-efficient way over the past two years?'

Column 3. How has your firm acted with regard to this factor? You now need to view this factor from the standpoint of whether your firm has kept abreast of any changes and been able to utilise this factor properly so as to offer legal services to clients in a client-oriented, competitive and cost-efficient way. When asking yourself the following question you need compare your firm to the 'ideal' firm.

> 'How has our firm over the last two years reacted, compared with the way in which the 'ideal solicitors' firm' would have reacted, to exploit this factor to offer legal services to clients in the optimum client-oriented, competitive and profitable way?'

Are you weak or strong with regard to this factor?

Having examined the latter two questions, you now need to set a level of how well you have compared to the 'ideal solicitors' firm' with regard to this factor. You need to compare your firm's achievement against that of the ideal firm and give yourself a score as to how close you have come to the 'ideal solicitors' firm' (10) or how far from that ideal you are (1) (**Column 4**). If you feel you have scored 8 or over, this is a strength, but if you have scored below this, it is a weakness (**Column 5**).

❏ Fill in **Table 46**.

Table 46 Is your firm strong or weak with regard to internal factors?

Legal service: _____

Column 1	Column 2	Column 3	Column 4	Column 5
Internal factor	How has factor affected way in which the 'ideal solicitors' firm' is able to offer a client-oriented, competitive and profitable service over the past two years?	How has your firm reacted to this factor over the past two years?	How does your firm compare with the 'ideal solicitors' firm'?	Is your firm strong or weak?

❑ Print this table from the disk for each legal service. Give a score out of 10 in columns 2–5 for each internal factor.

Opportunities and threats

After establishing where your firm stands in comparison to the 'ideal solicitors' firm' with regard to different internal factors, this exercise aims to establish whether these factors represent opportunities or threats to your firm's ability to offer legal services to your clients in a client-oriented, competitive and cost-effective way in the future.

For the majority of strengths and weaknesses you identify there are likely to be corresponding opportunities and threats. To identify strengths and weaknesses, you looked back over the past two years to the present. With opportunities and threats, you need to project those factors forwards and determine whether they do, or might, constitute a threat to your existing business or an opportunity to increase that business.

Table 47 has been set out for you to use to establish whether a factor represents an opportunity or a threat. In doing this it is first of all helpful to return to the 'ideal solicitors' firm' and view it from their standpoint. Again, there are questions that you can ask yourself to identify whether a factor is an opportunity or threat.

Guidelines for completing Table 47

Column 2. Ask yourself the following question:

'Over the next two years, will the 'ideal solicitors' firm' benefit from increasing investment in this area and will it improve their ability to offer legal services in a client-oriented, competitive and cost-effective way?'

If the answer to this question is 'yes', then this factor represents an opportunity for solicitors. If the answer is 'no', then you need to ask the question below to understand whether this factor could represent a threat.

'Over the next two years, if the 'ideal solicitors' firm' does not increase investment in this area, will it become unable to offer legal services in a client-oriented, competitive and cost-effective way in the market place?'

If the answer is 'yes' to the above question, then this factor could pose a threat to your firm's ability to offer this legal service to clients in the future.

Column 3. What are the opportunities or threats? Having established whether this factor represents an opportunity or threat for the 'ideal solicitors' firm' you now need to identify what these opportunities or threats are for them.

Ask yourself the following questions:

'What opportunities might arise in the future from this factor for the 'ideal solicitors' firm'?'

'What threats are likely to arise that might affect the 'ideal solicitors' firm' in the future?'

❏ Fill in **Table 47** below.

Table 47 Do internal factors represent opportunities or pose threats to the 'ideal solicitors' firm' in the future?

Legal service: _____

Column 1	Column 2	Column 3	
Internal factor	**Does this factor represent a threat or opportunity for the 'ideal solicitors' firm'?**	**What are the opportunities and threats?** **O = opportunity T = threat**	
		O	
		T	
		O	
		T	
		O	
		T	
		O	
		T	

❏ Print this table from the disk for each legal service.

Understanding whether internal factors represent opportunities or threats for your firm in the future (Table 48)

Having worked through the effect of the factor on the 'ideal solicitors' firm', you now need apply those factors to your firm taking into account the firm's capabilities and situation. The threats and opportunities may be the same, more serious or less serious due to the firm's standing.

Column 2. To understand whether an internal factor represents a threat or opportunity to your firm in the future you need to ask yourself the following questions:

'Are there any opportunities arising from this factor we will be able to take advantage of?'

'Are there any threats arising from this factor that will affect our business?'

Column 3. You now need to identify those opportunities and threats.

'What are the opportunities represented that we are in a position to be able to take advantage of?'

'What are the threats posed that will directly affect our firm?'

You then input these into Table 48.

Column 4. Measuring the intensity of that threat or opportunity on your firm. After identifying whether the different factors will affect solicitors and how they will do so, you now need to measure the intensity of the effect on your firm. This can be done by scoring them. It is suggested that you give each threat or opportunity a score out of 10, with 10 being a serious threat or excellent opportunity, and 1 being either a negligible threat or negligible opportunity because you judge that they will either have very little effect on you or because you are unlikely to be able to take advantage of the opportunity.

Remember: when looking at the threats and opportunities, you need to project forwards over the next two years.

❏ Fill in **Table 48**, on p. 109.

Table 48 Do internal factors represent opportunities or pose threats to *your firm* in the future?

Legal service: _____

Column 1	Column 2	Column 3	Column 4
Internal factor	**Does this factor represent a threat or opportunity for your firm?**	**What are the opportunities and threats?** **O = opportunity T = threat**	**What level of threat or opportunity does it represent? (score out of 10)**

❏ Print this form from the disk for each legal service.

Actions to bring your firm closer to the 'ideal solicitors' firm' and help negate threats or enable you to take advantage of opportunities

> You have identified the internal factors and how they have affected the market place and your firm and what the future effects from them are likely to be. You now need to identify what actions you might take within each legal service to begin to move your firm closer to the 'ideal solicitors' firm' and help negate threats or take advantage of opportunities.

> To do this look through the suggested actions (pp. 110–20) and outline those you think would help in Tables 49 and 50.

> Against each, it is suggested that you identify the level of threat or opportunity it is meeting which will help identify the priorities of the actions.

Checklist 4 Actions to strengthen a weak area, build on a strong area, negate a threat or take advantage of an opportunity

❏ Please photocopy or print these pages from the disk for each legal service.

Legal service: _____

On the following pages each internal factor identified in this section has a statement next to it in italics outlining the reason for improving that factor. The actions listed under these objective statements suggest activities that could be used to introduce or improve that factor in the firm. You may have other ideas about what to include.

As can be expected with internal factors, the actions suggested are internal to the firm and include planning, research, communication and investment actions.

Planning (P): This indicates that planning is one of the key elements of this action.

Research (SR) or (CR): This might be researching staff views (SR) or client research (CR).

Consultation (IC) or (EC): This might involve consulting within (IC) or external to (EC) the firm.

Investment (TI) or (FI): This might involve time investment (TI) or financial investment (FI).

Technology

This refers to the technological resources available to solicitors' firms which might be utilised in the supply of this legal service either as an internal system or as client facing system.

Planning (P), Staff Research (SR) or Client Research (CR), Internal Consultation (IC) or External Consultation (EC), Time Investment (TI) or Financial Investment (FI)

Internal factor	Suggested actions
Word processing software	*Improve software to ensure maximum efficiency* Upgrade software (FI) Ensure best use is being made of existing software (SR) + (EC)
Specific precedents software	*Utilise precedents where they will improve and streamline the service we are offering clients* Send out an internal request for information on software that might be of use (SR) Purchase appropriate software and training (FI) Share information amongst fee earners (IC) + (TI)
Computers	*Make computers available to all those who need them to efficiently service clients' needs* Employ a consultant to review existing arrangements and recommend changes (EC) Ask staff for their views and requirements (SR) Draw up a plan of computer requirements to be implemented over a period of time (P) + (TI)
Time-recording systems	*Ensure full use is being made of the system and investigate the full scope of system* Analyse current use and potential of the system (IC) + (EC)
Client database system	*Understand more about the clients of this legal service* Examine existing systems and review their capability and the information already held or that would be required (IC) + (EC) Research the different databases available and their compatibility with existing systems (IC) + (EC) Bring in consultant to check compatibility of systems and to assess your firm's requirements (FI) + (EC)
Client contact	*Present the firm in a consistent and professional manner to clients* Review use of, or create templates for, different letter or communication requirements (IC) + (P) + (TI) + (SR)
The Internet	*Identify ways in which the Internet can help the firm better understand and communicate with clients* Review how having web pages might help your firm; are they required? ask for staff views (SR) + (IC) + (TI) Invite a design and support company to come and outline what is entailed and how a web site can help (EC)

Other:

Other:

Fee earners' skills

This refers to the skills mix required of fee earners working within each legal service your firm offers.

> Planning (P), Staff Research (SR) or Client Research (CR), Internal Consultation (IC) or External Consultation (EC), Time Investment (TI) or Financial Investment (FI)

Internal factor	*Suggested actions*
Management skills	*Increase the management skills of individual fee earners to help improve the service to clients*
	Review fee earners' management experience (IC)
	Research fee earners' views of their own capabilities (SR)
	Outline needs (P)
	Research training courses (TI)
	Send fee earners on training courses (IC) + (FI) + (TI)
Client care skills	*Focus fee earners on the need for client care and improve their skills to enable them to do this*
	Research fee earners' attitudes to client care (SR) + (IC) + (TI)
	Review fee earners' approach to client care (P) + (TI)
	Undertake client research to measure fee earners' success at client care (CR) + (FI) + (TI)
	Outline needs (P)
	Research training options (EC) + (SR)
	Train fee earners (FI)
Administrative skills	*Improve fee earners' administrative skills to help improve the service to clients*
	Review fee earners' administrative skills (SR) + (IC)
	Research fee earners' views of their own capabilities (SR)
	Outline needs (P)
	Arrange for internal fee earners training where required (FI)
Planning skills	*Make this legal service more proactive to meeting client needs by increasing the amount of planning undertaken by all fee earners*
	Review fee earners' planning experience (SR) + (IC)
	Research fee earners' views of their own capabilities (SR)
	Review reporting structure (IC)
	Outline needs (P)
	Introduce reporting and planning structure (IC) + (P) + (TI)

Market knowledge

Increase the level of market knowledge fee earners have so that they can more closely meet clients' requirements

Ask fee earners about their market knowledge (SR) + (IC)

Set up feedback system so that any changes or events can be fed quickly back to the management (P) + (IC)

Set up a bi-annual or other reporting structure (P) + (TI) + (IC)

Computer literacy

Ensure computers are used to their full potential

Ask fee earners about their competency with the different systems (SR)

Organise training for those who require it (FI)

Sales ability

Become more proactive in converting enquiries into clients

Ask fee earners how confident they feel about converting enquiries into clients where opportunities arise (SR) + (IC)

Identify sales hooks and supply fee earners with prompt sheets outlining the firm's experience and benefits of using the firm (CR) + (TI)

Research and undertake training where required (P) + (FI)

Other:

Other:

Management time and systems

This refers to the management time available to undertake planning and anlysis and look at the broader aspect of each service to ensure the proper control is being imposed upon the supply to clients of each legal service. It also includes areas such as reporting methods.

Planning (P), Staff Research (SR) or Client Research (CR), Internal Consultation (IC) or External Consultation (EC), Time Investment (TI) or Financial Investment (FI)

Internal factor

Suggested actions

Planning time

Make better use of planning time and formalise it to integrate it into the management of the firm on a regular basis

Review planning requirements (IC)

Review frequency of reviews (IC) + (P)

Set annual planning structure (P) + (IC)

Allocate planning time and functions to individuals (IC) + (P)

Analysis time

Keep up to date with developments in this legal service on a regular basis

Identify information required (IC)

Identify information gathering methods (IC) + (P)

Allocate time to carry out (P)

People management time

Utilise management time to greater effect

Identify management functions and time required (IC) + (P)

Identify reporting structures (IC) + (P)

Allocate appropriate time (P)

Training time

Undertake to ensure that everyone is appropriately trained for the needs of their job

Identify management training needs (IC) + (P)

Allocate time (P) + (TI)

Marketing implementation time

Improve marketing activity effectiveness by formalising the time to be spent

Identify marketing needs (P) + (IC)

Identify the cost in money and time of the marketing activity (P)

Allocate individuals to undertake marketing actions (IC) + (P)

Set up marketing activity reporting structure (P) + (TI)

Other:

Other:

Administration staff skills

This refers to the capabilities of administration staff and their ability to contribute to the servicing of clients and processing of administrative matters.

Planning (P), Staff Research (SR) or Client Research (CR), Internal Consultation (IC) or External Consultation (EC), Time Investment (TI) or Financial Investment (FI)

Internal factor	*Suggested actions*
Computer literacy	*Ensure computers are used to their full potential*
	Send out internal questionnaire about systems to evaluate literacy (SR) + (TI)
	Research cost- and time-effective training options (EC) + (TI)
	Undertake training (FI)
Familiarity with firms' systems	*Ensure everyone utilises the firm's systems to their greatest benefit*
	Have each fee earner evaluate administrative staff's familiarity with the firm's systems (SR) + (IC)
	Undertake training where required (FI)
Ability to work under own initiative	*Increase the productivity of each member of the team and their contribution to bringing in revenue*
	Identify opportunities where this might be of use, with fee earners (IC)
	Ask staff for their evaluation of their own abilities (SR) + (IC) Undertake training (FI)
Understanding of work being done	*Increase the productivity of each member of the team and their contribution to bringing in revenue*
	Ask staff to evaluate their understanding of work being undertaken (SR)
	Ask fee earners for their evaluation of staff's understanding (IC)
	Identify ways in which staff can improve their understanding (IC)
Ability to take repetitive tasks away from fee earners	*Increase the productivity of each member of the team and their contribution to bringing in revenue*
	Research with different fee earners opportunities to do this (SR) + (IC)
	Discuss with administrative staff and outline competency requirements and responsibility levels, and organise admin staff and fee earner work modes and set parameters (IC) + (SR) + (P)

Ability to discuss matters over the telephone	*Improve communications with clients*
	Identify opportunities where this might be of use, with fee earners (SR) + (TI)
	Ask staff for their evaluation of their own abilities (SR) + (IC)
	Undertake training (FI)
Ability to work with all fee-earners in the firm	*Improve commumications within the firm*
	Undertake staff research to identify whether communications are good or not (CR) + (FI) + (TI)
	Identify key staff and encourage them to communicate (SR) + (CR)
	Undertake training where required (FI)
	Put in place tools to keep staff informed, i.e. bulletin board, e-mail updates, staff briefings (P) + (TI)

Other:

Marketing systems

This refers to the client information systems and client communication systems in place to encourage business growth, such as cross-selling, newsletters, promotional activities.

> Planning (P), Staff Research (SR) or Client Research (CR), Internal Consultation (IC) or External Consultation (EC), Time Investment (TI) or Financial Investment (FI)

Internal factor	*Suggested actions*
Systems to exploit cross-selling opportunities	*Use the client base for each legal service as prospective clients for others*
	Identify cross-selling opportunities and numbers (IC)
	Identify method of approaching clients, i.e. letter, telephone call, and time-frame and cost implications (CR) + (IC)
	Set up systems to ensure implemented (P) + (TI)
	Set up reporting and evaluation system (P) + (TI)
	Implement (TI)
Targeted client newsletters	*Promote to increase client loyalty*
	Ask clients whether they would like to receive a newsletter (CR)
	Identify client groups to whom newsletter should be sent (CR)
	Undertake cost analysis of newsletter and establish frequency and format (P) + (IC)
	Research staff views on having a newsletter (SR)

Set up systems to implement the newsletter (P) + (IC)

Set up system to research and evaluate the contents and effect of the newsletter (CR) + (TI) + (FI)

Targeted promotions to gain new clients

Expand the existing client base

Research optimum ability of existing structure for providing a legal service, i.e. how many more clients are required or can be coped with (IC) + (P)

Identify desirable clients (CR) + (IC)

Identify best method of approaching these prospective clients (CR) + (IC)

Identify method of evaluating promotion and reporting structure (P) + (TI)

Undertake promotions (FI) + (TI)

Targeted promotions to expand business from existing clients

Utilise the client base to expand the firm's fee income

Identify opportunities and numbers (CR) + (IC)

Identify method of approaching clients, i.e. letter, brochure/leaflet/advert, telephone call, etc. and time-frame and cost implications (CR) + (EC)

Set up systems to track and implement promotions (P) + (TI)

Set up reporting and evaluation system (TI)

Implement (FI)

Targeted promotions to encourage referral business

Utilise the client base to bring in new clients

Identify clients to target promotion to (CR) + (IC)

Identify method of approaching clients i.e. letter, brochure/leaflet/advert, telephone call, etc. and time-frame and cost implications (CR) + (IC)

Set up systems to ensure implemented (P) + (TI)

Set up reporting and evaluation system (P) + (TI)

Implement (FI) + (TI)

Promotions targeted at connector organisations

Increase the number of connector organisations we work with and expand the work we receive from existing ones

Identify organisations at which to target promotion (CR) + (IC)

Identify method of approaching them, i.e. letter, telephone call, visit, and time-frame and cost implications (CR) + (IC)

Set up systems to ensure implemented (P) + (TI)

Set up reporting and evaluation system (P) + (TI)

Implement (FI) + (TI)

Public relations exercises	*Create and ensure we take advantage of all public relations opportunities*
	Identify methods, i.e. events, newspapers etc. (P) + (TI) + (IC)
	Identify messages/aim of exercise (IC) + (CR)
	Identify cost implications (P) + (TI)
	Identify implementation structure (P)
	Set evaluation criteria and timeframe (P)
	Implement (FI) + (TI)
Promotions aimed at passers-by to encourage them to drop in	*Bring in more business from passers-by*
	Identify opportunities (CR) + (IC)
	Identify approach (CR) + (IC)
	Research cost implications (P)
	Set evaluation criteria (P)
	Implement (FI) + (TI)
Promotions targeted at raising the firm's profile	*Raise the firm's profile*
	Identify messages to put across (CR) + (IC)
	Identify methods (CR) + (EC) + (IC)
	Research cost implications (P)
	Set evaluation criteria (P)
	Implement (FI) + (TI)
Promotions aimed at encouraging client loyalty and maintaining contact with clients	*Maintain existing clients*
	Identify clients who would benefit from such attention (CR) + (P)
	Put together an ongoing communication plan (P) + (TI)
	Put into action (FI) + (TI)
Investment in marketing activities	*Plan our marketing spend to ensure we achieve the greatest return*
	Collate total marketing spend and/or allocated budget (P)
	Research historical return on investment (P) + (TI)
	Target all promotions to cover costs and make profit, i.e. treat marketing investment as a profit centre (P)
	Ensure appropriate reporting structures and budget control in place (P) + (TI)

Other:

Other:

Client care systems

This refers to the systems required or the approach needed to enable and ensure a consistent level of client care such as standardised letters, quotations, updates and information dissemination.

Planning (P), Staff Research (SR) or Client Research (CR), Internal Consultation (IC) or External Consultation (EC), Time Investment (TI) or Financial Investment (FI)

Internal factor	*Suggested actions*
Telephone manner	*Improve the quality of telephone contacts with clients*
	Undertake client research to identify whether the overall approach is good or not (CR) + (IC)
	Identify key reminders and collate prompt sheets (CR) + (TI)
	Undertake training where required (FI)
Quotations	*Improve our client communications at the start of any work to help bring clients to the firm*
	Identify charging methods for each legal service (IC)
	Formulate a format for quotations (P) + (IC)
	Undertake cost analysis of sending out quotations (P)
	Set up templates to be used (TI)
Update letters	*Improve the service clients feel they are receiving*
	Identify requirement and frequency for each legal service (CR)
	Ask clients when and what they would like to see (CR)
	Set up system to trigger letters to be sent (P) + (TI)
	Outline format of letters and information that needs to be included (IC) + (CR)
	Undertake cost analysis (P)
Prompt service targets	*Improve the service clients feel they are receiving from us*
	Identify average time taken for each transaction (IC) + (P)
	After consultation with fee earners, set targets of time per transaction (IC) + (P)
Updating clients about changes in the law that affect them	*Increase client contact to promote client loyalty where possible*
	Identify numbers of clients to whom this would be of benefit (CR) + (IC)
	Identify method to be used (CR) + (IC)
	Undertake cost analysis (P)
	Outline format of updates (P) + (IC)

Information telephone lines	*Introduce new client-oriented services*
	Identify areas in which it could be used (CR) + (IC)
	Identify viability and cost and manpower implications (P) + (EC)
	Plan how lines should be introduced or promoted (P) + (IC)
	Set out evaluation structure (P)
	Undertake pilot test of telephone lines (P) + (TI)
Client-friendly complaints systems	*Improve the service clients feel they are receiving from us*
	Identify existing system and compliance with Rule 15 (IC)
	Research existing client satisfaction with system (CR) + (IC)
	Identify where system might be automated (SR) + (IC)
	Set up evaluation structure (P) + (TI)
	Communicate systems to all fee earners (IC) + (TI)
Research into clients' needs	*Become more client-oriented*
	Identify client groups and research requirements (CR) + (IC)
	Identify methods that might be used and cost implications (IC)
	Undertake research (CR) + (FI)

Other:

Other:

Assessing opportunities and threats (Tables 49 and 50)

> **Column 1.** Identify factor.
>
> **Column 2.** Give score as shown in column 4, Table 48.
>
> **Column 3.** Identify actions to be undertaken.
>
> **Column 4.** Using column 2, identify the order of the actions with the greatest threat or opportunity being the first ranked priority and then in descending order to the least threat or least achievable opportunity.

❑ Fill in the columns in **Tables 49 and 50** as shown for each legal service then fill in **Tables 51 and 52** for each legal service.

Table 49 *Opportunities* from internal factors and actions you might take to bring your firm closer to the 'ideal solicitors' firm' and take advantage of those opportunities

Legal service: _____

Column 1	Column 2	Column 3	Column 4
Internal factor	Score (from Table 48, Column 4)	Action you might take to bring your firm closer to the 'ideal solicitors' firm' and take advantage of opportunities	Level of opportunity (rank 1–10)

Note: See list set out on pp. 110–20 for actions you might take in Column 3.

❑ Print this table from the disk for each legal service.

Table 50 *Threats* from internal factors and actions you might take to bring your firm closer to the 'ideal solicitors' firm' and negate those threats

Legal service: _____

Column 1	Column 2	Column 3	Column 4
Internal factor	Score (see Table 48, Column 4)	Action you might take to bring your firm closer to the 'ideal solicitors' firm' and negate any threats	Level of threat (rank 1–10)

Note: See list set out on pp. 110–20 for actions you might take in Column 3.

❏ Print this table from the disk for each legal service.

Table 51 Actions prioritised according to the level of *opportunity* they represent

Legal service: _____

	Internal factor	Actions to be taken	Type Planning (P) Research (SR) or (CR) Consultation (IC) or (EC) Investment (TI) or (FI)	Level of opportunity ranked 1–10 (from Table 49, Column 4)
1				
2				
3				
4				
5				
6				
7				
8				
9				
10				
11				
12				

Note: Under 'type' of action, use the following codings: P = planning, SR = staff research,
CR = client research, IC = internal consultation, EC = external consultation, TI = time investment,
FI = financial investment

> ❏ Please print this table from the disk for each legal service and to enable
> each value factor to be filled in.

Table 52 Actions prioritised according to the level of *threat* they represent

Legal service: _____

	Internal factor	Actions to be taken	Type Planning (P) Research (SR) or (CR) Consultation (IC) or (EC) Investment (TI) or (FI)	Level of threat ranked 1–10 (from Table 51, Column 4)
1				
2				
3				
4				
5				
6				
7				
8				
9				
10				
11				
12				

❑ Please print this table from the disk for each legal service and to enable each value factor to be filled in.

Section 1(d)

Analysing your competitors

The previous exercises have focused on your perceptions of what your clients are likely to want and an objective view of how your firm meets those needs.

In section (d) the emphasis is on your competitors: who they are, where they are and how they approach the market place.

As a useful exercise to start off with, simply list in Table 53 all of the firms or organisations that you feel compete with yours, noting their geographical location in relation to your firm.

This might include an organisation other than another law firm, e.g. licensed conveyancers, who could be seen to be in competition if they have any effect on your potential market.

How to research your competitors

If you are unsure about your competitors and their approach to the market place the following provide good sources of information about them.

Yellow Pages

These will prove a good place for you to start by counting all the companies in your area that provide services in competition with yours. Simply make a list of them together with their address and telephone details.

The Law Society's Directory of Solicitors and Barristers

This gives information about solicitors' firms in different areas, indicates their size, and lists the legal services they provide.

Contact your competitors

If you do not hold any information about your competitors, a good way of finding out more is to get hold of their firm's brochure (if they have one). Telephone and ask for one (you may prefer to hint that you are a potential client and ask them to post any information to your home) or visit their offices and pick up a brochure with details of the services they offer. You could send another member of the firm on a fact-finding mission.

Knowledge within your firm

In all likelihood, other fee earners in your firm will know something about those who compete with them for legal services. It is a good idea to pass the tables in this section to all fee earners and ask them to fill in what they know.

Once you have this information, which should be updated on a regular basis to keep tabs on your competitors, you are in a position to assess how your competitors approach their market place. Indeed, the very fact that they do not have a brochure or one that is badly produced will give you an initial feel for their approach, as will the speed with which they send you their materials and their manner on the telephone.

❏ Complete **Table 53** on p. 127.

Table 53 Your competitors and their geographical location in relation to your firm

Name of firm	Legal services in which the firm competes with yourselves	Location of the competing firms (local/provincial/national)

Key
Local   – indicates a firm being based within a one-mile radius.
Provincial – indicates a firm not operating nationally and based over one mile away.
National   – indicates a firm that is part of a national organisation or a very large firm operating nationally.

Having listed your immediate competitors, the following exercises will guide you through identifying further details about their nature. Many of your answers are likely to be instinctive or educated guesses.

Circulate copies of Tables 54–8 and completed copies of Table 53 to other fee earners to check and complete for the legal services they work within.

Gauging how active your competitors are in gaining business

For the purpose of this exercise your competitors can be classified as either 'aggressive', 'active' or 'passive'. The parameters for these classifications are set out below.

Aggressive: This would indicate that the competitors are undercutting on price to attract greater numbers of new clients, their philosophy being to take a loss in the short term but build their client base and future work. This might be having the effect of forcing you to drive your prices down in order to remain competitive.

Another way in which a competitor might be aggressive is by establishing strong relationships with sources of work such as 'connector' organisations, which will reduce your opportunities to gain work in those areas.

Active: This indicates that your competitors are competitive and have a proactive approach to their market place. This might involve them using promotional tools such as newsletters, brochures, seminars and advertising.

Passive: This indicates that your competitors are not actively working to increase their client base but existing on work that 'walks through the door'. They might be seen by yourselves as perhaps vulnerable to attack or even merger.

Table 54 also asks you to indicate whether your competitors are local, provincial or national. Please use the outline of these classifications on the previous page.

❏ Complete **Table 54** on p. 129.

Table 54 Approaches and location of competing firms

Legal service: _____

Name of competing firm	Aggressive	Active	Passive	Local	Provincial	National
TOTAL						

❑ Please print this table from the disk for each legal service.

Pigeonholing your competitors

This exercise simply asks you to summarise in one descriptive sentence each of your competitors. The purpose of this exercise is to 'pigeonhole' or neatly categorise your competitors.

The descriptive phrase that first springs to your mind to describe your competitors is usually the most useful phrase and is the one that your colleagues are likely to think of as well, because it will be obvious.

Example

XQZ Solicitors: 'a large and successful firm with an extremely strong commercial property practice and good contacts in the local business community'.

❏ Complete **Table 55** below. To ensure you have the correct view you should hand these forms to your colleagues to see whether their perceptions of your competitors differ.

Table 55 Pigeonholing your competitors

Name of competitor	Descriptive sentence

Assessing different aspects of your competitors' services

You were asked in Tables 26–36 to assess the factors your clients value from a law firm when purchasing legal services, and how your firm objectively presents itself with regard to those factors. In Table 41 you looked at how connector clients present their services to clients.

Using those same factors, the aim of Table 56 is to assess how your competitors perform in the market place with regard to these factors.

At the beginning of this section (p. 126), it was suggested that you obtain copies of your competitors' brochures to find out how they present themselves to the market place. These brochures will enable you to understand, to some degree, how these firms present themselves with regard to the different value factors set out in Table 56. You can also check their web sites for this information.

> ❑ Copy **Table 56** on pp. 132–3 and pass it to other fee earners for them to complete for the legal services they work within. Start by identifying whether an aspect is present in each competitor's approach along the whole column. If it is, rate its importance according to the weight that factor is given from the information you have. Number the factors according to the number of aspects identified as being present ('1' is the least important, '8' out of eight aspects is the top of the scale).

Table 56 Identifying the way in which your competitors present competing legal services with regard to value factors

Legal service: _____

Aspect of the service they present to their clients	Name of competitor: _____		Name of competitor: _____		Name of competitor: _____	
	Is this aspect identified in their client information? ✔ ✗	How important is this aspect? (Rating)	Is this aspect identified in their client information? ✔ ✗	How important is this aspect? (Rating)	Is this aspect identified in their client information? ✔ ✗	How important is this aspect? (Rating)
Do they promote the convenience of their offices or ease of reaching their offices?						
Do they promote the benefits of being a large organisation?						
Do they promote the benefits of being a small organisation?						
Is the way in which they present themselves high quality?						
Do they present their local knowledge as a benefit?						
Do they promote their reputation?						
Do they use testimonials to recommend themselves?						
Do they promote the friendliness and approachability of their staff?						
Do they promote the fact they have specialist knowledge?						
Do they promote their organisation's experience? For example, 'established for over x years'						

Note: Rate all aspects of their organisation, staff or service according to the number of aspects identified, i.e. on a scale '1–8' if eight aspects are identified, with '1' the least important.

❏ Please print this table from the disk for each legal service.

Table 56 *Continued*

Legal service: _____

Aspect of the service they present to their clients	Name of competitor: _____		Name of competitor: _____		Name of competitor: _____	
	Is this aspect identified in their client information? ✔ ✗	How important is this aspect? (Rating)	Is this aspect identified in their client information? ✔ ✗	How important is this aspect? (Rating)	Is this aspect identified in their client information? ✔ ✗	How important is this aspect? (Rating)
Do they promote their staff's experience?						
Ease of contact – do they promote 24-hour contact open seven days a week, web site for service, etc.?						
Do they package their service as a one-price item?						
Do they promote a quotation or estimating service?						
Do they promote or identify how clients will be kept up to date with the service?						
Do they promote the way in which they price their service?						
Do they promote the fact their service is value for money?						
Do they offer any guarantees or warranties?						
Do they clearly explain the service they offer?						
Do they promote speed as an aspect of their service?						
Other:						

❏ Please print this table from the disk for each legal service.

Identifying how you can combat or improve upon your competitors' approach to their clients

Having analysed your competitors' approach to their clients and the qualities they highlight, you need to identify how you can match or improve on their approach. In Table 56, you were asked to rate aspects according to their importance in your competitors' approach to their clients. Using those ratings, list the top four aspects for each competing organisation in Table 57 and next to it identify how your firm can improve/combat that approach.

> ❏ Complete **Table 57** below. Copy this table for each competitor.

Table 57 Identifying ways your firm can combat/improve on competing organisations' approach to their clients

Name of competitor: _____

Legal service(s) that could be threatened by their approach: _____

_____

Top-ranked four aspects of competitors' approach	Description of how your firm can combat/improve upon this approach
1	
2	
3	
4	
Secondary aspects (those ranked below the top four)	**Description of how your firm can combat/improve upon this approach**
5	
6	
7	
8	

Section 1(e)

Setting objectives and creating an action plan

After analysing your firm, clients, market place and competitors, you need to compile, from the information you have gathered, a list of actions and objectives for your firm over the next 12–36 months.

This section aims to guide you through doing this. There are two steps to the process:

- identifying and setting objectives;
- setting actions to achieve those objectives.

Identifying and setting objectives

What are objectives?

Objectives are the broad goals you set for your firm. They are statements of your intention to change, improve, grow, redirect or reduce a service you offer.

You can set objectives according to the main areas you have already analysed. Read back through the tables to give you a background and feel for realistic and worthwhile objectives. In some of the sections you have checklists of possible actions you can take for each legal service. Read through these lists before setting your objectives as they will help you identify what you might want to do.

The tables referred to above that might be particularly helpful are Tables 32–3, 38, 42, 45, 51–2 and 57.

The following are possible headings to put objectives under for each legal service:

1. Income and profitability
2. Your clients
   - Client types
   - Client lifespans/activity levels

- Alignment of your firm with clients' priorities/expectations
- Connector clients

3. External factors and internal factors
4. Competitors

For example you might set the following list of objectives for conveyancing:

1. Increase fee income.
   Streamline the service, reduce costs and increase profitability.
2. Reduce number of ST clients by selling and promoting other services to them.
   Contact all passive clients to encourage client loyalty.
   Change service to more closely meet clients' requirements and promote changes.
   Increase number of connector clients.
3. Become more market-reactive.
   Pre-empt market trends and promote to take advantage of those trends if appropriate.
   Increase knowledge of market through market and client research.
   Undertake full management review.
   Research staff capabilities.
   Increase staff training.
4. Pitch service to combat competitive organisations and actively promote the service you offer.

Long-term and short-term objectives

After identifiying objectives for your firm you now need to put them in a time-frame. There are two types of objectives: long-term objectives which are objectives which take longer than 12 months to achieve, and short-term objectives which are achievable within 12 months. For the purpose of this exercise it is suggested that long-term objectives are achievable in three years (12–36 months) and short-term objectives achievable in 12 months.

Short-term objectives might support long-term objectives or might stand alone.

> ❏ List the different objectives you want to set for a legal service, in **Table 58** on p. 137. It is important that you set yourselves realistic time periods in which to achieve the objectives you are aiming for.

Table 58 Objectives for each legal service

Legal service: _____

	Description of objective	Time-frame 0–12 or 12–36 months
1		
2		
3		
4		
5		
6		
7		
8		
9		
10		
11		
12		
13		
14		
15		

❏ Please print this table from the disk for each legal service.

Actions to meet those objectives

Having identified the objectives for each legal service, under each one you need to identify the actions that you might take to meet those objectives and set a deadline by which you plan to have achieved those actions. The deadline should be within the time-frame set to achieve the objective the actions support.

It is important that you set yourself realistic deadlines for these actions. You need to take into account the other work you are undertaking and the other actions you are proposing.

Table 59 on p. 139 enables you to collate those action points under the appropriate objectives and to set a deadline to them.

Again Tables 32–3, 38, 42, 45, 51–2 and 57 will prove valuable as you have already identified actions on them.

The action points identified will probably include those intended to bring your firm closer to your clients' requirements (internal, communication and promotion, p. 72), those which take advantage of any opportunities or negate threats with regard to external factors (p. 97), and those suggested by your analysis of internal factors (planning, research, consultation, investment, pp. 110–24).

This is the stage where you bring together the action required with the objectives identified in Table 58. Each objective may require a simple action point or a number of different approaches over a period of time, i.e. undertake client research; work to increase connector clients; change the message in your brochures; send out a specific mail shot; introduce a newsletter, seminar or surgery; make use of public relations.

It is useful to look at what is required to achieve each objective from three angles: internal, communication and promotional, as outlined below.

Internal requirements

You may need to put together a working group, ask someone to carry out further analysis, carry out internal staff research, create standard templates, or redecorate your reception area.

Communication requirements

What and how do you need to communicate with your clients and/or staff to achieve the objective identified? For example, to give your clients certain information you could review your firm's brochures, leaflets or web site. You could also examine the way in which you present a particular service and incorporate appropriate messages and information in any promotional materials you produce, or perhaps focus on an issue in a newsletter (if you produce one).

Promotion requirements

To achieve an objective, do you need to undertake promotion? You could invest in promotion to increase the number of clients and encourage referrals. You could also repackage and promote an existing service or change the image of the firm and promote that change.

Part 3 of this manual gives you an outline of different promotional approaches and when it is best to use them.

❑ Copy Tables 59–61 on the following pages according to the number of objectives you identified, and complete for each legal service.

Table 59 Actions required to meet the identified objective for each legal service

Legal service: _____

Objective		Time-frame 0–36 months
Actions		

Objective		Time-frame 0–36 months
Actions		

Objective		Time-frame 0–36 months
Actions		

Objective		Time-frame 0–36 months
Actions		

❏ Please print this table from the disk according to the number of objectives you identify for each legal service.

Table 60 Short-term objectives and action points

Legal service: _____

Objective		Time-frame 0–12 months

Objective		Time-frame 0–12 months
Actions		

Objective		Time-frame 0–12 months
Actions		

Objective		Time-frame 0–12 months
Actions		

❏ Please print this table from the disk according to the number of objectives you identify for each legal service.

Table 61 Long-term objectives and action points

Legal service: _____

Objective		
Actions		

Objective		**Deadline** 12–36 months
Actions		

Objective		**Deadline** 12–36 months
Actions		

Objective		**Deadline** 12–36 months
Actions		

> ❏ Please print this table from the disk according to the number of objectives you identify for each legal service.

The action plan

Now you have identified the objectives for your firm and the actions you wish to take to meet those objectives. Before you begin work on those action points you need to set them into a working plan or production timetable.

The action plan is where you take those action points and identify the processes required to carry out those actions against deadlines, e.g. if you wish to undertake a direct mail promotion in May, you will need to initiate the work on it in March to ensure that it is posted in May. If you wish to introduce standard letters, you will need investigate which to standardise beforehand and give yourself enough time to research and collate those standard letters.

For further information about how to implement different marketing initiatives please see the promotional section of this manual.

Planning your actions

Transfer the actions identified in Tables 59–61 onto the Action Plan in Table 62 under the months in which you wish to initiate those actions and indicate when those actions are to take place.

Please be sure to spread the work so that you are not overloaded at one time.

❑ Complete Table 62 on p. 143.

Table 62 *Action plan* [for 12-month period]

Legal service: _____

	January Month No.:	February Month No.:	March Month No.:
Short-term objectives			
Actions			
Long-term objectives			
Actions			

	April Month No.:	May Month No.:	June Month No.:
Short-term objectives			
Actions			
Long-term objectives			
Actions			

(*Continued overleaf*)

Table 62 *Continued*

	July Month No.:	August Month No.:	September Month No.:
Short-term objectives			
Actions			
Long-term objectives			
Actions			

	October Month No.:	November Month No.:	December Month No.:
Short-term objectives			
Actions			
Long-term objectives			
Actions			

❏ Please print this table from the disk for each legal service.

Section 1(f)

Collating your marketing report

Introduction

This is the final section in Part 1 'Marketing planning' and it is here that you will pull together much of the information that you have collated in the tables, to form a coherent report on your firm and each of the different legal services your firm offers.

As you will see, the beginning of the report focuses on the firm as whole and then moves quickly to each specific legal service, using the following figures:

- legal services offered and fee income: **Tables 1 and 2**;
- numbers and activity levels of clients: **Tables 1, 4 and 5**;
- fee income/hours taken per client type: **Tables 7, 13, 20 and 22**;
- analysis of clients' characteristics. **Tables 23-25**,
- outline of clients' priorities/requirements against your firm's performance: **Tables 26, 27, 37 and 38**;
- information on connector clients: **Tables 39, 40 and 42**;
- external factors and their effect on your firm: **Tables 44–46**;
- analysis of the firm's internal resources and performance: **Tables 46–48, 51 and 52**;
- competitor analysis: **Tables 45, 55 and 57**;
- objectives and action plan: **Tables 60–62**.

All the information you have collated in the preceding sections are put together with narrative in a report that you can use as a basis for future marketing activity.

Part 2 of this manual outlines ways in which you can research information you have had to estimate until now, and the final part sets out different promotional approaches and what they can achieve.

Putting your report(s) together

One way of pulling the report together is to use the example as a script that you could dictate and arrange to have typed up. Alternatively you could use the file on the disk and fill in the blanks by pasting in information from the tables where indicated.

Example marketing report

Introduction

[*Name of firm*] was established in [*date*]. There are [*number*] partners and [*number*] fee earners at this time.

The firm offers clients the following legal services:

[*List legal services the firm offers, as indicated in Table 1.*]

The financial year runs from [*give dates*] and during the 12 months from [*month, year*] to [*month, year*], the total fee income was [*? see Table 2*]. This breaks down between the different legal services in the following way:

Legal service	Percentage of firm's fees for the 12-month period	Fee income – £
[*Table 3*]		

The purpose of this report is to analyse the different legal services offered by [*name of firm*] as separate products.

Each of the legal services [*name of firm*] offers has been assessed and information gathered on the different aspects as listed below:

1. Where the fee income is generated.
2. The numbers and activity levels of clients.
3. The types of client who purchase this legal service and income from each type.
4. A study of the average hours taken to service each client type.
5. An analysis of clients' characteristics.
6. Different clients' priorities/requirements and a comparison of the firm's performance against these.
7. An analysis of 'connector clients' for this legal service.
8. An analysis of the effects that external factors might have on the firm's ability to offer this legal service followed by conclusions on how the firm might combat any negative effects or take advantage of any opportunities.
9. An analysis of the firm's internal resources and how these affect this legal service.
10. An analysis of actions that might be undertaken to improve the firm's performance with regards to internal factors.
11. An analysis of competitors to the firm for this legal service.

The purpose of these analyses has been to gather enough information and draw conclusions that feed in to setting short- and long-term objectives for each legal service and the actions to achieve them.

In the following pages the different legal services have been analysed separately.

A marketing analysis and plan for [Legal service]
Date: [day, month, year]

This report has been created after working through *Marketing Your Law Firm: A Solicitor's Manual*. In the absence of client research experience, estimates and assumptions have been used.

The aim of this report is to promote understanding of the value of this legal service to the firm and provide an analysis of [*xyz*] legal service that can be used for planning purposes and to help us improve the way in which we offer this service to the market place.

Further information can be found in the full tables used in the analysis which have been put into Appendix 1.

Our firm

[*Name of*] firm has been offering [*xyz*] service to clients for [*number*] years. At present the department has [*number*] fee earners and is supported by [*number*] administrative staff.

[*Give a description of service offered to clients.*]

The income in this area over the last three years has steadily [declined/seen a sharp down turn/remained steady/grown]. [*Base this on fee income figures over the last three years if available.*]

Over the last 12 months this legal service has bought in £ [*see Table 1*] which is equivalent to [*X*]% [*see Table 2, column 2*] of the firm's overall fee income. The service is [loss-making/break-even/profitable/very profitable]. [*See Table 2.*]

Our clients

The client base for this service is [*number – see Table 1*]. We have analysed the client base in a number of different ways:

1. We have split clients according to their lifespans and activity levels to identify whether there are any particular buying patterns for this legal service [*see Table 4*].

Passive clients:	[*number*]
Single transaction clients:	[*number*]
Active clients:	[*number*]

This indicates that we have the following scope for action with regard to these clients:

(a) To sell other services to the ST clients. [*List possible other services.*]
(b) To sell other services to passive clients. [*List possible services.*]
(c) To encourage ST and active clients to refer the firm.

2. We also split the client base according to whether clients are private, legal aid or commercial. The split was as follows [*see Table 5*]:

Private clients:	[*number*]
Legal aid clients:	[*number*]
Commercial or business clients:	[*number*]

The income generated from these clients and their call on the firm's time can be seen below:

	Fee income	Average income per client per 12-month period	Average hours
Private clients	[*Table 7*]	[*Table 13*]	[*Table 20*]
Legal aid clients	[*Table 7*]	[*Table 13*]	[*Table 20*]
Business or commercial clients	[*Table 7*]	[*Table 13*]	[*Table 20*]

This shows that [*type*] clients are the most valuable over a 12-month period. In addition we worked out an average hourly charge for the different client types. These were:

	Average hourly charge
Private clients	[*Table 22*]
Legal aid clients	[*Table 22*]
Business or commercial clients	[*Table 22*]

This indicates that [*type*] clients are the highest yielding clients as they show the highest average fees per hour.

Characteristics and needs of our clients

An initial analysis of our clients revealed that the majority of individual clients show the following characteristics:

[*Insert Tables 23–5 with totals for client characteristics*]

This has identified that we have a predominance of [*gender, age, social group, locality*] as clients for this firm.

We then looked more closely at clients having certain characteristics to try to arrive at a conclusion as to whether they have differing priorities, needs or expectations from us.

Needs, priorities and expectations

We looked at the expectations of passive, active and ST clients [*Table 26*].
We looked at the expectations of different client types [*Table 27*].

After looking at our clients' needs we turned our focus to the firm and identified how we think the firm performs with regard to those value factors. Having established some judgement on this we compared our performance with what we perceived to be our clients' needs and found that the firm was weak in some areas and strong in others, as shown in the lists below.

Strong   **Weak**

[*List strong and weak factors from Table 37.*]

These are the areas we propose should be investigated through research as soon as is practicably possible.

However, there are a number of actions we can take to improve the firm's performance where it is weak and to build upon strong areas. These actions fall into three categories: internal action, communication action and promotional action. The table below indicates which actions it is proposed we take immediately and the time-frame for putting them into place.

Value factor   **Action**   **Category of action**   **Priority**

[*Insert action list and priority order from Table 38.*]

Connector clients

In addition to individual clients and commercial clients, we identified connector clients. These are organisations who pass, or could pass, clients to us. They were identified as the following.

Names of connector clients   **Type of organisation**   **Pigeonhole description**
[*Tables 39 and 40*]

From research we conducted into the approach of connector clients to their market place, we have established our best approach to them for referrals. We have done this by identifying how we can tailor our service, or the way we present our service, so that it has resonance with the way they approach their clients, as seen in the list below.

[*List connector clients, and top four aspects of service and ways to match our service to theirs, from Table 42.*]

Our environment

External factors affecting legal service

To understand the pressures on us when offering [*name*] legal service, we looked at some of the factors outside this firm that have an impact on our ability to offer this legal service.

The factors we examined were:

[*List factors analysed from Table 46.*]

Each factor was analysed with regard to its past/present effect on the market place and our firm's performance. We then looked at the effect that each factor might have on the firm's ability to offer our clients this legal service in the future. Finally, we identified actions we might take to combat the negative effects or realise the opportunities offered by this factor.

[*Factor*]

[*Effect on the firm over the last two years, from Table 44, Part 1*]

[*Effect on the firm over the last two years, from Table 44, Part 2*]

[*Actions that could be taken to combat negative effects or take advantage of opportunities, from Table 45.*]

Internal factors affecting the way we offer this legal service

We carried out a review of a number of internal factors (over which we have some control), to establish how our firm stands with regard to these factors at present, and to see whether they will have an effect in the future.

[List factors, from Table 46, column 1]
[Effect on solicitors over the past two years, from Table 46, Column 2]
[Whether our firm is strong or weak, from Table 46, Column 5]
[Opportunities or threats from factors, from Table 47]

Having identified the possible effects from these internal factors, we looked at actions that we might take to improve the firm's performance with regard to each of them. These actions took the form of planning (P); research (SR) or (CR); consultation (IC) or (EC); or investment (TI) or (FI).

ACTIONS TO TAKE ADVANTAGE OF OPPORTUNITIES

Internal factor [Table 51]	Opportunity identified	Action identified	Type of action

ACTIONS TO NEGATE THREATS IDENTIFIED

Internal factor [Table 52]	Threat identified	Action identified	Type of action

Competitor analysis

An initial analysis identified the following organisations as competing with us for clients:

[List competitors and give descriptive phrase from Table 55.]

We conducted further research into the way that these competitors approach the market place and found the following:

Name of competitor [Table 54]	How active they are in getting clients

Further research revealed that these competitors use the following sales messages to approach their market place and we also identified how we could best combat their approach:

Name of competitor	Top four aspects	Our approach to combat competitors

[*Table 57*]

Objectives and action plan

All of the information we examined led us to formulate the following objectives and action plan.

[*Insert Tables 60–62.*]

Part 2

Market and client research

Section 2(a)

Approaching a research project

Research is one of the most valuable tools you can use when making management decisions. Researching your market, your clients and those who are not your clients can give you valuable information on which to base future activity and decisions.

Your market place

There are two main approaches to this research: analysing trends in the overall market for legal services, and analysing the characteristics and any trends in your client catchment area – your local market place.

Researching the trends in the overall markets for legal services

The Law Society publishes an Annual Statistical Report that can give a valuable insight into the present and future market trends for different legal services. Other sources of information are legal journals, including the Law Society's *Gazette*.

Researching your local market place

In addition to general trend information, it is useful to research your local area and analyse its characteristics. Much of this can be done from behind a desk by collating figures for the different services available in your locality. The list below suggests a number of different sources that you can use to give you top line numbers and a starting point to find further information:

■ Yellow Pages;
■ Business Pages;
■ Thomson Local;
■ local newspapers;
■ local authority publications.

You can get an idea of the levels of relevant activity in your local area by collating information about business sectors that connect or compete with your firm. For example, the numbers of local estate agents, financial advisers, competing solicitors and surveyors will give you an indication of the demand for their services in your locality, which should then link in with the demand for relevant legal services in the area. Reviewing and comparing these figures annually will enable you to build a picture of areas of increasing or decreasing activity. This information can then be translated to your business plans. For example, if the number of estate agents doubles in your area, you might forecast an upturn in conveyancing and act accordingly to fulfil this expected increase in demand.

In Part 1, section 1(c), Tables 43–5 guide you through the process of analysing the effect of different external factors on your firm.

Having identified organisations in your market, or that connect to and affect your market, a useful and informative exercise is to telephone them and request a leaflet or brochure about the services they offer. The information in these brochures and leaflets will give you an insight into the approach of these organisations to clients. This information will enable you to position your firm and legal services to complement and match their approach. Where they are competing with solicitors' firms, knowing how they approach the market will help you position your firm to combat them.

Researching potential and existing clients

Research into your existing client base can give you vital information about your clients, the services you offer and how your firm is viewed.

You can use a number of different methods to research your clients, including postal questionnaires, telephone research, focus groups and one-to-one interviews.

The method you use will depend on what you want to learn from the exercise, the resources you have available, the number you want to contact and the complexity of the research. These factors will also indicate whether you should employ a research agency or whether it may prove possible to carry out the research in-house.

A research exercise can be extremely sophisticated, or relatively simple. The aim of Part 2 is to provide you with an overall understanding of the research process and enough pre-prepared material to allow you to conduct your own postal research in-house with a measure of competency and accuracy.

Why postal research?

This method of research is the simplest to carry out in-house. It is an extremely effective way of gathering information and will frequently work out the least expensive. Other methods of research are also discussed, but not in as much detail, and this manual does not provide pre-prepared questionnaires for other methods.

Conducting research

How do you, as a non-research professional, go about deciding how, when and why research should be conducted?

The first thing you need to determine is what you want to learn and how research will help you. The following list identifies different reasons for carrying out research and some of the questions that research can answer.

- **To understand what your clients are looking for in a particular service.** You might want to look at the way in which you offer a particular legal service. Is the service you offer what your clients need, want or expect?

- **To find out what your clients think of you as a service provider.** What do clients think of the firm and the service you offer? Do they think your firm is expensive or inexpensive, well presented or not well presented, client-oriented or profit-oriented?

- **To look into the impression the members of staff are making on the clients.** How did your clients find the approach of the solicitor who carried out their work for them? What did they think of the secretarial and reception staff when in contact with your firm?

- **To find out what your clients know about you and the services you offer.** Are your clients aware of the different legal services your firm offers? Do they know about and have a need for these legal services?

- **To find out why your clients use you.** Why do your clients choose to use your firm for a legal service? What were the factors that encouraged them to use you? Where and how did they first hear of you?

- **To find out why your clients do not use you for all legal services.** Do clients have a legal requirement that is met by another firm? Why are clients not using your firm for this legal service?

- **To measure how important the different aspects of client care are to your clients.** Is client care important to your clients? What do they want? Do your clients recognise the client care you offer? How do they rate and value that client care?

- **As a means of advertising your firm.** Are clients aware of the services your firm offers and do they need them? By asking questions, i.e. 'Did you know that we offer the following …', you are advertising that you do offer those services.

- **As a means of finding the correct medium for advertising your firm.** Do clients notice advertisements? Have they noticed your advertisements? Would your advertisements influence their choice of solicitor? What sort of advertising would be most likely to persuade them to choose a solicitors' firm?

- **As a client care exercise.** Were clients happy with the service you provided? Are there any other services they would like to see? What changes would they make?

- **To look into new services.** Would your clients be interested in using a particular service? What would they expect from such a service? Have they heard of particular firms or organisations offering this service and and have they used them?

- **To look into the importance of existing service capability to your clients.** Do your clients feel it is important that you are able to provide a particular service?

- **To look into your pricing methods.** Do your clients perceive the service you offer as expensive, cheap or value for money? Does price have a great effect on their decision to use a particular firm for this service or not?

- **As an information verification exercise.** You might wish to verify or increase your knowledge of statistics about your clients. Do they own their own company? Are they home owners? How much do your clients earn? Do they have children? How old are they?

- **To reassure your clients and encourage client loyalty.** Researching clients' views on a topic or event, especially where there has been adverse publicity about solicitors, or a new law is passed that might affect your clients in some way, can help you gauge whether you need to take action to reassure or provide information to your clients. The act of asking your clients and confronting an issue can also have the effect of encouraging client loyalty by demonstrating you are in touch with your clients and their needs.

- **To be reassured.** You might have a fall-off in a legal service, and while you may be aware that the market is dictating this, you might want to make sure that this is the only reason.

- **To understand your competitors.** You may want to look at your clients' and non-clients' awareness and perception of your competitors in the area.

- **To understand how you measure against your competitors.** You might want to know how the services you offer measure up against those your competitors offer.

Many of the reasons for carrying out research identified in this list are not mutually exclusive of each other, and you will frequently find that you can incorporate several into a single research exercise.

However, you should be aware that research can create a 'Catch 22' situation, i.e. you may find that having more information about your clients and market place raises further questions and a need for more or further refined information. In addition, the nature of the research may raise expectations in clients' minds that you will not be able to meet, or it might prompt clients to ask unwanted questions about your firm and services.

Before undertaking research

Before conducting research, it is important that you have a clear and strong motivation for doing so, and you should be aware that:

- If you are undertaking research among your existing clients then you must be careful that you don't overburden them with unnecessary requests for information.
- Undertaking research is a resource-consuming process – do you have the human resources and time to allocate to this exercise?
- If you do choose to use an external research agency, it can prove expensive – what value does this research have for you? How will you use it?
- You must bear in mind that the way in which any questionnaire, telephone call or panel meeting is conducted is an advertisement for your firm.
- Those you ask will, in all likelihood, be able to determine your reasons for undertaking the research from the questions asked and information required. Do you want to draw attention to this topic with clients?

If, after bearing these factors in mind, you feel that the research you propose is appropriate, the next step is to look at how you should approach the research exercise.

Approaching a research project

If you intend to carry out the research in-house, you will find the following process useful when planning your research project.

1. Begin by outlining exactly what you want to achieve from the research project.
2. Identify who can supply the information you want.
3. Decide how the research is to be conducted.
4. Set out and agree the questions.
5. Produce your questionnaire.
6. Analyse the responses.
7. Draw conclusions from the results and prepare a report discussing them.

Outline exactly what you wish to achieve from the research project

A clear statement of what you want to know and why you want to know this information is the starting point of any research project.

In the Part 1, Marketing Planning, you were asked to make assumptions to your knowledge and that of your colleagues about your clients' values and your firm's standing. If you are basing decisions about the future of your business on these exercises and assumptions, it is advisable to carry out client research to verify your assumptions first.

One of the functions of research, apart from finding out new information, is to verify a theory or prove an assumption.

Identify who can supply the information you want

The reasons for undertaking the research will, in most cases, indicate to whom you need to send the questionnaires. For example, if your research is to investigate whether you should offer a new legal service, it would make sense to conduct research among those who are most likely to need or want that legal service.

Having identified your target group, if you cannot create a list or identify their characteristics from your database, you might send the questionnaire to a cross-section of your clients, but include verification questions on the questionnaire to allow you to differentiate your target audience from other respondents.

Identifying who the respondents are is important when assessing the results of a research project. For example, the response from 24–40-year-olds might not be the same as the response of 40–60-year-olds. Therefore, you need to be aware of their age to ensure you use the results of the research in the correct manner and do not use information from the younger respondents to set your strategy for approaching an older group.

The amount of information you can use to identify and define your target group will vary according to how much detail you hold about your clients on your database. In all likelihood, however, those who you ask will have some common values, i.e. they will have all used your firm for conveyancing, and will have only used your firm once. The greater number of common values you require the target audience to have, the more complex the research and the more specific the use of the information yielded, i.e. if you are researching customer satisfaction for a particular service, it would make sense to ask clients who have received that service from your firm. This is straightforward; however, it becomes more complex if you then sub-divide those persons according to their age, when they last used your firm, how much they spent, and so on.

When deciding who your research should target, the following questions are a good way of checking that your choice of recipients is sensible. Begin by listing those that you feel it would be useful to contact, then ask yourself the following questions:

'Will responses from these respondents give me useful and relevant information?'

'Can I identify this group and obtain their details?'

'Can I translate these respondents' answers into useful action?'

If the answer is 'yes' to these questions, then the likelihood is that they would be the appropriate audience for the research.

Decide how the research is to be conducted

Having identified what it is you want to find out from the research and who is able to supply the information to do this, you need to decide which research method to use and whether you can carry out the research in-house or whether it is more appropriate for a third party to carry out the research on your behalf.

The method you choose will vary according to the level of detail, the type of information you want, who you want to question, and the resources such as personnel and money you have available.

Research methods

A summary of each of the three main methods you might use to conduct your research, together with their pros and cons, have been identified below. The three methods are:

- postal research;
- telephone interviews;
- focus group interviews or one-to-one interviews.

Postal research

This is where a questionnaire is posted to a target audience. This type of questionnaire might also be inserted into local newspapers or magazines.

For:

- Economical to carry out as it can be done in-house (mostly).
- Can be used to reach and measure the response of a broad number of people.
- Is the least intrusive to the respondent.
- May be a one-stage process.

Against:

- The answers are, the majority of the time, formularised, forcing respondents into boxes.
- Those who choose to respond will be those most interested and you may miss a level of response from the disinterested.
- It is easy for people not to respond.
- You need to send the questionnaire to a large enough selection of potential respondents so that you have a chance of receiving enough responses to make the results representative and meaningful.

Telephone interviews

Where the questions are asked of the target audience over the telephone.

For:

- As long as your target audience can be contacted, this is a quick way of getting a response to your questionnaire.
- You can continue until you have achieved the correct number of responses.
- It is easy to review and adjust the questionnaire to adapt to the responses you receive in order to obtain the information required.
- Greater control over those who respond by asking them qualifying questions before completing the questionnaire.

Against:

- Can prove expensive as frequently an agency will be required to carry out the telephone calls.
- Can be seen as intrusive by respondents.
- Fewer questions can be asked and they should be shorter and less detailed.
- If you are using an agency, a third party is speaking to your clients and you have less control over the situation.
- This is a specialist area, and it is more appropriate to employ an agency than for some other forms of research which therefore has cost implications.

Focus groups

This is where groups of six to eight members of the target audience discuss and answer questions about the subject being researched.

For:

- You can gain a first-hand impression and response to your questions.
- You can ask in-depth questions.
- You can control the members of the group by inviting those who meet the required criteria.
- Your results will be three-dimensional as the interviewer will be able to measure a number of different responses to questions.

Against:

- Depending on the information being asked for, i.e. if you are asking the group to criticise or discuss the firm in some detail, it is advisable to use a third-party skilled interviewer as attendees are likely to be more honest in their answers.

However, where you are seeking the group's views on a potential service or idea, you can conduct the groups in-house. It can prove expensive to employ a skilled interviewer.

- Whoever is interviewing the group may have a personal bias which could influence respondents or the way in which responses are heard.
- You need to be very subject-specific and focus on one particular area in depth.
- They can be difficult and time-consuming to organise.

One-to-one interviews

This is where individual clients or past clients are interviewed to determine their views.

For:

- You can gain an immediate impression and response.
- The interviewer may ask in-depth questions.
- Your results will be three-dimensional as the interviewer will be able to measure a number of different responses to questions.

Against:

- You are only receiving the views of one person.
- The respondent is likely to be a willing or enthusiastic participant to have consented to the interview, and therefore the responses may not be representative of your whole client base.
- Depending on the information being asked for, i.e. if you are asking the individual to criticise or discuss the firm in detail, it is advisable to use a third-party skilled interviewer as that way the interviewee is likely to be more honest in his/her answers. However, where you are seeking an individual's views on a potential service or idea, you can conduct the interview yourself. It can prove expensive to employ a skilled interviewer.
- The interviewer may have a personal bias which could influence respondents.
- They can be difficult and time-consuming to organise.

None of these methods is necessarily exclusive of any other, and a research plan over the course of a year may use a mixture of methods to look at the different aspects of the service(s) on offer.

Example

Firm *XYZ* might have the following research programme:

- Short evaluation questionnaires to be sent to clients after the completion of their matter, i.e. after each conveyancing transaction. These questionnaires would simply ask for general details about the service received.
- A more detailed questionnaire sent to a cross-section of clients once a year to measure the overall impression clients have of the firm and the service provided.
- A focus group held to discuss a particular service, i.e. a group to discuss what clients might expect from their solicitor with regards to a conveyancing transaction.
- A telephone survey to find out the profile of the firm and its competitors.

The above example demonstrates how different methods of research might be used to obtain different information.

Which research method should you use?

The two methods that lend themselves most readily to carrying out research in-house are postal questionnaires and focus groups or one-to-one interviews.

It is often possible to answer your question(s) using one or a number of different research methods. As a basic guide, the reasons why you might undertake research (as listed on pp. 157–8) have been set out with the appropriate methods for conducting research identified below them.

KEY TO THE SYMBOLS

Under each question, symbols have been inserted to denote the most appropriate research method.

✉	postal research,
☎	telephone research,
☺☺	discussion groups
☺	one-to-one interviews.

✓✓ denotes appropriate method
✓ against the symbol denotes appropriate but not ideal approach
✗ not appropriate.

1. To understand what your clients are looking for in a particular service.
   📋 = ✓✓   ☎ = ✓   😊😊 = ✓✓   😊 = ✓✓

2. To find out what your clients think of you as a service provider.
   📋 = ✓✓   ☎ = ✗   😊😊 = ✓   😊 = ✓

3. To look into the impression the members of staff are making on the clients.
   📋 = ✓✓   ☎ = ✗   😊😊 = ✗   😊 = ✓

4. To find out what your clients know about you and the services you offer.
   📋 = ✓✓   ☎ = ✓   😊😊 = ✓   😊 = ✓

5. To find out why your clients use you.
   📋 = ✓✓   ☎ = ✗   😊😊 = ✗   😊 = ✗

6. To find out why your clients are not using your firm.
   📋 = ✓✓   ☎ = ✗   😊😊 = ✗   😊 = ✗

7. To measure how important the different aspects of client care are to your clients.
   📋 = ✓✓   ☎ = ✓   😊😊 = ✓   😊 = ✓

8. As a means of advertising your firm.
   📋 = ✓✓   ☎ = ✗   😊😊 = ✗   😊 = ✗

9. As a means of finding the correct medium for advertising your firm.
   📋 = ✗   ☎ = ✓   😊😊 = ✓✓   😊 = ✗

10. As a client care exercise.
   📋 = ✓✓   ☎ = ✗   😊😊 = ✗   😊 = ✓

11. To look into new services.
   📋 = ✓✓   ☎ = ✓   😊😊 = ✓✓   😊 = ✓

12. To look into the importance of existing service capability to your clients.
   📋 = ✓✓   ☎ = ✗   😊😊 = ✓   😊 = ✓

13. To look into your pricing methods.
   📋 = ✓✓   ☎ = ✓   😊😊 = ✗   😊 = ✗

14. As an information verification exercise.
   📋 = ✓✓   ☎ = ✓✓   😊😊 = ✗   😊 = ✗

15. To reassure your clients and encourage client loyalty.
   📋 = ✓✓   ☎ = ✓   😊😊 = ✗   😊 = ✗

16. To be reassured.
   📋 = ✓✓   ☎ = ✓✓   😊😊 = ✗   😊 = ✗

17. To understand your competitors.
   📋 = ✓✓   ☎ = ✓✓   😊😊 = ✓   😊 = ✗

18. To understand how you compare with your competitors.
   📋 = ✓✓   ☎ = ✓✓   😊😊 = ✗   😊 = ✗

If you want to obtain the answers to a number of questions in the same exercise, care should be taken as they may not mix well. Thus, the same research method might not be appropriate for all of them and you may need to conduct a second exercise.

In-house vs. research agency

It is recommended that a research agency is used when carrying out some types of research as set out below:

Box 6 When to use an outside agency to conduct research

Research method	Third party/agency	In-house
Postal research	✗	✓
Telephone research	✓	✗
Focus groups	✓✗	✓✗
One-to-one interviews	✗	✓

Key
✓ = Recommended.
✗ = Not necessary to involve a third party/agency or not advised to be carried out in-house.
✓✗ = Could be carried out depending on the subject, complexity or size of the research project and in-house resources available.

The following factors will also affect whether you carry out the research in-house or employ an agency.

YOUR RESOURCES

What resources do you have available for the research project? Can you afford to employ an agency? Is there anyone in the firm who can take charge of carrying out the research in-house and do they have the time and understanding to do so?

On this latter point, it is a worthwhile investment to send someone on a basic re-search training course – preferably a member of the firm with the time and inclin-ation to undertake a research project afterwards. This will be less expensive than using an agency for this or most other research projects. In addition, this manual provides you with sufficient information to undertake your own postal research.

HOW BIG IS YOUR TARGET AUDIENCE?

If there are thousands in your audience, it might make sense to employ an agency to send out the questionnaires and analyse the responses. However, you can get around this by splitting your research into manageable chunks, i.e. send out 200 questionnaires a fortnight over 10 weeks. In this way, the workload can be shared across your in-house resources.

WHAT DO YOU WANT TO ASK THE TARGET AUDIENCE?

The nature of the questions you want to put to the target audience might lend themselves to a particular research method.

In addition, and in some instances to get an objective view, it might be better if the research is carried out by a third party. For example, where you are carrying out in-house staff research, to gain the staff's trust and encourage honest answers it would make sense for a third party to carry out the research keeping names confidential. If you wanted to try to establish how your firm and your competitors compare or who has heard of you, by not identifying your firm as the organisation carrying out the research, you will get a more objective response.

WHAT CONTACT INFORMATION DO YOU HOLD ON THE TARGET AUDIENCE?

If you do not have telephone numbers it might not be possible to carry out telephone research. If you cannot identify the target audience on your database, you would waste too much time trying to identify them on the telephone, and a postal questionnaire including verification questions may thus prove more cost-efficient.

Box 7 Recommended research methods according to the target audience

Availability of respondents	Research method			
	Postal questionnaire	Telephone questionnaire	Focus groups	One-to-one interviews
Existing clients only	✓	✗	✓	✓
Non-clients only (those who have never, as far as you are aware, been clients of your firm)	✓	✓	✓✗	✗
Past clients (i.e. over three years since they have used your firm)	✓	✓	✓✗	✗
Mix of existing and non-clients	✓	✓✗	✓✗	✗
Local residents	✓ (inserted in local papers/magazines or distributed by Post Office to postcode areas)	✓ (telephone numbers obtained from list brokers or telephone books)	✗	✗

Key
✓ = This is a good method to use.
✗ = Not a particularly good method.
✓✗ = Can be used, but may be difficult to set up or for the target audience to be identified.

Numbers and quotas

It is useful here to discuss the numbers that should be used in different research projects.

In brief, the number of respondents contacted will depend on the way in which you plan to conduct the research.

There are no absolute numbers that must be contacted to give you a credible result. The guide below suggests how to identify the numbers of respondents that would be appropriate.

Postal questionnaires

These should be sent to a sufficient number so that the response you achieve is high enough to give you a representative number of your client base. It is important that the number of answers you analyse is enough to give you an indication of the majority opinion, i.e. there is no point in relocating your premises in the opinion of 10 clients when you have a client base of 500; however, if you get a 100 per cent positive response from 10 per cent of your client base, this might indicate that it would be a good idea.

In general, you should estimate a minimum response of 10 per cent and a maximum of around 40 per cent. The response rate will depend on factors such as how well your target audience know you, how relevant they feel the questionnaire is to them, etc. In addition, you might offer a prize draw to recipients to encourage them to return the questionnaire. Experience is the best indicator of the response you might expect, but if this is your first research exercise you can always send the questionnaire to an easily managed sample such as 100. The number of responses will indicate how many questionnaires you need to send out.

Telephone questionnaires

Quotas are usually used in telephone research. This is to maintain control over costs and to ensure you reach a representative number and profile of respondents.

If you want to conduct telephone research, it is advisable to go to an external research agency as they will have the telephone operative set-up and expertise to handle the research.

Focus groups/interviews

These might be one-to-one or in groups. If you are holding a focus group you do not want too many people at any one time as this will limit discussion – perhaps six to eight attendees. The number of one-to-one interviews you conduct will depend on the variety of views that you get. If you conduct 10 and they all say the same thing, you may not want to undertake any more.

Setting out and agreeing the questions

The number and type of questions that you ask will be dictated by the research method you choose.

Postal research

You should ask a maximum of 12 questions, not including verification questions, or enough questions to fill one side of two A4 sheets with the questions comfortably spaced.

The questions should have controlled optional answers.

Example:

Do you think that the service we provide is:

	Very	Quite	Not very	Not at all
1. Efficient	❑	❑	❑	❑
2. Good value for money	❑	❑	❑	❑

Or:

Looking at [*service*], please indicate how strongly you agree or disagree with the statements on a scale of 1 to 5 ('1' is where you strongly disagree and '5' would indicate you strongly agree).

[*Statement*]   1 2 3 4 5
                                                    disagree → strongly agree

Or,

Please rate [*service*] out of 8 in the following aspects. (Please circle or cross the appropriate number; '1' is very poor, '8' is very good.)

[*Aspect of service*]   1 2 3 4 5 6 7 8

The aim is to arrive at a majority opinion about the service you offer; if you leave the questions open, you may receive 20 different responses. In addition, this makes it easier for the respondents to fill in – the easier a questionnaire is to answer, the more likely it is that people will take the time to complete it. It is important that you do not mix different scales or change the rank of '1' from being good to being poor on the same questionnaire as this will confuse respondents.

It is also best if the questionnaire has a theme to it, i.e. looking at a specific legal service your firm offers, as this helps focus the recipient's mind when answering.

PUTTING TOGETHER THE QUESTIONS FOR YOUR POSTAL QUESTIONNAIRE

The following steps will help you to begin putting together the questions for your postal questionnaire.

1. Identify the area you want to research, e.g. conveyancing as a service.
2. Identify what you want to learn from the research. For example, the value factors identified in Part One are factors that you might want to research in order to verify any assumptions you have made, such as your clients' attitude to the prices you charge, whether they think you offer value for money, and whether the locality of your firm is important.
3. Identify the active descriptions of these different aspects. For example, the active description of 'price' might be 'expensive', 'inexpensive', 'value for money', or the active description of 'locality' might be to ask clients' views about whether they think local knowledge is important, and whether they think your firm is a local firm.
4. Write the question based on the key you have identified, for example:

   'Do you think that our conveyancing service is value for money?'
   very good value, quite good value, satisfactory, not good value, poor value

   OR

   'Do you think that local knowledge is important in conveyancing?'
   very important, quite important, not at all important

5. Look at all of the questions: can they be categorised according to service, price, presentation, etc? If they can, group them together on the questionnaire.
6. Check that the questions will yield useful information. Do you need to verify the respondents by age, social group, etc. to give their answers more meaning?
7. Check for any ambiguity.

Once you have assembled your questionnaire then it is a good idea to test it to measure how easy it is to fill in, and to check the questions make sense and that there is no ambiguity. This can easily be accomplished by asking one of your colleagues to role-play as a recipient of the questionnaire.

Telephone interviews

Telephone questionnaires should be no longer than 10 questions. The questions should be straightforward so that the respondent can easily understand and answer them. It is strongly advised that you use a research agency for this type of research as it is a specialist area.

Discussion group interviews/one-to-one interviews

These should be used where you have a specific service or item that you wish to research. For example, you might discuss a new service you are proposing to introduce, asking the group for their views of your plans and ideas of what they would like to see.

Group discussions and interviews will normally ask for a judgement about something specific that has been presented to them.

You can conduct this type of research yourself. However, depending on what you want to research it may be advisable for a research agency to carry it out on your behalf. You need also to be aware that you may bring a bias to the way you present your ideas to the group and note their responses.

This manual concentrates on postal research questionnaires. It is the simplest method of research to carry out in-house, an extremely effective way of gathering information, and it will frequently work out the least expensive.

Producing your postal questionnaires

Having decided on your questions, it is now time to turn your attention to producing your questionnaire.

There are a number of factors that you will want to take into account when producing your questionnaires:

- Which statements and elements should you include in the questionnaire?
- Do you want to personalise the letter and/or questionnaire?
- How are you planning to have them returned to you?
- Do you need to know who has returned the questionnaire to you?
- How do you propose to print them?

Statements and elements that should be included in the questionnaire

The most important thing to remember about a postal questionnaire is that it needs to be easy to read, follow and return. You want to remove as many barriers to response as possible.

There are several elements or statements every questionnaire should include:

- an introductory letter or paragraph including a request for the respondent to fill in and return the questionnaire;
- questions to verify the status and profile of the respondent;
- unambiguous and relevant questions set out in an uncluttered and easy-to-read style;
- space for respondents to comment freely;
- a statement about the confidentiality of the information given;
- instructions about returning the questionnaire and a stamped, self-addressed envelope if appropriate;
- respondents should be thanked for their time;
- details of any prize draw into which the questionnaires are to be entered;
- details of any time limits for the questionnaire to be returned;
- respondents' details on the questionnaire (where appropriate), and an opportunity for them to indicate any change or amendment to those details.

Do you personalise the letter and/or questionnaire?

It is always a good idea to personalise the letters, unless you are sending out several thousand and costs prohibit it. There are various ways you can personalise the letters and/or questionnaires:

1. Mail merge the address details onto a letter and/or questionnnaire (where single-sheet A4) which has been printed out from the PC, or photocopied onto headed paper.
2. Print out address labels and stick them on the letter and/or onto the questionnaire in an appropriate space.
3. Give a disk with the target address details, together with headed paper (or printed letters), and questionnaires to a fulfilment house (frequently contacted through printers) who can then print the letters and have them inserted and sent out for you. This is probably only worthwhile where you plan to send out several thousand letters.

It might make sense to hire a temp (perhaps a student) for one or two days, to collate and send out the questionnaires.

How will the questionnaires be returned to you?

An extremely important element of your questionnaire is the response mechanism. This usually takes the form of an envelope included with the questionnaire. The envelope might be freepost, postage paid or stamped and self-addressed. It is important not to ask the respondents to pay to return a questionnaire as this will create a barrier to their responding.

Freepost. You apply to the Post Office for a freepost address and then pay according to the number of replies received. You can then print the envelopes or labels to go onto the envelopes in the office. Telephone your local post office to find out how to apply and the costs involved.

Postage paid. Again you will need to telephone your local post office to find out what you need to do. This usually involves having the envelopes properly preprinted.

Stamped self-addressed. You will need to self-address envelopes and stick stamps onto them – you can now buy self-adhesive stamps from the post office.

If your questionnaire is A3 folded to A4, you can have a fold mechanism printed onto the back page showing how to fold it to postcard size. A freepost address can be printed in the appropriate place, so that when folded it shows on one side. This approach can be used where the questionnaire is being inserted loose in a magazine or local paper, rather than sent in an envelope that could contain other items or a return envelope. In addition, the questionnaire will need to be printed on heavy paper to give it sufficient substance to be put into the post.

Do you need to know who has returned the questionnaire to you?

Depending on the aim of the research, it might be more or less appropriate to identify the respondents so that you know who they are when they return their questionnaire.

If you are verifying your database, knowing who the respondents are is the key to your research. For example, if you are asking questions about whether the target audience would be interested in attending a seminar and what they would like to gain from it, obviously you will want to know who the respondents are so that you can fulfil their potential orders.

However, if you want to learn about the services you offer and clients' views of your firm, it is not so important to know names, but it is important to ensure you know appropriate facts about them such as their age, the size of their business, etc.

How do you propose to print the letters and questionnaires?

The cost-effectiveness of different printing methods will depend on the number of questionnaires you are planning to send out, whether you want to personalise them, the budget available and level of quality you want them to impart to the target audience.

A guide to the different printing methods and where they are cost effective is set out in Box 8.

Box 8 Different methods of producing questionnaires and letters

Questionnaire and letter production method	Number to be sent out				
	50 and under	51–100	101–250	251–1000	1000+
Produced and printed on in-house PC ■ Can be personalised through mail merge ■ Takes time and effort in-house ■ Limited on format, i.e. single-sheet A4 ■ Limited on design and use of colour	✓	✓	✗	✗	✗
Photocopied ■ Can be personalised through mail merge – photocopy letter and put through laser printer for address details ■ Issues with quality ■ Limited on format, i.e. single-sheet A4 ■ Limited on design and use of colour	✓	✓	✗	✗	✗
Digitally printed ■ Can be personalised through mail merge – have the letter printed and then put through laser printer for address details ■ Will require setting by designer or printer ■ Not limited on format, i.e. A3 folded to A4, A4 folded to DL ■ Not limited on design and use of colour	✓✗	✓✗	✓	✓✗	✓
Two- or four-colour printers ■ Can be personalised through mail merge – have the letter printed and then either put them through laser printer, via mail merge or send labels or a disk to a finishing house – will depend on numbers ■ Will require setting by designer or printer ■ Not limited on format, i.e. A3 folded to A4, A4 folded to DL ■ Not limited on design and use of colour	✗	✗	✗	✓✗	✓

Key
✓ = This is a cost-effective approach.
✗ = Not likely to be particularly cost-effective.
✓✗ = Borderline – might or might not prove the most cost-effective approach.

Collating and analysing the responses

This can be very labour intensive. Research bureaus have specialist software that allows them to cross-analyse and collate results easily. It is, however, unlikely that a solicitors' firm will have this software. The software itself is not particularly expensive but it does require the person operating it to understand the language associated with the discipline of research.

It is quite possible to analyse the responses by using spreadsheets. In general, this entails a straight count and then a percentage of those who answered, i.e. 'of the 35 respondents, 53 per cent felt that we offered very good value for money, 27 per cent felt we offered moderately good value for money, and 20 per cent felt that we offered poor value for money'.

Always work to the total of respondents answering the question, i.e. if only 30 of the 35 answer a particular question, then 30 respondents for that question equal 100 per cent, not the total of 35 from whom the questionnaire was received.

It becomes more difficult to analyse the responses where you want to cross-analyse the questions.

Where a question asks for a rating, take the value of the ratings selected, add them all up and divide by the number of respondents.

Example

If 13 rate a service as '6', 12 as '8', 10 as '10', the overall rating is $13 \times 6 + 12 \times 8 + 10 \times 10 = 274/35 = 7.8$.

Therefore the service being asked about has achieved an overall rating of 7.8.

If you have more than 50 questionnaires to analyse, it may be easier to ask a research company to undertake the analysis for you.

Preparing the report

Once you have analysed and counted the responses, they are then put with words into a final report. This entails pulling together the top line results and drawing conclusions from them.

The report should include the following sections:

1. **An introduction,** which should include:
   - the reason why you undertook the research;
   - an outline of how the questionnaire was produced and who it was sent to, including details of any incentive used;
   - an outline of the level of response received and how the analysis was carried out.

2. **An outline of the responses received.** This is often set out as a number of short paragraphs with summary tables giving the number and views of respondents. Each table should contain the all notable results discussed.
3. **A conclusion** drawing together any actions arising from the research such as promotional activities or further research, etc.
4. **A copy of the questionnaire** should be attached as an appendix, as should any tables analysing the results of the questionnaires.

Pre-prepared questionnaires

In the following pages a selection of different postal questionnaire blueprints have been collated. These should not be used as they are because they are far too long. Use them rather as a guide to producing your own questionnaire, as a shopping list of questions that might be asked.

Complexity

The blueprint questionnaires have been split into three categories.

Category A: Simple

In this category, fairly straightforward questionnaires can be sent out to clients with their bills about a specific service they have just received or to verify their information for your database.

- Overall service evaluation cards to be sent or given to clients on the conclusion of different matters.
- General verification questionnaire.

Category B: General

These are more complex questionnaires that might be sent out for a specific exercise to understand more generally how the firm is viewed.

- Basic general questionnaire that may be used to find out what clients think of your firm.
- Questionnaire that might be utilised to understand what non-clients look for in a solicitors' firm and to establish selling hooks.
- Questionnaire to measure clients' reactions to staff.

Category C: In-depth and specific

These are questionnaires that look in greater depth at a specific service, or aspect of your firm or the service you offer clients.

- Questionnaire to investigate clients' reactions to a specific service.
- Questionnaire to measure awareness/reaction to a newsletter distributed by the firm.
- Questionnaire to measure clients' reactions to seminars/surgeries conducted by the firm.
- Questionnaire to measure awareness of competitors by both clients and non-clients.

Verification questions

At the start or end of a questionnaire, it is a good idea to include one or two questions to verify certain details about the respondent.

The answers to these questions will enable you to identify whether the respondents demonstrate any trends, i.e. all those aged over 50 think your firm is unfriendly, whereas those aged under 30 think it is very friendly.

These questions will also give you information that you can use when analysing your clients (see Part One, section 1(a)).

Remember, you do not want to overburden recipients with questions, so only the most relevant verification questions should be asked.

Questionnaire 1 Example verification questions

Private clients

Q. Please verify that the name and address shown on this questionnaire are correct.

Q. Which age band do you fall within:

18–24 ❑   25–34 ❑   35-44 ❑   45–64 ❑   65+ ❑

Q. Please tick the box that best describes your job:

Professional/senior/middle management   ❑
Junior management/office worker   ❑
Skilled manual worker   ❑
Semi-skilled and unskilled manual workers/unemployed   ❑

Q. Do you own your own property?

Yes ❑   No ❑

Q. Do you have a private pension?

Yes ❑   No ❑

Q. Prior to this have you used the services of [*your firm's name*] in the last:

one year ❑   two years ❑   three years ❑   five years ❑   ten years ❑

Q. How many times have you used the services of this firm in the last three years?

_____

Q. What were your reasons for using a solicitor in the last three years? Please list below:

_____
_____
_____
_____

Q. Would you shop around for a solicitor?

Yes ❑   No ❑

Q. If yes, where would you begin looking:

Yellow Pages   ❑
Citizens' Advice Bureau   ❑
Ask friends   ❑
Respond to advertisements   ❑

Other (please specify) _____

Q. Would like to receive a newsletter updating you about legal matters that could have an effect on your daily life?

Yes ❑   No ❑

Q. Would you be willing to take part in further research exercises?

Yes ❑   No ❑

Commercial clients

Q. Please verify that the name and address shown on this questionnaire are correct.

Q. Please tick the box that best describes your job title:

Professional/senior management   ❑
Administration   ❑
Finance   ❑
Marketing   ❑

Q. Are you responsible for purchasing legal services?

Yes ❑   No ❑

If 'No', state who is responsible:

Name/job title: _____

Q. Please indicate which describes your business:

Sole trader   ❑
Partnership   ❑   Number of partners: _____
Limited company   ❑
Public limited company   ❑

Other (please specify): _____

Q. Please indicate how many employees there are in the business:

2–6   ❑
7–20   ❑
21–50   ❑
51–100   ❑
100–500   ❑

Other (please specify): _____

Q. Please indicate the turnover of the business:

£0–250,000 ❑
£250,000–1 million ❑
£1–5 milllion ❑
£5 million + ❑

Q. Prior to this, have you used the services of [*your firm's name*] in the last:

One year ❑
Two years ❑
Three years ❑
Five years ❑
10 years ❑

Q. How many times have you used the services of this firm in the last three years?

_____

Q. What were your reasons for using a solicitor in the last three years? Please list below:

_____

_____

_____

Q. Please indicate whether you would like to receive a newsletter updating you about legal matters of relevance to your business.

Yes ❑   No ❑

Q. Please indicate whether you would be willing to take part in further research exercises.

Yes ❑   No ❑

Section 2(b)

Example questionnaires

Category A: Simple

This category includes straightforward questionnaires that can be sent to clients with their bills asking them about the service for which they have just employed your firm, and a verification questionnaire that can be used to verify and gather information about them for your database.

Questionnaire 2 Overall service evaluation card

We recently [*identify the work that was done*] for you. Now that this work has finished we would like to ask for a little of your time to fill in this questionnaire. We are constantly reviewing and trying to improve the service we offer you, and in order to do this we need your feedback.

Thank you for your time.

Please indicate a score for each of the questions by circling the appropriate number. The top rating is '5' and indicates that the service was good, descending to '1' which indicates that the service was not satisfactory.

Q1.   Did you find the person who advised you helpful?   5 4 3 2 1
                                                          extremely → not at all

If the score is below '3', is there any particular reason?

_____
_____
_____

Q2.   Did you find letters well written and easy to understand?   5 4 3 2 1
                                                          extremely → not at all

If the score is below '3', is there any particular reason?

_____
_____
_____

Q3.   Did you find the people who advised you easy to contact? 5 4 3 2 1
                                                          extremely → not at all

If the score is below '3', is there any particular reason?

_____
_____
_____

Q4.   Did the person who advised you explain your matter to you clearly?
                                                             5 4 3 2 1
                                                          extremely → not at all

If the score is below '3', is there any particular reason?

_____
_____
_____

Q5. Was your matter dealt with over a satisfactory period of time?

5 4 3 2 1
extremely → not at all

If the score is below '3', is there any particular reason?

_____
_____
_____

Q6. Did you find our charges:

Good value	❏
Reasonable	❏
High	❏
Very high	❏

Q7. How helpful was the receptionist?

5 4 3 2 1
extremely → not at all

If the score is below '3', is there any particular reason?

_____
_____
_____

Q8. How comfortable did you find our waiting area?

5 4 3 2 1
extremely → not at all

If the score is below '3', is there any particular reason?

_____
_____
_____

Q9. When you telephone, do we answer quickly?

5 4 3 2 1
extremely → not at all

Q10. Would you use us again on another matter?

Yes, definitely ❏   Maybe ❏   No ❏

Q11. Would you recommend us to friends, family or colleagues?

Yes, definitely ❏   Maybe ❏   No ❏

Q12. Are there any other comments you would like to make?

_____
_____
_____

Thank you for taking the time to complete and return this questionnaire.

Questionnaire 3 General verification questionnaire

We would like to ask for your help. We are updating our records and we would appreciate your assistance in answering the following questions.

The information you give us will be kept strictly confidential and will contribute towards our offering a service that is relevant and useful to you.

Thank you for your time.

Q1. **Please confirm that the name and address shown on this questionnaire are correct and mark any changes in the space provided.**

Q2. **Which age band do you fall within:**

18–24 ❏   25–34 ❏   35–44 ❏   45–64 ❏   65+ ❏

Q3. **Are you:**

Single ❏   Married ❏   Co-habiting ❏   Divorced ❏   Widowed ❏

Q4. **Please tick the box that best describes your job:**

Professional/senior/middle management ❏
Junior management/office worker ❏
Skilled manual worker ❏
Semi-skilled and unskilled manual workers/unemployed ❏

Q5. **Would you make the decision to use a particular solicitor alone?**

Yes ❏   No ❏

If 'no' please give the name/names of those who would be involved in the decision.

_____

_____

Q6. **Do you own your own property?**

Yes ❏   No ❏

Q7. **Do you have a private pension?**

Yes ❏   No ❏

Q8. **Have you used the services of a solicitor in the last:**

One year ❏   Two years ❏   Three years ❏   Five years ❏   10 years ❏

How many times have you used the services of a solicitor in the last three years?_____

What is/are the name of the solicitors' firm(s) you used?

_____

Q9. What was your reason for using a solicitor in the last three years?

Home sale/purchase (conveyancing) ❑
Death of a friend or relative ❑
To make a will ❑
To obtain compensation for an injury ❑
A domestic dispute ❑
A dispute with neighbours ❑
Landlord and tenant relations ❑
Criminal proceedings ❑
Motoring offences ❑
Financial/tax advice ❑
Employment contract or dispute ❑
Matrimonial or family reasons ❑
Other (please state): _____

Q10. Would you, or have you, shopped around for a solicitor?

I have ❑   I have not ❑
I would ❑   I would not ❑

Q11. **In this question, we are trying to understand how important different factors are in your choosing a solicitors' firm.** Please rate each of the following ten factors in order of importance 1–10 with regard to when you first choose a solicitor, '10' being the most important, descending to '1' being the least important.

[*Use 10 from this list*]

A recommendation from someone ❑
I know/knew someone in the firm ❑
They are well established in the local area ❑
They have a good reputation ❑
They are inexpensive ❑
Friends use them ❑
I have used them in the past ❑
They had a good telephone manner when I called them ❑
They gave me a clear explanation about their services on the phone ❑
They sponsor local charities in the area ❑
The initial consultation was free ❑
People and colleagues I know use them ❑
They can demonstrate experience ❑
They have specialist knowledge ❑

They package their services in a user-friendly way ❏
They have a good approach to client care ❏
The firm is large and can offer a broad range of legal services ❏
The firm is small and friendly ❏
The approach of the reception staff ❏
Their offices are convenient ❏
They offer good value for money ❏

Q12. Would like to receive a newsletter updating you about legal matters that could have an effect on your daily life?

Yes ❏   No ❏

Q13. Would you be willing to take part in research exercises we conduct from time to time?

Yes ❏   No ❏

Thank you for taking the time to complete and return this questionnaire.

Category B: General

These are more complex questionnaires that might be sent out to clients and non-clients to obtain their general views on an area.

Questionnaire 4

Used to find out what clients think of your firm   p. 187

Questionnaire 5

Used to measure clients' reactions to staff   p. 193

Questionnaire 6

Used to understand what non-clients look for in a solicitors' firm
and establish selling hooks   p. 199

Questionnaire 4 What clients think of your firm

Q1. Are you currently using the services of [*your firm's name*]?

Yes ❑   No ❑

Q2. Are you using the services of any other firm of solicitors or legal services provider at present?

Yes ❑   No ❑

If Yes, please state name of organisation/service provider:

_____

Q3. Have you used the services of [*your firm's name*] in the last:

One year ❑   Two years ❑   Three years ❑   Five years ❑   10 years ❑

How many times have you used the services of this firm in the last three years? _____

Q4. Did you obtain or apply for legal aid? [*Only use if appropriate.*]

Yes ❑   No ❑

Q5. What was your reason for using [*your firm's name*] in the last three years?

[*Please use as appropriate: 'personal reasons' for questionnaires sent to private clients and 'business reasons' for questionnaires sent to business or commercial clients.*]

Personal reasons:

Home sale/purchase (conveyancing)	❑
Death of a friend or relative	❑
To make a will	❑
To obtain compensation for an injury	❑
A dispute with an individual	❑
A dispute with an organisation	❑
Landlord and tenant relations	❑
Criminal proceedings	❑
Motoring offences	❑
Financial/tax advice	❑
Employment contract or dispute	❑
Divorce or separation	❑
Debt or hire purchase problems	❑
Faulty goods or services	❑

Other (please state): _____

Business reasons:

Setting up a business	❑
Sale/acquisition of a business	❑
Sale/purchase of business premises	❑

Debt collection ❏
Insurance claim ❏
Customer–supplier relations ❏
Employment contracts and disputes ❏
Tax advice ❏
Contract drafting requirements ❏
Trademark application/dispute ❏
Patent application/dispute ❏
Other intellectual property dispute ❏
Planning application/dispute ❏

Other (please state): _____

Q6. **How did you hear about** [*your firm's name*]?

[*Please pick those that could be relevant to your firm from this list.*]

Advertising in local newspapers/local magazines ❏
From the Yellow Pages/Thompson Local ❏
Through brochures or newsletters mailed to me ❏
Through being mentioned in papers or magazines ❏
From sponsorship of sports or the arts ❏
Appearing in legal directories ❏
Professional recommendation (i.e. bank, building society) ❏
Recommendation from a friend or relative ❏
Seeing the offices ❏
From the Citizens' Advice Bureau ❏
Referral from another solicitor ❏
Through a charity, special interest group or other agency ❏
From an invitation to a seminar/reception at the firm ❏
From a personal contact with the firm ❏

Other (please state): _____

Q7. **In this question, we are trying to understand how important different factors are in your choosing a solicitors firm.** Please rate each of the following ten factors in order of importance 1–10 with regard to when you first choose a solicitor, '10' being the most important, descending to '1' being the least important.

[*Use 10 from this list*]

A recommendation from someone ❏
I know/knew someone in the firm ❏
They are well established in the local area ❏
They have a good reputation ❏
They are inexpensive ❏
Friends use them ❏
I have used them in the past ❏
They had a good telephone manner when I called them ❏
They gave me a clear explanation about their services on the phone ❏

They sponsor local charities in the area ❑
The initial consultation was free ❑
People and colleagues I know use them ❑
They can demonstrate experience ❑
They have specialist knowledge ❑
They package their services in a user-friendly way ❑
They have a good approach to client care ❑
The firm is large and can offer a broad range of legal services ❑
The firm is small and friendly ❑
The approach of the reception staff ❑
Their offices are convenient ❑
They offer good value for money ❑

Q8. Did you consider other firms?

Yes ❑   No ❑

If 'Yes', please list the other firms you considered:

_____

_____

Q9. How would you describe the approach of the solicitors who looked after your matter? Please tick a box for each description listed.

[Use five from this list.]

	Very	Quite	Not at all
Professional	❑	❑	❑
Disorganised	❑	❑	❑
Arrogant	❑	❑	❑
Caring	❑	❑	❑
Experienced	❑	❑	❑
Good explainer	❑	❑	❑
Patient	❑	❑	❑
Quick	❑	❑	❑
Slow	❑	❑	❑
Confident	❑	❑	❑

Q10. How would you describe the approach of those in reception and secretaries in the firm with whom you were/are in contact?

[Use five from this list.]

	Very	Quite	Not at all
Professional	❑	❑	❑
Disorganised	❑	❑	❑
Arrogant	❑	❑	❑
Caring	❑	❑	❑
Experienced	❑	❑	❑
Good explainer	❑	❑	❑
Patient	❑	❑	❑
Quick	❑	❑	❑
Slow	❑	❑	❑
Confident	❑	❑	❑

Q11. Did you feel that the service provided by the firm offered you good value for money?

Very good value for money ❏
Good value for money ❏
Adequate value for money ❏
Poor value for money ❏

Q12. How well informed did you feel about the progress of your matter?

Very well informed at all stages, i.e. given regular updates
  without the need to prompt ❏
Quite well informed, i.e. occasionally given information
  without the need to prompt ❏
Informed when asked for information ❏
Reluctantly informed when asked for information ❏

Q13. Were you given a quotation/estimate before work began?

Yes ❏   No ❏

Q14. How well informed or updated were you on the costs involved during the progress of your matter?

Very well informed at all stages, i.e. given regular updates
  without the need to prompt ❏
Quite well informed, i.e. occasionally given information
  without the need to prompt ❏
Informed when asked for information ❏
Reluctantly informed when asked for information ❏

Q15. Have you used another firm of solicitors in the past?

Yes ❏   No ❏

If yes, how did the service provided by this firm compare:

Very well ❏
Quite well ❏
About the same ❏
Poorly ❏

Q16. How likely are you to recommend this firm to colleagues and/or friends?

Very likely ❏
Quite likely ❏
Unlikely ❏
Very unlikely ❏

Q17. **How likely would you be to use** [*your firm's name*] **again in the future?**

Very likely ❏
Quite likely ❏
Unlikely ❏
Very unlikely ❏

Q18. **As far as you are aware, with which of the following services is** [*your firm's name*] **able to provide help to clients?**

[*Please use as appropriate: 'personal reasons' for questionnaires sent to private clients and 'business reasons' for questionnaires sent to business or commercial clients.*]

Personal reasons:
Home sale/purchase (conveyancing) ❏
Death of a friend or relative ❏
To make a will ❏
To obtain compensation for an injury ❏
A dispute with an individual ❏
A dispute with an organisation ❏
Landlord and tenant relations ❏
Criminal proceedings ❏
Motoring offences ❏
Financial/tax advice ❏
Employment contract or dispute ❏
Divorce or separation ❏
Debt or hire purchase problems ❏
Faulty goods or services ❏

Other (please state): _____

Business:
Setting up a business ❏
Sale/acquisition of a business ❏
Sale/purchase of business premises ❏
Debt collection ❏
Insurance claim ❏
Customer–supplier relations ❏
Employment contracts and disputes ❏
Tax advice ❏
Contract drafting requirements ❏
Trademark application/dispute ❏
Patent application/dispute ❏
Other intellectual property dispute ❏
Planning application/dispute ❏

Other (please state): _____

Q19. Looking at the firm generally, please indicate how strongly you agree with the following statements about the firm. A score of '5' indicates you agree strongly with the statement, descending to '1' where you disagree strongly with the statement.

[*Please pick the 10 most relevant to your firm from this list.*]

	Agree → Disagree
The firm has a professional approach	5 4 3 2 1
The firm is not client-oriented	5 4 3 2 1
The billing information is clear	5 4 3 2 1
Documentation from the firm is well presented	5 4 3 2 1
The firm is well run and organised	5 4 3 2 1
The staff were professional and friendly	5 4 3 2 1
I would be happy to work with any solicitor in the firm	5 4 3 2 1
The offices are in need of modernisation	5 4 3 2 1
They are well established in the local area	5 4 3 2 1
They send me information about their services	5 4 3 2 1
They are inexpensive	5 4 3 2 1
They gave me a clear explanation over the phone	5 4 3 2 1
The approach of the reception staff is welcoming and helpful	5 4 3 2 1
The firm is not wholly profit-oriented	5 4 3 2 1
The firm has a caring culture	5 4 3 2 1
The firm is involved in the local community	5 4 3 2 1

Q20. Finally, if there are any comments you would like to make about [*your firm's name*] we would be glad to hear them.

_____
_____
_____
_____
_____
_____
_____
_____

Thank you for your time

Questionnaire 5 Measuring clients' reactions to staff

Q1. Are you currently using the services of [*your firm's name*]?

Yes ❑   No ❑

Q2. Have you used the services of [*your firm's name*] in the last:

One year ❑   Two years ❑   Three years ❑   Five years ❑   10 years ❑

How many times have you used the services of this firm in the last three years? _____

Q3. What have been your reasons for using [*your firm's name*] in the last three years?

[*Please use as appropriate: 'personal reasons' for questionnaires sent to private clients and 'business reasons' for questionnaires sent to business or commercial clients.*]

Personal reasons:
Home sale/purchase (conveyancing)   ❑
Death of a friend or relative   ❑
To make a will   ❑
To obtain compensation for an injury   ❑
A dispute with an individual   ❑
A dispute with an organisation   ❑
Landlord and tenant relations   ❑
Criminal proceedings   ❑
Motoring offences   ❑
Financial/tax advice   ❑
Employment contract or dispute   ❑
Divorce or separation   ❑
Debt or hire purchase problems   ❑
Faulty goods or services   ❑

Other (please state): _____

Business:
Setting up a business   ❑
Sale/acquisition of a business   ❑
Sale/purchase of business premises   ❑
Debt collection   ❑
Insurance claim   ❑
Customer–supplier relations   ❑
Employment contracts and disputes   ❑
Tax advice   ❑
Contract drafting requirements   ❑
Trademark application/dispute   ❑
Patent application/dispute   ❑
Other intellectual property dispute   ❑
Planning application/dispute   ❑

Other (please state): _____

Q4. How did you contact this firm in the first instance?

By telephone ❑
By letter ❑
By visit ❑

Q5. When you telephone the firm, is the phone generally answered:

Quickly, i.e. within three rings ❑
Moderately quickly, i.e. between three and six rings ❑
Fairly slowly, i.e. between six and nine rings ❑
Slowly ❑

Q6. When you telephone the firm between working hours, i.e. 9 a.m. to 5.30 p.m., is the telephone ever:

	Frequently	Occasionally	Never
Not answered	❑	❑	❑
Engaged	❑	❑	❑
On answering machine	❑	❑	❑

Q7. When you have to leave a message, how confident do you feel that the message will be relayed correctly?

Very confident ❑
Quite confident ❑
Not very confident ❑
Not at all confident ❑

Q8. How knowledgeable is the person on the switchboard about the movements of the solicitors in the firm and when they might be available?

Very knowledgeable ❑
Quite knowledgeable ❑
They don't seem sure ❑
They have no idea ❑

Q9. Generally how satisfied are you with the speed with which your call is returned?

Very satisfied ❑
Quite satisfied ❑
Not very satisfied ❑
Dissatisfied ❑

Q10. How would you sum up the general telephone manner of the switchboard and secretaries to whom you speak? Please indicate whether you agree or disagree with the following descriptions by circling the appropriate number – '5' indicates you agree, descending to '1' indicating you disagree.

[Use five from this list]

	Switchboard Agree→disagree	Secretaries Agree→disagree
Helpful	5 4 3 2 1	5 4 3 2 1
Courteous	5 4 3 2 1	5 4 3 2 1
Efficient	5 4 3 2 1	5 4 3 2 1
Obstructive	5 4 3 2 1	5 4 3 2 1
Professional	5 4 3 2 1	5 4 3 2 1
Pleasant	5 4 3 2 1	5 4 3 2 1
Off-hand	5 4 3 2 1	5 4 3 2 1
Abrupt	5 4 3 2 1	5 4 3 2 1
Knowledgeable	5 4 3 2 1	5 4 3 2 1
Unhelpful	5 4 3 2 1	5 4 3 2 1
Rushed	5 4 3 2 1	5 4 3 2 1

Q11. When you have written to the firm requiring a response, how quickly has someone responded to you?

Very quickly, i.e. on the day letter received ❏
Moderately quickly, i.e within 2 days ❏
Fairly slowly, i.e. between two and five days. ❏
Slowly, i.e over five days ❏

Q12. How have they responded?

By letter ❏   By telephone ❏

Q13. Has the solicitor responded or his/her secretary?

Solicitor ❏   Secretary ❏

Q14. How satisfied have you been with this response?

Very satisfied ❏
Quite satisfied ❏
Not very satisfied ❏
Dissatisfied ❏

Q15. When visiting the firm, how do you usually travel to the firm's offices?

By bus ❏   By train ❏   By taxi ❏
On foot ❏   By car ❏

Q16. When first travelling to the firm, how easy was it to find?

Very easy	❏
Quite easy	❏
Difficult	❏
Very difficult	❏

Q17. If you travelled by car, how easy was it to park?

Very easy	❏
Quite easy	❏
Difficult	❏
Very difficult	❏

Q18. When attending the offices for an appointment, how long do you usually have to wait once the allotted time of your appointment arrives?

I go straight in	❏
Under five minutes	❏
Over five but under 10 minutes' wait	❏
Over 10 but under 15 minutes' wait	❏
Over 15 but under 30 minutes' wait	❏

Q19. Do you find the waiting area/reception area comfortable?

Very comfortable	❏
Quite comfortable	❏
Adequate	❏
Uncomfortable	❏

Q20. How do you find the other rooms/offices you have visited in the firm?

Very comfortable	❏
Quite comfortable	❏
Adequate	❏
Uncomfortable	❏

Q21. As far as you are aware, with which of the following services is the firm able to provide help to clients?

[*Please use as appropriate: 'personal reasons' for questionnaires sent to private clients and 'business reasons' for questionnaires sent to business or commercial clients.*]

Personal reasons:

Home sale/purchase (conveyancing)	❏
Death of a friend or relative	❏
To make a will	❏
To obtain compensation for an injury	❏
A dispute with an individual	❏
A dispute with an organisation	❏

Landlord and tenant relations ❑
Criminal proceedings ❑
Motoring offences ❑
Financial/tax advice ❑
Employment contract or dispute ❑
Divorce or separation ❑
Debt or hire purchase problems ❑
Faulty goods or services ❑

Other (please state): _____

Business:
Setting up a business ❑
Sale/acquisition of a business ❑
Sale/purchase of business premises ❑
Debt collection ❑
Insurance claim ❑
Customer–supplier relations ❑
Employment contracts and disputes ❑
Tax advice ❑
Contract drafting requirements ❑
Trademark application/dispute ❑
Patent application/dispute ❑
Other intellectual property dispute ❑
Planning application/dispute ❑

Other (please state): _____

Q22. Looking at the firm generally, please indicate how strongly you agree with the following statements about the firm. A score of '5' indicates you agree strongly with the statement, descending to '1' where you disagree strongly with the statement.

	Agree → Disagree
The firm has a professional approach	5 4 3 2 1
The firm is not client-oriented	5 4 3 2 1
The firm is well run and organised	5 4 3 2 1
The staff were professional and friendly	5 4 3 2 1
I would be happy to work with any solicitor in the firm	5 4 3 2 1
The offices are in need of modernisation	5 4 3 2 1
They are well established in the local area	5 4 3 2 1
They send me information about their services	5 4 3 2 1
They gave me a clear explanation over the phone	5 4 3 2 1
They treat me like a valued client	5 4 3 2 1

Q23. **How did you hear about** [*your firm's name*]?

[*Please pick those that could be relevant to your firm from this list.*]

Advertising in local newspapers/local magazines	❏
From the Yellow Pages/Thompson Local	❏
Through brochures or newsletters mailed to me	❏
Through being mentioned in papers or magazines	❏
From sponsorship of sports or the arts	❏
Appearing in legal directories	❏
Professional recommendation (i.e. bank, building society)	❏
Recommendation from a friend or relative	❏
Seeing the offices	❏
From the Citizens' Advice Bureau	❏
Referral from another solicitor	❏
Through a charity, special interest group or other agency	❏
From an invitation to a seminar/reception at the firm	❏
From a personal contact with the firm	❏

Other (please state): _____

Q24. **Finally, if there are any comments you would like to make about** [*your firm's name*] **we would be glad to hear them.**

_____
_____
_____
_____
_____
_____
_____
_____

Thank you for your time

Questionnaire 6 Understanding what non-clients look for in a solicitors' firm and establishing selling hooks

Q1. Are you currently using the services of a solicitor?

Yes ❑   No ❑

Q2. Have you used the services of a solicitor in the last:

One year ❑   Two years ❑   Three years ❑   Five years ❑   10 years ❑

How many times have you used the services of this firm in the last three years? _____

Q3. How long have you used the services of the solicitor you are employing at present or have employed in the past?

One year ❑   Two years ❑   Three years ❑   Five years ❑   10 years ❑

Q4. What have been your reasons for using a solicitor in the last three years?

[Please use as appropriate: 'personal reasons' for questionnaires being sent to private clients and 'business reasons' for questionnaires being sent to business or commercial clients.]

Personal reasons:
Home sale/purchase (conveyancing)	❑
Death of a friend or relative	❑
To make a will	❑
To obtain compensation for an injury	❑
A dispute with an individual	❑
A dispute with an organisation	❑
Landlord and tenant relations	❑
Criminal proceedings	❑
Motoring offences	❑
Financial/tax advice	❑
Employment contract or dispute	❑
Divorce or separation	❑
Debt or hire purchase problems	❑
Faulty goods or services	❑

Other (please state): _____

Business:
Setting up a business	❑
Sale/acquisition of a business	❑
Sale/purchase of business premises	❑
Debt collection	❑
Insurance claim	❑
Customer–supplier relations	❑
Employment contracts and disputes	❑
Tax advice	❑

Contract drafting requirements ❑
Trademark application/dispute ❑
Patent application/dispute ❑
Other intellectual property dispute ❑
Planning application/dispute ❑

Other (please state): _____

Q5. **How did you hear about the solicitor you are using at present or have used in the past?**

[*Use those relevant to your firm from this list.*]

Advertising in local newspapers/local magazines ❑
From the Yellow Pages/Thompson Local ❑
Through brochures or newsletters mailed to me ❑
Through being mentioned in papers or magazines ❑
From sponsorship of sports or the arts ❑
Appearing in legal directories ❑
Professional recommendation (i.e. bank, building society) ❑
Recommendation from a friend or relative ❑
Seeing the offices ❑
From the Citizens' Advice Bureau ❑
Referral from another solicitor ❑
Through a charity, special interest group or other agency ❑
From an invitation to a seminar/reception at the firm ❑
From a personal contact with the firm ❑

Other (please state): _____

Q6. **How many firms do you think you would consider when looking?**

1 ❑
2 ❑
3 ❑
4 + ❑

Q7. **In this question, we are trying to understand how important different factors are in your choosing a solicitors firm.** Please rate each of the following ten factors in order of importance 1–10 with regard to when you first choose a solicitor, '10' being the most important, descending to '1' being the least important.

[*Use 10 from this list*]

A recommendation from someone ❑
I know/knew someone in the firm ❑
They are well established in the local area ❑
They have a good reputation ❑
They are inexpensive ❑
Friends use them ❑
I have used them in the past ❑

They had a good telephone manner when I called them ❑
They gave me a clear explanation about their services on the phone ❑
They sponsor local charities in the area ❑
The initial consultation was free ❑
People and colleagues I know use them ❑
They can demonstrate experience ❑
They have specialist knowledge ❑
They package their services in a user-friendly way ❑
They have a good approach to client care ❑
The firm is large and can offer a broad range of legal services ❑
The firm is small and friendly ❑
The approach of the reception staff ❑
Their offices are convenient ❑
They offer good value for money ❑

Q8. **How important are the following aspects of a solicitors' firm, or the service they offer, in your remaining loyal to the firm. Please rate each aspect 1–10, '10' being very important descending to '1' being the least important.**

[*Use 10 from this list.*]

They send me information about their services ❑
The approach of the reception staff is always welcoming ❑
Their offices are convenient ❑
They offer good value for money ❑
They keep me informed and updated about my matter ❑
They offer a broad range of services and expertise ❑
They package their services in a user-friendly way ❑
They invite me to seminars ❑
They know who I am when I see them ❑
They send me a newsletter ❑
They send me information brochures ❑
They explain what is happening clearly ❑
I would feel happy about working with any solicitors in the firm ❑
They keep in contact even when there is no work to do ❑
I view the firm as my family's solicitor ❑

Q9. **What would make you stop using the services of a solicitors firm? Please indicate how likely you would be to stop using a firm if each aspect were true by giving each aspect a score. A score of 10 is an aspect that alone would make you stop using a solicitor, down to 1, not really a strong effect.**

[*Use 10 from this list.*]

An off-hand approach by the reception staff ❑
Their offices are awkward to get to ❑
Untidy and uncomfortable offices ❑
I had to constantly chase to find out what was happening ❑
I found them arrogant ❑
They did not keep in touch with me after the initial work was completed ❑

They didn't explain my matter and their actions clearly ❑
They made no effort to sell their services to me ❑
Their services seemed to be expensive ❑
They didn't quote for their work ❑
They didn't appear sympathetic to my situation ❑
They didn't make me feel important to them ❑
The solicitor was often said to be too busy to see me for a while ❑
The solicitor did not make me feel confident ❑

Q10. In general, what is your impression of solicitors on the whole?

	Agree → Disagree
They are efficient and work hard for their money	1 2 3 4 5
They really listen and understand	1 2 3 4 5
They are well respected	1 2 3 4 5
They are approachable/easy to talk to	1 2 3 4 5
One can trust them to do their best	1 2 3 4 5
They are in touch and up to date	1 2 3 4 5
They are intelligent	1 2 3 4 5
They are mainly after your money	1 2 3 4 5
They are not as honest as they might be	1 2 3 4 5
They are pompous and have a condescending manner	1 2 3 4 5
Their charges are too high for the work they do	1 2 3 4 5
They do not value their clients	1 2 3 4 5
They sit back and let the work come to them	1 2 3 4 5
They are not commercially aware	1 2 3 4 5
They are old-fashioned on the whole	1 2 3 4 5
They depend on the old boys' network	1 2 3 4 5

Q11. Would like to receive a newsletter updating you about legal matters that could have an effect on your daily life?

Yes ❑   No ❑

Q12. Would you be willing to take part in research exercises we conduct from time to time?

Yes ❑   No ❑

Q13. Finally, if there are any comments you would like to make about [*your firm's name*] we would be glad to hear them.

_____
_____
_____
_____
_____
_____
_____
_____

Thank you for your time

Category C: In depth and specific

These are questionnaires that look in greater depth at an area and are generally more specific than the other questionnaires.

Questionnaire 7

Used to investigate clients' reactions to a specific service   p. 204

Questionnaire 8

Used to measure awareness/reaction to a newsletter distributed
by the firm   p. 208

Questionnaire 9

Used to measure clients' reactions to seminars/surgeries conducted
by the firm   p. 212

Questionnaire 10

Used to measure awareness of competitors by both clients and
non-clients   p. 216

Questionnaire 7 Investigating clients' reactions to a specific service

You recently employed this firm to undertake the following on your behalf:

_____

To ensure we are at all times offering you the best service available, we are sending out this questionnaire to all those who employ us for legal services. We would be grateful if you would complete and return it to us in the envelope provided.

Thank you for your time and help.

Q1. How many times have you used the services of this firm in the last three years?

_____

Q2. Please state the reasons for employing the services of this firm in the last three years. i.e. to write a will, because of a motoring offence, etc. [*Please change for business/commercial clients.*]

1. _____

2. _____

3. _____

4. _____

5. _____

Q3. Did you obtain or apply for legal aid? [*Only include if appropriate.*]

Yes ❑   No ❑

Q4. How professional did/do you find the approach of the solicitors in the firm with whom you were/are in contact?

Very professional ❑
Quite professional ❑
Not very professional ❑
Poor ❑

Q5. How professional did/do you find the approach of the reception and secretaries in the firm with whom you were/are in contact?

Very professional ❑
Quite professional ❑
Not very professional ❑
Poor ❑

Q6. Did you feel that the service provided by the firm offered you good value for money?

Very good value for money ❏
Good value for money ❏
Adequate value for money ❏
Poor value for money ❏

Q7. How well informed did you feel about the progress of your matter?

Very well informed at all stages, i.e. given regular updates
without the need to prompt ❏
Quite well informed, i.e. occasionally given information
without the need to prompt ❏
Informed when asked for information ❏
Reluctantly informed when asked for information ❏

Q8. Were you given a quotation/estimate prior to work commencing?

Yes ❏   No ❏

Q9. How well informed or updated were you on the costs involved during the progress of your matter?

Very well informed at all stages, i.e. given regular updates
without the need to prompt ❏
Quite well informed, i.e. occasionally given information
without the need to prompt ❏
Informed when asked for information ❏
Reluctantly informed when asked for information ❏

Q10. Were there any areas of the service provided that in your view could be presented in a more convenient and compact manner? If there were, please could you outline which areas and how, below:

_____
_____
_____

Q11. As far as you are aware, with which of the following services is the firm able to provide help to clients?

[*Please use as appropriate: 'personal reasons' for questionnaires sent to private clients and 'business reasons' for questionnaires sent to business or commercial clients.*]

Personal reasons:
Home sale/purchase (conveyancing) ❏
Death of a friend or relative ❏
To make a will ❏
To obtain compensation for an injury ❏
A dispute with an individual ❏

A dispute with an organisation ❑
Landlord and tenant relations ❑
Criminal proceedings ❑
Motoring offences ❑
Financial/tax advice ❑
Employment contract or dispute ❑
Divorce or separation ❑
Debt or hire purchase problems ❑
Faulty goods or services ❑

Other (please state): _____

Business:
Setting up a business ❑
Sale/acquisition of a business ❑
Sale/purchase of business premises ❑
Debt collection ❑
Insurance claim ❑
Customer–supplier relations ❑
Employment contracts and disputes ❑
Tax advice ❑
Contract drafting requirements ❑
Trademark application/dispute ❑
Patent application/dispute ❑
Other intellectual property dispute ❑
Planning application/dispute ❑

Other (please state): _____

Q12. **Looking at the firm generally, please indicate how strongly you agree with the following statements about the firm. A score of '5' indicates you agree strongly with the statement, descending to '1' where you disagree strongly with the statement.**

	Disagree ↔ agree
The firm has a professional approach	1 2 3 4 5
The firm is not client-oriented	1 2 3 4 5
The firm is well run and organised	1 2 3 4 5
The staff were professional and friendly	1 2 3 4 5
I would be happy to work with any solicitor in the firm	1 2 3 4 5
The offices are in need of modernisation	1 2 3 4 5
They are well established in the local area	1 2 3 4 5
They send me information about their services	1 2 3 4 5
They gave me a clear explanation over the phone	1 2 3 4 5
The approach of reception staff is welcoming and helpful	1 2 3 4 5

Q13. Finally, if there are any comments you would like to make about [*your firm's name*] we would be glad to hear them.

_____
_____
_____
_____
_____
_____
_____
_____

Thank you for your time

Questionnaire 8 Measuring awareness/reaction to a newsletter distributed by the firm

Q1. **Are you currently using the services of** [*your firm's name*]?

Yes ❏ No ❏

Q2. **Have you used the services of** [*your firm's name*] **in the last:**

One year ❏
Two years ❏
Three years ❏
Five years ❏
10 years ❏

How many times have you used the services of this firm in the last three years? _____

Q3. **What was/were your reason(s) for using** [*your firm's name*] **in the last three years?**

[*Please use as appropriate: 'personal reasons' for questionnaires sent to private clients and 'business reasons' for questionnaires sent to business or commercial clients.*]

Personal reasons:
Home sale/purchase (conveyancing) ❏
Death of a friend or relative ❏
To make a will ❏
To obtain compensation for an injury ❏
A dispute with an individual ❏
A dispute with an organisation ❏
Landlord and tenant relations ❏
Criminal proceedings ❏
Motoring offences ❏
Financial/tax advice ❏
Employment contract or dispute ❏
Divorce or separation ❏
Debt or hire purchase problems ❏
Faulty goods or services ❏

Other (please state): _____

Business:
Setting up a business ❏
Sale/acquisition of a business ❏
Sale/purchase of business premises ❏
Debt collection ❏
Insurance claim ❏
Customer–supplier relations ❏
Employment contracts and disputes ❏

Tax advice ❏
Contract drafting requirements ❏
Trademark application/dispute ❏
Patent application/dispute ❏
Other intellectual property dispute ❏
Planning application/dispute ❏

Other (please state): _____

Q4. **Do you receive [*newsletter name*] on a regular basis?**

Yes ❏   No ❏

Q5. **On average, how much of each newsletter would you say you read?**

One page ❏
Two pages ❏
Half ❏
Three-quarters ❏
From cover to cover ❏

Q6. **What impression does the newsletter give you about the firm? Please indicate how strongly the following impressions come across from the newsletter:**

	Weak ↔ Strong
The firm is professional	1 2 3 4 5
The firm is client-oriented	1 2 3 4 5
The firm is aware of client requirements	1 2 3 4 5
The firm is well run	1 2 3 4 5
The firm is expensive	1 2 3 4 5
The firm gives good value for money	1 2 3 4 5
The firm is not approachable	1 2 3 4 5
The firm is up to date with changes in the law	1 2 3 4 5
I trust them more	1 2 3 4 5

Q7. **In the last two issues, which of the following articles, features or sections did you read?**

[*Name of article here*] ❏
[*Name of article here*] ❏
[*Name of article here*] ❏
[*Name of article here*] ❏
[*Name of article here*] ❏
[*Name of article here*] ❏
[*Name of article here*] ❏

Q8. How interesting did you find these articles, features or sections?

	Very Interesting	Quite Interesting	Not at all Interesting
[*Name of article here*]	❏	❏	❏
[*Name of article here*]	❏	❏	❏
[*Name of article here*]	❏	❏	❏
[*Name of article here*]	❏	❏	❏
[*Name of article here*]	❏	❏	❏
[*Name of article here*]	❏	❏	❏
[*Name of article here*]	❏	❏	❏

Q9. Did you feel that the articles were written in a style easy to understand´?

	Very well written	Quite well written	Badly written
[*Name of article here*]	❏	❏	❏
[*Name of article here*]	❏	❏	❏
[*Name of article here*]	❏	❏	❏
[*Name of article here*]	❏	❏	❏
[*Name of article here*]	❏	❏	❏
[*Name of article here*]	❏	❏	❏
[*Name of article here*]	❏	❏	❏

Q10. Was the information in the article, feature or section of use to you?

	Very useful	Quite useful	Not at all useful
[*Name of article here*]	❏	❏	❏
[*Name of article here*]	❏	❏	❏
[*Name of article here*]	❏	❏	❏
[*Name of article here*]	❏	❏	❏
[*Name of article here*]	❏	❏	❏
[*Name of article here*]	❏	❏	❏
[*Name of article here*]	❏	❏	❏

Q11. Do you keep your copy of the newsletter?

Yes ❏   No ❏

Q12. Please indicate below if there are any areas you would like to see further information about in the newsletter. Please give a mark out of 10, '10' being very interested and '1' being not at all interested.

Personal subjects:
Purchasing/selling a house (i.e. conveyancing)   ❏
Probate on the death of a friend or relative   ❏
What is involved in making a will   ❏

How and when you can obtain compensation for an injury ❏
What actions can be taken regarding a domestic dispute ❏
What actions can be taken regarding a dispute with neighbours ❏
What your responsibilities and rights are as a landlord ❏
What your responsibilities and rights are as a tenant ❏
What is involved in criminal proceedings ❏
How a solicitor can help with motoring offences ❏
Financial/tax advice ❏
Employment contract or dispute ❏
What is the present approach to matrimonial or family issues ❏

Other (please state): _____

Business-related subjects:
What legal requirements there are in setting up a business ❏
How to approach the sale/acquisition of a business ❏
How to approach the sale/purchase of business premises ❏
What your legal position is with regards to debt collection ❏
What the common problems are when faced with an
    insurance claim ❏
How the law can help with customer/supplier relations ❏
Employment contracts and disputes ❏
Tax advice ❏
Contract drafting requirements ❏
The process involved in a trademark application/dispute ❏
The process involved in a patent application/dispute ❏
Other intellectual property dispute ❏
The process involved in a planning application/dispute ❏

Other (please state): _____

Q13. **Finally, if there are any comments you would like to make about the design or contents of the newsletter, we would be glad to hear them.**

_____
_____
_____
_____

Thank you for your time

Questionnaire 9 Measuring clients' reactions to seminars/surgeries conducted by the firm

Q1. **Are you currently using the services of** [*your firm's name*]?

Yes ❑ No ❑

Q2. **Have you used the services of** [*your firm's name*] **in the last:**

One year ❑ Two years ❑ Three years ❑ Five years ❑ 10 years ❑

How many times have you used the services of this firm in the last three years? _____

Q3. **What was/were your reason(s) for using** [*your firm's name*] **in the last three years?**

[*Please use as appropriate: 'personal reasons' for questionnaires sent to private clients and 'business reasons' for questionnaires being sent to business or commercial clients.*]

Personal reasons:

Home sale/purchase (conveyancing)	❑
Death of a friend or relative	❑
To make a will	❑
To obtain compensation for an injury	❑
A dispute with an individual	❑
A dispute with an organisation	❑
Landlord and tenant relations	❑
Criminal proceedings	❑
Motoring offences	❑
Financial/tax advice	❑
Employment contract or dispute	❑
Divorce or separation	❑
Debt or hire purchase problems	❑
Faulty goods or services	❑

Other (please state): _____

Business:

Setting up a business	❑
Sale/acquisition of a business	❑
Sale/purchase of business premises	❑
Debt collection	❑
Insurance claim	❑
Customer–supplier relations	❑
Employment contracts and disputes	❑
Tax advice	❑
Contract drafting requirements	❑
Trademark application/dispute	❑
Patent application/dispute	❑

Other intellectual property dispute ❏
Planning application/dispute ❏

Other (please state): _____

Q4. Which of the following seminars/surgeries have you attended over the last 12 months?

[Name of seminar/surgery and date] ❏
[Name of seminar/surgery and date] ❏

Q5. How interesting did you find the seminar/surgery?

	Very Interesting	**Quite Interesting**	**Not at all Interesting**
[Name of seminar/surgery and date]	❏	❏	❏
[Name of seminar/surgery and date]	❏	❏	❏

Q6. Was the information in the seminar/surgery of use to you?

	Very useful	**Quite useful**	**Not at all useful**
[Name of seminar/surgery and date]	❏	❏	❏
[Name of seminar/surgery and date]	❏	❏	❏

Q7. What impression did the seminar/surgery give you about the firm? Please indicate how strongly the following impressions come across.

	Weak ↔ Strong
The firm is professional	1 2 3 4 5
The firm is client-oriented	1 2 3 4 5
The firm is aware of client requirements	1 2 3 4 5
The firm is well run	1 2 3 4 5
The firm is expensive	1 2 3 4 5
The firm gives good value for money	1 2 3 4 5
The firm is not approachable	1 2 3 4 5
The firm is up to date with changes in the law	1 2 3 4 5
I trust them more	1 2 3 4 5
The solicitors in the firm are expert in their field	1 2 3 4 5

Q8. How likely would you be to attend a seminar/surgery again in the future?

Very likely ❏
Quite likely ❏
Unlikely ❏
Very unlikely ❏

Q9. Please indicate below if there are any areas for which you would like a seminar. Please give a mark out of 10, '10' being very interested and '1' being not at all interested.

Personal subjects:
Purchasing/selling a house (i.e. conveyancing) ❏
Probate on the death of a friend or relative ❏
What is involved in making a will ❏
How and when you can obtain compensation for an injury ❏
What actions can be taken regarding a domestic dispute ❏
What actions can be taken regarding a dispute with neighbours ❏
What your responsibilities and rights are as a landlord ❏
What your responsibilities and rights are as a tenant ❏
What is involved in criminal proceedings ❏
How a solicitor can help with motoring offences ❏
Financial/tax advice ❏
Employment contract or dispute ❏
What the present approach is to matrimonial or family issues ❏

Other (please state): _____

Business-related subjects:
What legal requirements there are in setting up a business ❏
How to approach the sale/acquisition of a business ❏
How to approach the sale/purchase of business premises ❏
What your legal position is with regard to debt collection ❏
What the common problems are when faced with an insurance
    claim ❏
How the law can help with customer–supplier relations ❏
Employment contracts and disputes ❏
Tax advice ❏
Contract drafting requirements ❏
The process involved in a trademark application/dispute ❏
The process involved in a patent application/dispute ❏
Other intellectual property dispute ❏
The process involved in a planning application/dispute ❏

Other (please state): _____

Q10. How likely are you to recommend the seminars/surgeries run by this firm to colleagues and/or friends?

Very likely   ❏
Quite likely   ❏
Unlikely   ❏
Very unlikely   ❏

Q11. Finally, if there are any comments you would like to make about the seminars/surgeries, we would be glad to hear them.

_____
_____
_____
_____

Thank you for your time

Questionnaire 10 Measuring awareness of competitors by both clients and non-clients

[You may choose to send this out anonymously and include your own firm as one of the three or more competing firms mentioned in Q5.]

Q1. **Are you currently using the services of a solicitor?**

Yes ❏ No ❏

Q2. **Have you used the services of a solicitor in the last:**

One year ❏ Two years ❏ Three years ❏ Five years ❏ 10 years ❏

How many times have you used the services of a solicitor in the last three years? _____

Q3. **What have been your reasons for using a solicitor in the last three years?**

[Please use as appropriate: 'personal reasons' for questionnaires sent to private clients and 'business reasons' for questionnaires being sent to business or commercial clients.]

Personal reasons:

Home sale/purchase (conveyancing)	❏
Death of a friend or relative	❏
To make a will	❏
To obtain compensation for an injury	❏
A dispute with an individual	❏
A dispute with an organisation	❏
Landlord and tenant relations	❏
Criminal proceedings	❏
Motoring offences	❏
Financial/tax advice	❏
Employment contract or dispute	❏
Divorce or separation	❏
Debt or hire purchase problems	❏
Faulty goods or services	❏

Other (please state): _____

Business reasons:

Setting up a business	❏
Sale/acquisition of a business	❏
Sale/purchase of business premises	❏
Debt collection	❏
Insurance claim	❏
Customer–supplier relations	❏
Employment contracts and disputes	❏
Tax advice	❏

Contract drafting requirements ❏
Trademark application/dispute ❏
Patent application/dispute ❏
Other intellectual property dispute ❏
Planning application/dispute ❏

Other (please state): _____

Q4. **In this question, we are trying to understand how important different factors are in your choosing a solicitors firm.** Please rate each of the following ten factors in order of importance 1–10 with regard to when you first choose a solicitor, '10' being the most important, descending to '1' being the least important.

[Use 10 from this list]

A recommendation from someone ❏
I know/knew someone in the firm ❏
They are well established in the local area ❏
They have a good reputation ❏
They are inexpensive ❏
Friends use them ❏
I have used them in the past ❏
They had a good telephone manner when I called them ❏
They gave me a clear explanation about their services on the phone ❏
They sponsor local charities in the area ❏
The initial consultation was free ❏
People and colleagues I know use them ❏
They can demonstrate experience ❏
They have specialist knowledge ❏
They package their services in a user-friendly way ❏
They have a good approach to client care ❏
The firm is large and can offer a broad range of legal services ❏
The firm is small and friendly ❏
The approach of the reception staff ❏
Their offices are convenient ❏
They offer good value for money ❏

Q5. **Please indicate if you have heard of the following firms of solicitors:**

[Name of competing solicitors' firm] ❏
[Name of competing solicitors' firm] ❏
[Name of competing solicitors' firm] ❏

Q6. Please indicate if you have used the services of any of these solicitors, either at present or in the past:

	Use at present	Have used in the past
[*Name of competing solicitors' firm*]	❑	❑
[*Name of competing solicitors' firm*]	❑	❑
[*Name of competing solicitors' firm*]	❑	❑

Q7. How satisfied were you with the service you received from these solicitors?

	[*Name of competing solicitors' firm*]	[*Name of competing solicitors' firm*]	[*Name of competing solicitors' firm*]
Very satisfied	❑	❑	❑
Satisfied	❑	❑	❑
Not very satisfied	❑	❑	❑
Very dissatisfied	❑	❑	❑

Q8. Please indicate which of the following services you are aware each firm is able to offer:

	[*Name of competing solicitors' firm*]	[*Name of competing solicitors' firm*]	[*Name of competing solicitors' firm*]
Home sale/purchase (conveyancing)	❑	❑	❑
Death of a friend or relative	❑	❑	❑
To make a will	❑	❑	❑
To obtain compensation for an injury	❑	❑	❑
A dispute with an individual	❑	❑	❑
A dispute with an organisation	❑	❑	❑
Landlord and tenant relations	❑	❑	❑
Criminal proceedings	❑	❑	❑
Motoring offences	❑	❑	❑
Financial/tax advice	❑	❑	❑
Employment contract or dispute	❑	❑	❑
Divorce or separation	❑	❑	❑
Debt or hire purchase problems	❑	❑	❑
Faulty goods or services	❑	❑	❑

Other (please state): _____

	[Name of competing solicitors' firm]	[Name of competing solicitors' firm]	[Name of competing solicitors' firm]
Business:			
Setting up a business	❏	❏	❏
Sale/acquisition of a business	❏	❏	❏
Sale/purchase of business premises	❏	❏	❏
Debt collection	❏	❏	❏
Insurance claim	❏	❏	❏
Customer–supplier relations	❏	❏	❏
Employment contracts and disputes	❏	❏	❏
Tax advice	❏	❏	❏
Contract drafting requirements	❏	❏	❏
Trademark application/dispute	❏	❏	❏
Patent application/dispute	❏	❏	❏
Other intellectual property dispute	❏	❏	❏
Planning application/dispute	❏	❏	❏

Other (please state): _____

Q9. **Please indicate, for those firms you have heard of, which of the following statements you would associate with them. Indicate by circling the number how strongly you agree ('5') or disagree ('1') that the statements apply to each firm.**

	[Name of competing solicitors' firm]	[Name of competing solicitors' firm]	[Name of competing solicitors' firm]
The firm is professional	1 2 3 4 5	1 2 3 4 5	1 2 3 4 5
The firm is client-oriented	1 2 3 4 5	1 2 3 4 5	1 2 3 4 5
The firm is aware of client requirements	1 2 3 4 5	1 2 3 4 5	1 2 3 4 5
The firm is well run	1 2 3 4 5	1 2 3 4 5	1 2 3 4 5
The firm is expensive	1 2 3 4 5	1 2 3 4 5	1 2 3 4 5
The firm gives good value for money	1 2 3 4 5	1 2 3 4 5	1 2 3 4 5
The firm is not approachable	1 2 3 4 5	1 2 3 4 5	1 2 3 4 5
The firm is up to date with changes in the law	1 2 3 4 5	1 2 3 4 5	1 2 3 4 5
They are a key part of the local community	1 2 3 4 5	1 2 3 4 5	1 2 3 4 5
The solicitors in the firm are expert in their field	1 2 3 4 5	1 2 3 4 5	1 2 3 4 5
Using the firm adds status to my business dealings	1 2 3 4 5	1 2 3 4 5	1 2 3 4 5

	[Name of competing solicitors' firm]	[Name of competing solicitors' firm]	[Name of competing solicitors' firm]
They are in a good location	1 2 3 4 5	1 2 3 4 5	1 2 3 4 5
I have only heard good said of them	1 2 3 4 5	1 2 3 4 5	1 2 3 4 5
The firm has a clear identity and image	1 2 3 4 5	1 2 3 4 5	1 2 3 4 5

Q10. How did you hear about the solicitors' firms mentioned

	[Name of competing solicitors' firm]	[Name of competing solicitors' firm]	[Name of competing solicitors' firm]
Advertising in local newspapers/ local magazines	❏	❏	❏
From the Yellow Pages/Thompson Local	❏	❏	❏
Through brochures or newsletters mailed to you	❏	❏	❏
Through being mentioned in papers or magazines	❏	❏	❏
From sponsorship of sports or the arts	❏	❏	❏
Appearing in legal directories	❏	❏	❏
Professional recommendation (i.e. bank, building society)	❏	❏	❏
Recommendation from a friend or relative	❏	❏	❏
Seeing the offices	❏	❏	❏
From the Citizens' Advice Bureau	❏	❏	❏
Referral from another solicitor	❏	❏	❏
Through a charity, special interest group or other agency	❏	❏	❏
From an invitation to a seminar/ reception at the firm	❏	❏	❏
From a personal contact with the firm	❏	❏	❏

Other (please state): _____

Q11. In general, what is your impression of solicitors on the whole?

	Disagree ↔ Agree
They are efficient and work hard for their money	1 2 3 4 5
They really listen and understand	1 2 3 4 5
They are well respected	1 2 3 4 5
They are approachable/easy to talk to	1 2 3 4 5
One can trust them to do their best	1 2 3 4 5
They are in touch and up to date	1 2 3 4 5
They are intelligent	1 2 3 4 5
They are mainly after your money	1 2 3 4 5
They are not as honest as they might be	1 2 3 4 5
They are pompous and have a condescending manner	1 2 3 4 5
Their charges are too high for the work they do	1 2 3 4 5
They do not value their clients	1 2 3 4 5
They sit back and let the work come to them	1 2 3 4 5
They are not commercially aware	1 2 3 4 5
They are old-fashioned on the whole	1 2 3 4 5
They depend on the old boys' network	1 2 3 4 5

Q12. Finally, if there are any comments you would like to make about any of the solicitors' firms mentioned, we would be glad to hear them. Please indicate which firm you are commenting on.

_____
_____
_____
_____

Thank you for your time.

Part 3

Promotion

Using different promotional methods

Introduction

Before you start

Before you begin to promote your firm and the legal services you offer, there are a number of preliminary considerations:

- your firm's image;
- maintaining a continuity in your approach;
- your reason for promoting;
- your promotional budget;
- the people factor;
- evaluating your promotions.

Your firm's image

What is the image of your firm? What are you saying to your clients with your offices, your logo and printed materials, your client care systems, your overall approach and the approach of your fee earners?

Your firm's image has different aspects to it. There is the visual image communicated through your logo, the firm's stationery, brochures, any media you use and your offices. Then there is the image or impression given to clients when interacting with your firm, such as the approach of fee earners and staff and the client care systems your firm has in place.

If you want to find out how your firm's image is perceived, the first place to start is to find out more about your existing clients, who they are and what they think of you. (Part 1 of this manual guides you through evaluating and understanding your client base and Part 2, the research section, shows you how to find out what your clients think through client research.) Knowing about the type of clients you have will give you an idea of the way your firm is perceived.

You then need to ask yourself:

- Do you have an image as such and what is it?
- Is your current image appropriate for your locality?
- Is your current image attracting the sort of clients you want?
- Is your image appropriate for your firm and the personalities in the firm?
- Is your image visible to your clients and potential clients?

With answers to these questions you might decide you need to strengthen your existing image or perhaps change it to appeal to a wider audience or different clients. Whatever your motivation, before considering promotion, you need to appreciate that image can be a delicate thing.

Actions such as improving or changing your internal client care systems, the approach of staff and the look of your offices, can all affect the impression your clients have of you when working with you. However, though these actions may strengthen your service to existing clients and inspire greater client loyalty, they may not be sufficiently visible to attract new groups of clients. You may also need to alter the way your firm projects itself in the market place by changing your visual approach such as your logo and the look of any promotional materials or letterheads.

If you are changing the image of your firm, it is useful to note the following:

- Try to ensure that any changes you make are logical extensions of your existing approach because if you radically change your image overnight you run the danger of alienating existing clients.
- Research clients' views (usually only necessary where you are making radical changes). You can do this quickly and easily by holding focus groups to discuss the impression that your proposed new visual approach gives your clients – or you might want to present a number of different approaches and measure their response to each.
- Having decided on a new approach, you should then introduce it to clients with caution. Perhaps send a letter to them to explain why you have changed your approach – this is a good client contact opportunity.

Whichever approach you take, you should make sure that your existing clients are not alienated and kept on board selling them the positive side of any changes and keeping them fully informed.

Continuity of approach

One of the most important aspects of your firm's promotional activity is that there is a continuity of approach to the visual aspects and the facts and messages contained in written information. Continuity is extremely important as the repetition of images and information will encourage recognition of your firm and acceptance of the messages you are giving.

The importance of continuity across all promotional activities and materials cannot be stressed enough.

Maintaining continuity throughout your visual and written approach need not be restrictive, and it can also make life easy not to have to 'rewrite the book' every time.

There are a couple of different approaches you might adopt for the visual presentation of your firm's image and the image of each of your legal services:

- One image suits all. Create a single image that covers all legal services.
- The firm has an overall image and each legal service has its own image that has a family resemblance to the overall image. This might be achieved through using symbols, colour coding, or some other design element.

When approaching written information you can ensure you maintain continuity by setting out the facts and messages that apply to each legal service – a simple crib sheet giving the firm's approach to offering each legal service, and the way you want to present the firm as a whole. Part 1 is useful in helping you do this.

Your reason for promoting

Before undertaking any promotional activity, you need to have a very clear reason for the promotional activity. (See p. 135 on setting objectives and actions for further guidance.) If you know why you are promoting you will be able to prioritise any expenditure or investment needed and you will be able to evaluate the success of the promotion.

Your promotional budget

It would be simple to state that you should allocate a percentage of your annual turnover to promoting and marketing your firm; however, the budget you need will vary according to what you are trying to achieve.

The best way to approach setting a budget is to begin by identifying your objectives for the next three years and then the actions you need to take in the next 12, 24 and 36 months to contribute towards achieving those objectives. (See p. 135 of this manual about setting objectives and actions.)

As well as allowing for actions to achieve specific objectives, you should allow for ongoing activities such as cross-selling, client loyalty promotions, researching your clients' needs and your firm's performance, to name a few.

A good way of setting the budget is to identify different types of expenditure for different areas of activity. Three suggested areas of activity are:

- new client promotions;
- client loyalty work and referral incentives;
- cross-selling promotions to existing clients.

You should also be aware, year on year, how the work you do in one year will affect the work in following years. New customers you gain from one promotion may require promotional investment in the following year, such as investment in sending them newsletters to encourage loyalty or promotions selling other services your firm offers to take advantage of cross-selling opportunities.

Another example would be that if you invest a great deal and produce an elaborate brochure one year, you have set a precedent and would be ill-advised to lower your standard to a cheap and cheerful production the next year.

When setting a promotional budget you need to be aware of the possible returns you might expect from the promotion, what your targets are, and what you can afford.

The people factor

It is important that everyone in the firm is made aware of any promotions being undertaken and that they have a clear understanding of why, where and how they are taking place.

This is so that if a client, or potential client, rings up in response to the promotion, everyone in the firm is able to explain how the promotion works, why the promotion might not apply to them and what its aims are. A quick and concise answer will ensure that any potential respondent is encouraged and anyone who may not qualify for the promotion is pacified.

In addition, everyone should be aware of which clients have responded to a promotion so that if any specific offer has been made, for example '10 per cent off if you present this letter when purchasing our services', they are correctly billed minus the discount.

Evaluating your promotion

This is the single most vital aspect of any promotional work. You must identify the effect and results of any promotional work you undertake. Any information you gain from a promotional activity is important for planning promotions in the future so that you can promote your firm efficiently and effectively, with least wastage of resources.

Whatever you invest in promoting your firm should be examined for a return. This might be in the form of money, in a change in your clients' perception of your firm (evidenced through research) or in the profile of your clients.

Some promotions will be easy to evaluate. How many new customers did the promotion generate and how much they are worth to the firm's bottom line? Others will be less clear cut. For example, it may not be easy to identify how well received a newsletter is and you will probably have to conduct specific research.

It may also be difficult to identify the results of a promotion quickly. Some promotions might have a long-term effect while others have a short life. A referral promotion might have a long response time, whereas a direct mail promotion might ask for an immediate response.

The most important thing is to establish whether the promotion was a success for your firm or not. A promotion that cost £3,000 and brings in only three new clients might be a success if each new client is worth over £1,000 to the firm. However, if the aim was to bring in nine new clients then you may not judge the promotion a success and another method may prove more appropriate in this instance.

The benchmarks for success are usually set by the reason for carrying out the promotional activity.

Methods of evaluating different promotional approaches are discussed in the relevant sections.

How promotion can help

Is promotion a good idea for solicitors' firms?

People expect to be sold to, and a product to be marketed. If someone doesn't make the effort to sell their services, a potential client may simply shrug their shoulders and take their custom to someone whom they perceive wants their business and money. People see and accept the sales pitch, in whatever form it takes, as an integral part of the product or service they are purchasing.

This approach applies to legal services as with any other service or product. Increased competition from non-traditional legal service providers together with a loosening of professional practice rules to enable solicitors to undertake marketing promotions, has kick-started marketing for solicitors. The public and the majority of the legal profession no longer think marketing and selling different legal services inappropriate. Solicitors now have the opportunity to go out and get clients, rather than waiting for them to walk through the door.

How can promotion influence clients?

To understand how promoting the legal services your firm offers may help increase the number of clients your firm handles, it is useful to take a quick look at the decision-making process that individuals and organisations go through when purchasing a service or product.

The following diagrams show an interpretation of the stages an individual or an organisation might go through when deciding what needs to be purchased and which supplier they want to use.

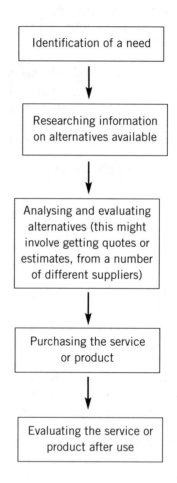

Figure A Individual purchasing decision.

Figure A illustrates that there are a number of different stages an individual may go through when making a purchasing decision. The stages might be undertaken to a greater or lesser extent, depending on whether it is:

■ The first time the product or service has been purchased.
■ The re-purchase of a product or service but from a different supplier.
■ The re-purchase from the same supplier of the same product or service.
■ The re-purchase from the same supplier of a different product or service.

Figure B Organisational purchasing decision.

Figure B represents where one business purchases the product or service supplied by another.

As with individuals the stages might be entered into, to a greater or lesser extent, depending on whether it is:

- The first time the product or service has been purchased.
- The re-purchase of a product or service but from a different supplier.
- The re-purchase from the same supplier of the same product or service.
- The re-purchase from the same supplier of a different product or service.

Understanding the decision-making process that your clients, or potential clients, may go through when selecting a firm of solicitors, enables you to identify when it might be a good idea to promote your firm and what type of message you should be giving to effectively influence them to purchase your products.

Each stage shown in the purchase decision-making process has been set out below with examples of ways in which promotion can be used to influence the purchaser.

Box 9 Purchase decision stages

Individual	Organisational	Examples of ways that promotion can be used to influence purchase decision or need
Indentification of need	Identification of need/problem Investigating and developing possible solution to problem and identifying parameters of purchasing service	■ Creates a need through advertising and educating clients about possibilities and options available to them ■ Creates a need for expertise by advertising the benefits of using a firm with a specialisation or experience
Researching information on alternatives available	Search for possible service suppliers	■ Ensures that your firm's capabilities in different areas are placed so that buyers have ready access to them ■ Provides buyers with general information about the area in question to position yourself as an expert ■ Encourages existing clients to promote your firm

Box 9 *Continued*

Individual	Organisational	Examples of ways that promotion can be used to influence purchase decision or need
Analysing and evaluating alternatives	Evaluating the alternative service providers available to see how they meet specifications	■ Ensures that your firm is in a position to provide clear information covering all of the needs of a client and containing the factors that might affect their purchasing decision ■ Ensures that clients have a good initial impression of your firm through the offices, telephone manner and speed of response to queries ■ Ensures that the image and profile of your firm matches buyers' expectations and creates confidence in them that your firm is able to provide the service to the level required
Purchasing the service	Purchasing the service	■ Gives clear explanations of costs and extent of service supplied ■ Gives clear explanations of any formalities required ■ Ensures you are in a convenient position to supply clients' needs ■ Gives clear explanations of any contractual obligations
Evaluating the service after use	Ongoing evaluation of the supplier's performance	■ Provides clients with the level of communication they require ■ Ensures that any client care exercise undertaken is recognised and valued by the client ■ Ensures that the supply of the service you provide has a two-way communication ability, i.e. ask your clients what they want and make them aware of all aspects of the service they have received

Ways in which promotion can be used to help your business

There are a number of ways that promotion can be used to affect your business.

1. PROMOTING YOUR FIRM TO GAIN COMPLETELY NEW CLIENTS

To obtain new clients is perhaps the most obvious reason why products are promoted. However, to use promotion effectively, you need to know who you want as new clients and how to reach them.

The question of 'who you want', can be answered by looking at your existing clients and identifying which are most valuable to you.

The question of 'how to reach them' can be answered by asking these 'valuable' existing clients a number of pertinent questions such as where they heard about you and their buying habits.

There are also a number of other reasons you might choose to promote to get new clients. Perhaps one of the legal services you offer needs more clients to bring overheads per client down and increase the profit margin for that legal service. You may need more clients to keep a solicitor fully employed.

Whatever your reason, before promoting you need to consider:

- how many new clients you want;
- how many new clients your firm can handle;
- how valuable each of those clients might be in the short and long term;
- how much you can afford to invest in any promotional activity.

2. CROSS-SELLING

In section 1(b) you were asked to identify whether your clients are 'passive', 'active' or 'single transaction (ST) clients'. See Box 1 on p. 13 to identify what these descriptions mean.

Promotions to each of these three client categories should aim to encourage them to purchase from you again. Once someone has purchased from you, every effort should be made to maintain them as clients unless they did not like the service you offered and this is made clear. At some stage, you have probably heard someone say that it is far cheaper to keep an existing client than get a new one – this is nearly always correct.

Ideally, all of your clients should fall within the 'active' category. Realistically, many of them will fall into the 'passive' category. Everyone who has purchased from you is a prospect to purchase again, even those who you think are 'ST clients'. All new clients are 'ST clients' until they purchase from you a second time and then they are 'active' or may fall into 'passive'. All should receive promotional attention and no one who has used your services should fall out of a promotion loop altogether.

Passive clients:

- need to be encouraged to use your firm if or when they next need legal services;
- need to be made aware of a need by creating that need in them;
- need to be reminded of your existence and the services you offer;
- need to be told about any new services you introduce, or changes to existing services;
- will be more likely to use you again if you maintain regular contact with them.

ST clients:

- should be promoted to, and encouraged to use other services your firm offers, e.g. if they have bought a house, they may need a will written, etc.;
- should have new services promoted to them;
- should be given every opportunity to become 'passive' or 'active' clients by your maintaining regular contact with them for a certain period of time to encourage them to think of you as their solicitor;
- should be strongly encouraged to refer new potential clients to you.

Active clients:

- promotion will encourage them to use your firm when they next need legal services;
- promotion will encourage them to continue to use your firm;
- promotion will help you to combat any promotion by your competitors;
- promote new services to them;
- promote to them as a client care exercise and to maintain regular contact with them;
- promote to encourage them to refer potential clients to you.

As far as possible you should tailor any promotions to the nature of clients and the aims of the promotion.

The aim with cross-selling is to encourage repeat business from existing clients with the least promotional expenditure on your part. Decisions will need to be made, based on results, about the best time-frame to promote to different client types to keep them loyal or sell them new services.

3. ENCOURAGING LOYALTY AMONGST EXISTING CLIENTS

This type of promotion would aim to maintain contact with clients in ways such as sending them newsletters, inviting them to lunches, seminars or parties.

4. COMBATTING COMPETITION FROM OTHER SOLICITORS OR ORGANISATIONS

If an area of your income is under threat from competitors, rather than cutting costs, it is often a good tactic to invest in promoting to the target audience under threat to combat the competitors' actions. In addition, if you consistently promote to a particular target audience it can create a barrier to entry by a competitor.

5. RAISING THE PROFILE OF YOUR FIRM

By promoting to educate your clients about the services you offer, you can ensure that your firm is the one that springs to mind should they require a particular service.

6. NEGATING BAD PRESS

If your firm receives bad press you might advertise or write to your clients to dispel any rumours, contradict negative comments and rebuild your reputation.

7. POSITIONING OR RE-POSITIONING THE IMAGE OF YOUR FIRM

If research indicates that you need to re-position or change the image of your firm and the services you offer, you should promote your new approach to clients and sell it to them. See pp. 225–6 where image is discussed.

8. ENSURING YOU ARE ABLE TO ATTRACT HIGH QUALITY STAFF

The image of your firm and the level of activity undertaken to build the number of clients may make a difference to the staff that you are able to attract. The quality and amount of promotional activity you undertake says a lot about the attitude of your firm to the future and may enable you to recruit high quality staff or even make your firm appear desirable as a merger partner.

9. INFORMING CLIENTS AND POTENTIAL CLIENTS OF NEW SERVICES

This is an obvious time to promote to build awareness and clients in a new area of business.

Who do you promote to?

It depends on what you are aiming to achieve. You might promote to increase business or keep in touch with existing active, passive or ST clients. Or you might promote to gain new clients. A good promotional plan should include a mix of all four target audiences.

'Promotion means expenditure that we cannot afford!'

Often promotion is thought of as too expensive, both in terms of time and money. However, promotion of your firm should be viewed as an investment and be judged in the same way. All promotional activities should be properly analysed and evaluated to measure their return on investment, which should then be clearly quantified in terms of the bottom line.

Promotion should be viewed as a fee earner in its own right!

Determining your promotional messages

Having identified possible communication opportunities for you to influence potential purchasers and contact your clients, you now need to try to identify the messages to communicate. The message you give to clients will depend on what you want the promotion to achieve and what will motivate the different client types and potential clients to respond.

What you want the promotion to achieve

If you want a client to come to a seminar, you need to invite them; if you want them to use your firm for conveyancing, you need to tell them. The reason for contacting your client should be made crystal clear to them. Don't be afraid of telling them you want them to call you – they won't know if you don't say so. See Section 1(f) in Part 1 on objectives and actions to help identify the messages you might want to put across in promotional materials.

How to encourage a reaction

In section 1(b) of this manual, exercises focused on making assumptions and trying to determine what clients for the different legal services want from that service. Although in many instances this information will have been assumed, it can provide the basis of promotions to clients and potential clients. By using client values in any promotional message, you are more closely aligning your firm to their desires and encouraging the recipient to react by making it more attractive for them to do so. Client research (see Part 2) can provide you with valuable information on what clients or potential clients are looking for.

One promotional message, i.e. low price or experienced solicitor, will not necessarily fit all services or all client types as the main motivational message. You might need to change your message because, although there will often be common themes, clients for different services might have different priorities when purchasing different services and will therefore be influenced by different messages from your firm. For example, the primary concern of someone purchasing your conveyancing services might be price; the experience of the solicitor may be important but not nearly as important, whereas the experience of a solicitor undertaking a medical negligence case may well be key to the choice of solicitor.

If you have not undertaken client research you will need to draw conclusions and make assumptions using your perceptions and experience of clients in consultation with other fee earners.

Section 3(b)

The promotional tools

Introduction

Once you have established why you want to promote your firm's services, and decided what you want to say and who you want to promote to, the burning question is 'which promotional method do I use?' In the following section a selection of promotional methods are explained with the following outlined for each:

- when you should use this promotional tool;
- the characteristics of each one;
- how to create this promotional tool;
- how to evaluate its use.

Summary of the promotional methods

1. Brochures, leaflets and other printed materials

The quality of your brochures, leaflets and other printed materials such as letterhead is of great importance in presenting your firm. These may be produced for a number of reasons:

- for a specific promotion such as a direct mailshot or for a seminar;
- as a general communication tool to give clients and potential clients more information about your services;
- to be displayed in reception for anyone interested to take;
- to be distributed to intermediary organisations to distribute.

Whatever they are used for, it is important that they are well produced, accurate and reflect the image of the firm.

2. Public relations

This is an extremely broad heading and will cover many of the seminars, events, sponsorship, advertising and client care initiatives that you undertake. However, the best known form of public relations is the press release that can be used to specifically target information to a particular market or respond to specific issues or events.

3. The Internet

This can be used as an information source and means of communication with your clients. It should always be remembered that a lot of people still do not have access to the Internet so any web site should always be used as one element within a number of different promotional approaches.

The section starting on p. 262 gives you a guide to how you might use the Internet as a marketing tool.

4. Newsletters

Newsletters are most commonly used as a client care promotional tool to maintain contact with clients, educate them and inform them of any changes in the law or in your firm that might affect them.

They may also be used as a subtle selling tool if sent to non-clients on a regular basis ensuring that your firm and work is known to them.

5. Direct mail letters

This method of promotion can be used when conveying a specific message and will normally ask the recipient to respond in some way.

They are best used where it is possible to identify, isolate and locate a specific profile of recipients, the target audience.

6. Seminars

These should be used as a positioning and public relations exercise, as well as an opportunity to meet potential new clients.

By presenting a seminar on a specific subject of concern or interest, you will position your firm as experts in the field and as a central source of information should the seminar attendees require help in this area. In addition, you are presenting yourself as an organisation in touch with the needs of those attending.

7. Sponsorship

This is usually used as a method of raising the profile of a firm in a local area and to provide public relations opportunities.

The sponsorship package should be directed towards some activity that attracts your target audience.

8. Advertising

You might use advertising in a number of different ways and to produce a number of different results. It is an extremely flexible promotional tool. It may be used to back up another promotional exercise or for any of the following reasons:

- to generate a response;
- to ensure your presence stands out, for example, in directories;
- as a part of a general awareness campaign;
- as a part of a positioning exercise.

The effectiveness of advertising can often be difficult to evaluate. However, as a medium, if properly handled, it is a very good way of reaching a wide audience outside of and including your existing client base.

9. Client entertaining and open days

The purpose of client entertaining and holding open days, is to build relationships with existing clients and to introduce yourself to potential new clients and the local community.

Different approaches to client entertaining are identified together with hints and tips on how to ensure the day or event is successful.

Brochures, leaflets and other printed materials

Your brochures, leaflets, and branded office stationery present the outward image of your firm. The way in which they are produced, the format of your logo, the images you choose and the colours you use, all make a statement about your firm.

One of the most important things about your printed materials is that they should show consistency in the use of your logo, quality and the information given.

This section aims to give you a clear understanding of how to produce printed materials.

The following are discussed:

- assessing printed materials;
- choosing an appropriate designer;
- your logo;
- producing stationery;
- producing brochures and leaflets.

Assessing printed materials

An important aspect of producing printed materials is understanding why one piece is good and another not. Whether you like the design of a particular piece of printed material is subjective. However, there are aspects of all printed materials that can be viewed objectively to determine whether they achieve what you intended. When you look at the piece in question, there are a number of questions you can ask.

Business cards and stationery

■ Do they look professional, serious, authoritative, trustworthy – what impression do they give of the organisation?

■ Do the different elements look well balanced on the paper and do they look neat and tidy?

■ What is the quality of print and production?

■ Do they reflect the profile of the organisation they represent?

Brochures and leaflets

■ Are they appropriate for the audience to whom they are directed? Can you tell by looking at them to whom they are directed?

■ Do the pages have a balance to them with regard to the quantity of copy and images?

■ Are the pictures used appropriate, well positioned and well set?

■ Do the contents and style of copy work well with the design?

■ Is the text accurate and spelling correct?

■ Do the colours create the right atmosphere?

■ Is there a message in the use of colour?

■ Does the paper used contribute or detract from the item?

■ Is the item a cohesive production?

■ Who is the item aimed at?

■ Is the impression they give appropriate for the organisation that produced it?

■ Is the item appropriate for the industry of the organisation that produced it?

Take the time to review your firm's printed materials and ask these questions about each individual piece.

In addition, collect together all of your printed materials and set them out on a desk or table next to each other. Viewing the whole group, ask yourself:

■ Are they recognisable as coming from one organisation?

- Are they consistent with regard to quality, feel and impression?
- Is their use of colour consistent or complementary with each other?
- Do they all sit comfortably together?

All of your printed materials should sit well together and demonstrate a family resemblance. This does not mean that one design fits all, it means that you need to have a visual theme across all of them. If your printed materials do not sit well together, make sure that when you come to reprint you have them redesigned to do so.

Working with designers

Analysing their work

Before launching into the nuts and bolts of producing printed materials, it will be helpful to discuss how you can pick a designer who will be able to produce appropriate designs for your firm.

The first thing to do is to invite a couple of local designers to show you their portfolios and discuss your needs. Whether or not you like a designer's work is subjective, but as you look through their portfolio ask yourself the same questions about their work as you did about other promotional materials (see 'Assessing printed materials' on p. 242).

In addition, at the presentation you should ask the designer questions about the brief they were given for different items of work and how their design met the requirements of the brief. They will probably explain this automatically as they present their portfolio to you. Seeing what a designer has produced for other organisations will give you an insight into the tone and feel of their work and though your requirements will be quite different, this will help you judge how their approach might suit your firm.

Asking designers to pitch for your business

It is accepted practice to invite two or three designers to put together a pitch for the work you have in mind. However, there are a few points to note:

- The value of the project or longer-term work needs to be substantial enough to make it worth their while putting in the time. Coming up with ideas and making them work is approximately 80 per cent of the design process.
- Some designers may charge for this.
- Some may not be prepared to pitch against others.
- It is not a good idea, unless a very high value project, to ask more than three designers to pitch.
- Having a pitch will not reduce the final design cost; though if a designer charges for a pitch then this will usually be taken off the final bill.

- The designers may not have enough information to cover all of the text features or visual elements. The pitch is only an indication of the approach they suggest might be appropriate for you.
- If you are doing a brochure or newsletter, it is a good idea to ask for a front cover and an inside spread to see how the pages will run.

Getting a quote on the job

It is also important to ask them for an indication of how much they will charge you for the work you have in mind. To gain some insight into possible costs involved, ask them as they go through their portfolio to give you an indication of the costs of each piece that could be relevant to your project:

- how much the design cost;
- what the print run was and how much the print cost;
- if it was an item for a specific promotion, what the results of the promotion were.

Designers often calculate their costs according to an hourly rate (e.g. £30–90 per hour) and often, designers will ask you what budget you have. You could give them a ball park figure or state you still need to finalise the budget and ask them to put together a quote. In all likelihood they will not be able to give you a quote on the spot but having discussed your requirements, ask them their thoughts on possible approaches and ask them to quote on these. The quote should include:

- design cost (and any variation according to different sizes, etc.) including the number of proofs and corrections included in the price as this can change the final cost radically;
- any illustration or photographic costs, and options such as purchasing stock photography, using existing shots, etc.;
- a print cost.

It is also a good idea to ask for details of any extra costs or price reductions from including or leaving out different elements or variations, such as:

- the number of colours and price variation if one-colour, two-colour or four-colour;
- the type of paper they suggest;
- the number of pages and the size and format, i.e. A4, DL, A5 – landscape or portrait;
- any finishing variations such as lamination, varnish or embossing.

If you have never worked in this area before, when you are choosing a designer it is a good idea to pick one who will work closely with you and guide you through the process. Obviously they should show a clear understanding of your firm and why you want the brochure.

Your logo

Your logo is the symbol, words or visual repeated across all of your firm's materials to identify them as originating from your firm. If you already have a logo and you are not particularly happy with it, or it represents your firm 10 years ago, it is worthwhile having a designer look at it and quote on adjusting it or redesigning it to suit your firm today.

You should always be aware that your existing logo will identify your firm to past and existing clients and any new logo should be a logical extension of the old one so that it is not too drastic a change which might have the effect of raising a question in your clients' minds as to whether the firm is appropriate for them.

There are a number of things that it is useful to note about logos:

- they need to be clear and identifiable as a symbol;
- they need to reflect your firm and its standing;
- they need to be used consistently on all of the firm's materials;
- they should be practical and easy to use.

A logo needs to be clear and identifiable as a symbol. A logo could be a word, a visual symbol or a combination of both. Whatever it is, a logo needs to have its own identity on a page and stand out from copy and other visuals. Your logo should also stand out from the crowd and be easily recognisable.

A logo needs to reflect your firm and its standing. The style of logo you choose, such as the font you use if your logo is your firm's name, can indicate whether your firm is traditional, modern, a commercial or private practice by its look and feel.

Your logo needs to be used consistently on all of the firm's materials. It is vital that your logo is not redesigned on a regular basis. It should appear in the correct format, proportion and colour (if this is an issue) on all of the firm's communications. Organisations frequently prepare a document outlining how their logo must appear if used. This will identify colour options, sizes, etc.

Logos should be practical and easy to use. Logos need to be used everywhere and therefore should be adaptable. For example, if you have a very long horizontal logo, it might be difficult to balance other logos with it or put it onto portrait leaflets effectively. Remember that although a logo looks good on A4 letterhead, you also need to be able to reduce it or enlarge it to fit different items such as business cards, brochures, leaflets, web sites and office signs.

You also need to be aware of colours and ensure that your logo will work equally effectively in one-colour, two-colour and four-colour versions.

Producing printed materials

Stationery

The description 'stationery' includes letterheads, business cards, compliment slips, quotations, invoices and any other everyday branded stationery materials.

When you have your logo designed, the designer should indicate how your logo and firm's identity will work on these items.

Brochures and leaflets

It is useful here to draw a distinction between brochures and leaflets. Brochures are general publications about the firm or legal services, whereas leaflets are publications produced for a particular purpose such as a promotion.

WHEN TO USE BROCHURES

Brochures contain information about the firm, the services the firm offers, the people, the firm's philosophy and approach to clients. They are the printed embodiment of your firm's approach and have the following objectives.

1. To maintain or create an image of the firm through:

   - their design and appearance;
   - the presentation of information about the services the firm offers and the people in the firm.

2. To promote loyalty amongst existing or first time clients because:

   - the quality of a brochure can confirm a client's decision to choose your firm;
   - brochures can provide a point of reference for clients and give them useful information about the firm;
   - they provide an opportunity to communicate with clients, i.e. when a new brochure is distributed.

3. To increase work from existing clients through:

   - reminding clients of the firm's services;
   - maintaining an open dialogue with clients.

4. To gain new clients by:

   - presenting the firm to them;

- informing them about the firm's services.
- giving the firm credibility and presence.

CHARACTERISTICS OF BROCHURES

- Brochures can be any number of sizes, e.g. A4, A5, DL, and formats, e.g. square, landscape or portrait.
- They are put together by graphic designers.
- They are often printed on high quality paper, usually quite thick such as 150 gsm or higher.
- They reflect the image or position of the firm.
- They are distributed to old clients, new clients or potential clients.
- They contain information about the firm that will be relevant to the client.
- They are written in short sections, often with pictures or space around them.
- They will often contain photographs and/or illustrations.
- They are usually free to the client.

HOW TO CREATE YOUR BROCHURE

The visual quality of a brochure is of enormous importance. The visuals need to match the firm's image and appeal to the target audience.

Depending on the way in which you want to present your firm and the services you offer, you may opt for a single brochure covering all areas, or a series of brochures covering each of the different services the firm offers.

When producing brochures, it is recommended that you use a graphic designer and copywriter. They will work from the brief you give them. The steps to producing a brochure have been set out on the following pages.

1. Prepare a brief

The brief is the key to achieving a brochure that correctly reflects your firm and the image you want to give your clients and potential clients.

Creating a brief is fairly straightforward and the list below indicates what needs to be included in it:

- A background to the firm.
- A background of the people working in the firm.
- An outline of the specific services that your firm provides.
- An outline, with examples, of the firm's logo and any other advertising or brochures produced in the past.
- Examples of the firm's existing or past brochures and any mission statements.

- An outline of the target audience and client base and an explanation of the purpose of the brochure and the information needs of the target audience.

- Technical information such as the print run and the budget.

- An indication of how eye-catching or design-led you would like the brochure to be.

- A list of descriptive words indicating the image and impression you would like the brochure to give, i.e. business-like, fun, professional, young, trustworthy, caring, efficient, local, international, etc. (see the section on image on pp. 225–6).

- Any specifications that need be taken into account, i.e. the use of a particular font, accreditation logos, etc.

- Whether it is envisaged one brochure will be sufficient or if a family of brochures is required.

- Whether you will want to use the design for other marketing materials.

If you have worked with a designer before, unless you are radically changing your approach, they will already have some idea of what you like and you can abbreviate the brief to a certain extent. However, it is a useful exercise to work through and gather the information listed as it will help clarify your intentions and communicate them to the designer.

The brief will give the designer and copywriter enough to come up with some visuals and copy ideas that can then be discussed. When they have collated some ideas they will present them to you. Depending on the chain of approval and management set-up in the firm, you might choose to see them alone or have them present to the firm's management committee. If you have asked a number of designers to pitch for the work this may be logistically difficult and it may be better to have them present to you for you to circulate. The following is a quick list of questions you might like to ask of the designer(s) when discussing their ideas.

- Double check that it will be possible to produce the presented visuals within budget and that there aren't any extra costs or unknown costs such as photographic or illustrative costs.

- Check the print quote given and that the quantity is correct.

- Ask to see samples of the paper, if possible printed in four-colour (or the number of colours you are using) so that you can check for print show through. You might want to use environmentally friendly paper or recycled paper.

- Ask for any cost variations between the designs.

- Ask how the designer envisages the design working on other brochures, i.e. how the family of brochures will work.

Hint: If you see a brochure or leaflet that you admire and you feel has elements you would like integrated into your firm's brochure, it is a good idea to show this to the designer and identify why you like it and what you like about it. This will help the designer gain some insight into what you want.

2. Discuss the ideas and concepts presented by the designer and copywriter

After having the ideas presented to you by the designer, if you feel that they are workable, it is a good idea to present them to the fee earners in the firm to gain their comments (if necessary). You may also circulate or present them to other staff in the firm and ask their views.

If you have a choice of concepts and you know which you prefer, always ensure you have a well thought-out sales story with regard to your choice. Only ever present the design concepts you are happy with. You are the one who will need to produce the brochure and your input and enthusiasm will make a huge difference to it actually being produced and the accuracy and presentation of the finished article. Take detailed notes of any comments or suggestions made and discuss these with the chosen designer.

3. Finalise and agree the copy

Once you have agreed the concept, the most important thing to do is finalise and agree the copy. Depending on how you choose to approach it, you, or the copywriter, will have produced initial copy to go into the brochure. You now need to ensure that this copy is accurate and comprehensive. The copy also needs be agreed in principle by the relevant people in the firm (if necessary).

Having done this, the copy should be given to the designer.

4. Finalise the design approach

Any photographs and illustrations that are being used should be discussed in detail so that the designer can commission or source them.

5. The proofing process

Proof 1. The first proof will show you how the copy fits and works with the design. It might be too long, too short or the meaning might not flow once it is set out. The illustrations or photos might not look quite right and adjustments needed. After discussing any changes with the designer a second proof should be produced.

Proof 2. It is a good idea to circulate this proof to your colleagues for comment. Now is the time that you need to get sign-off on the copy (or make changes) by anyone else involved.

Pass any comments or changes to the designer.

Proof 3. This should be the final proof and again, it is a good idea to pass this to anyone else involved such as your colleagues, informing them that this is their last chance to make changes to the copy.

Again, pass any changes to the designer.

Sign-off. The designer will now give you a final proof to sign-off before he sends it off for reproduction and print.

You should not be editing or making changes after this, as it will add to the cost.

6. Reproduction ('repro')

Reproduction is where any pictures are scanned into the artwork at high resolution and films made that will be used to produce the plates for the printers. Most printers have their own repro capability in-house, or the artwork files may be sent out to a repro house to have scans put in and films made. The designer will manage this.

7. Colour proofs

There are various types of colour proofs which can be viewed as a guide once the final artwork has been sent to the printer or repro house.

'Cromalins' are proofs made up using the final film on special paper. They are produced to check four-colour work (i.e. from CMYK films). It is a good idea to see them, even though they are the most expensive type of colour proof. They enable you to check there have been no glitches after final film has been output from the designer's submitted files, i.e. that the images are in the right place at the appropriate resolution, the correct fonts have been used and the final printed version will look how you imagine. Cromalins appear glossy and the colours often look brighter than on the finished product. If there are any problems, the printer may need to re-run one or all of the films, which adds to the cost unless the error is the fault of the printer (or repro house).

There are cheaper types of colour proof, usually produced from an inkjet or laser printer before final film has been output. The colour is not usually as reliable as on a cromalin but they can be useful nevertheless, especially for two-colour work where a cromalin is not appropriate.

It is always a good idea for the designer to check the colour proofs. They will ask you to sign off the proof prior to 'passing for press'.

You should not be editing or making changes at this stage, it is purely a technical checking process.

8. Printing your brochure

Before signing off the final colour proof, it is worthwhile double-checking the print run and the paper that will be used with the printer. It is now time to 'pass for press' and print.

HOW TO EVALUATE YOUR BROCHURE

When you first see your printed brochures they will, it is hoped, not be any great surprise as you will have seen several proofs of them. However, now that you have them in your hands it is a good idea to find out what those in the firm and some of your clients think of them.

At the beginning of this section, a list of questions you can ask to help you evaluate brochures and printed materials has been set out (p. 242). This list can easily be used to create a questionnaire for the staff to give their views.

Then, obviously, you must try to establish how well the brochure was received by clients. Ask clients you see, or you could invite a number of clients to take part in a panel. Meetings of the panel should then be held in the early evening on a regular basis to discuss their view of the way your firm presents itself, and whether they have any comments about your brochures, etc. Alternatively, you might choose to send a questionnaire with some of the brochures you send to clients. Questionnaire 8 in Part 2 can be amended and used to research your clients' reactions and the impression they gain from your brochure (see Q6 on p. 209).

Leaflets

WHEN TO USE LEAFLETS

Leaflets can be produced for a number of different purposes.

1. To promote loyalty amongst existing clients by:
   - giving them useful information about the firm;
   - providing an opportunity to communicate with them, i.e. sending out a leaflet about a new service or offer.

2. To increase work from existing clients through:
   - reminding clients of the firm's services and telling them about new services;
   - maintaining an open line to clients.

3. To maintain or create an image of the firm through:
   - its design and appearance;
   - the presentation of information about the services the firm offers and any special offers or promotions.

4. To promote a service to gain new clients by:
   - describing the service;
   - outlining an offer or incentive to use the service.

CHARACTERISTICS OF LEAFLETS

- Leaflets tend to be A5 or DL (folded to fit a standard envelope).
- They will follow the firm's design style but might have their own theme relevant to the offer or service they are promoting.
- They are put together by graphic designers.
- They are often printed on less heavy paper than brochures.
- They should reflect the image or position of the firm.
- They are distributed to clients and non-clients.
- They can be used for a wide range of reasons: direct mail promotions, to promote a seminar, etc.
- They contain information about the firm that will be relevant to the client.
- They are written in short sections, often with pictures or space around them.
- They will often contain photographs and/or illustration.
- They will usually be distributed to a target audience either as part of a mail shot or as an insert in the media (see p. 315).
- They will usually have a finite life linked to the promotion or offer.

HOW TO CREATE YOUR LEAFLET

Follow the steps outlined for creating a brochure. The only major difference is that there will be an offer, a call to action, i.e. 'telephone now', and a sales message.

HOW TO EVALUATE YOUR LEAFLET

Again, are you happy with it?

If you use the leaflet for a direct mail promotion or other promotion, did it generate a response? What do staff think of it? Ask clients for their reactions – again, you might want to ask a panel of clients for their views. Was it the offer, the presentation of the offer, or the way in which it was distributed? There are a number of factors that might affect the result of a promotion. Please see 'Direct mail' on p. 293 where this has been discussed in more detail.

Public relations

Public relations is an extremely broad heading and can be used to cover a wide range of activities undertaken by your firm including seminars, parties, sponsorship, or client care initiatives. However, because these are discussed in separate sections of this manual, this section focuses on working and communicating with the public via the media and putting together press releases, articles and radio interviews.

Communicating with your local market place through the media is an important part of any law firm's promotional mix and though you are not paying for the column inches or radio time, they do have a cost attached, namely the cost of the time put in by members of the firm and any materials, such as stationery, used.

Depending on the information and messages given out by the firm, media relations can help the firm in the following ways:

1. To promote loyalty amongst existing clients by:

   - raising clients' confidence and confirming their decision to use your firm;
   - giving them useful information;
   - keeping clients up to date with activities the firm is undertaking.

2. To increase work from existing clients by:

   - reminding clients of the firm's services;
   - telling them about new or expanded services.

3. To gain new clients or help towards gaining new clients through:

   - putting your firm's name in front of a wide local audience;
   - positioning the firm as having expertise in a certain field;
   - giving the firm credibility;
   - giving the firm a place in the locality.

4. To maintain or create an image of the firm through:

   - raising awareness of the firm in the locality;
   - raising awareness of the services the firm offers;
   - positioning the firm through publicising its activities;
   - positioning the firm as a spokesperson on a particular area of law and giving the firm credibility as an expert in that area;
   - giving the firm credibility in the local area;
   - creating a proactive image of the firm.

5. To combat a negative image or bad press by:

   - giving you the opportunity to put the firm's side across and combat any bad press about the firm or any of its fee earners.

Press releases

These are a recognised method of sending information to the local press, specialist magazines or local radio stations.

Characteristics of press releases

- They are put onto identifiable press release paper, i.e. headed paper with a large heading 'Press release' or 'News'.
- They are set out in double line spacing.
- They should be no longer than one side of A4, though it is not fatal if it is necessary to run over.
- They should include quotes from named and relevant individuals where possible.
- They should include contact details.
- At the end, they should include factual background information or sources of further information for editors.
- They should be concise and include all relevant information.
- Their subject should be of interest to the readers of the targeted media with regard to a legal issue, an activity of the firm in the local area, in response to a broad national issue or in response to a highlighted problem of someone in the local area.

Working with the media

There are a number of things to be aware of with the press:

- Sending out a press release does not mean that it will be used.
- The press are looking for news and therefore a negative angle might be seen as more newsworthy than a positive one. It is important that a press release is checked in its own right for any negative aspects and also checked to ensure it is not contradicting any other press releases sent out or adding fuel to a recent or existing negative story. For example, it would be unwise to send out a press release about expanding your offices just after discussion on solicitors charging high fees has featured in the papers – the story that emerges might end up being about your firm obviously making large profits as it is rich enough to be able to expand.
- Quotes and stories will be chopped around to suit the story being written.
- The journalist might contact other relevant bodies for a quote or comment.
- You need always to be aware of the broad national view of solicitors to ensure that the press release is appropriate.

The above is not meant to put anyone off working with the media, merely to encourage caution. Nothing is 'off the record' and bad news is more newsworthy than good news.

Creating and sending out press releases

There are a number of steps which have been outlined below that will help you create and send out press releases.

1. TO WHOM DO YOU SEND PRESS RELEASES?

On the whole you will be sending out press releases to the following:

- local newspapers;
- local radio stations;
- national press;
- local magazines such as local authority publications or borough magazines;
- local TV news rooms where they feature the local news after the main news;
- trade publications;
- legal publications.

The main audiences for your regular press releases will tend to be your local press, radio stations, magazines or TV news rooms.

However, if your firm becomes the focus of the national press then you will need to deal with the national press and issue them press releases stating your firm's position, when and if it happens. In addition, if there is an issue of national concern about which you are commenting, you could send the press release to the national press. But unless you are a major player in the legal world, it is unlikely that your news will be of interest to the national press.

If you are specifically targeting a trade, you can send press releases to trade publications. However, they should be specifically relevant to their readers.

Announcements about the firm, the members of the firm or an initiative taken by the firm that you judge would be of interest to the legal world can be sent to legal publications. Again, the information would need to be relevant to others in the legal world, their readers.

The important rule to follow when deciding to which media you should send your press release, is that the information it contains needs to be of interest or newsworthy to their readers, viewers or listeners.

2. CREATE A MEDIA LIST

It is recommended that you create a media list of all of the media listed above relevant to your firm.

You can either purchase a copy of *British Rates and Data* (BRAD) from EMAP Business Communications for approximately £265 and look up all the information in there, or you can visit their web site at **www.brad.co.uk**. However, before you do so, you will need to telephone them and ask for their subscription services. They will give you a password to enter the site on a one-day trial, after which you might like to take out a subscription.

Note: Because of the expense, it would probably make sense to try to track down a copy of BRAD through your local library or ask around to see if anyone would lend you a copy. However, if you do decide to purchase a copy, BRAD will prove useful if you want to undertake any advertising or inserts.

Alternatively, you can undertake local searches as below.

Local newspapers

Details can be found in the Yellow Pages for your local area under 'Newspapers and magazines'. In addition, any local papers you or any of your fee earners receive might be appropriate.

Local radio stations

Details might be found in the Yellow Pages under 'Broadcasting services', or if you visit the Radio Authority's web site at **www.radioauthority.org.uk** you can see a list of all independent radio stations with their coverage areas. For local BBC radio stations, simply telephone the local BBC offices or the London offices to establish their details.

Local magazines

As with 'Local newspapers'.

Trade publications

Unless you know the different trade publications produced for different areas such as construction, plumbing, etc. it might be a good idea to get hold of a copy of BRAD to look them up, or you could look for the publications on the Internet. A number of them will have their own web sites.

Legal publications

You will probably be aware of the range of these available. Again their details will be available in BRAD.

Once you have established a list of the different media you could send press releases to, the next step is to establish the name and/or location of the person in those media who should receive your release. You can do this by telephoning and asking to whom you should send press releases and whether they would like to receive press releases via e-mail (some will prefer not to), fax or in the post. At the same time, it is a good idea to ask for editorial deadlines and if they are magazines or trade publications, ask about the editorial or forthcoming features schedule to see whether there are areas you can tie in with.

Using this information, you can now create a mailing list. You should try to update it on a regular basis.

Note: It is helpful to obtain copies of publications or newspapers that you want to target so that you can become familiar with their approach and style. The best way may be to have your firm put on their distribution lists where possible, or telephone them and ask them to send you a media pack or features list. If your firm is based outside the catchment area of a local publication, you can often pay a subscription to have the publications sent to you, or find out if anyone in the firm lives in the distribution area so that they may request to receive those publications. If you advertise with different publications, you will usually be put on a distribution list by the media sales executive.

3. DECIDING WHEN TO SEND OUT A PRESS RELEASE

There are two levels of press releases: planned press releases and reactionary press releases which are sent out in response to something happening.

Planned press releases

It is possible to plan press releases for the year in advance. These will tend to be press releases about a planned and diarised event, i.e. a seminar, an office move, the opening of a new department, a change in the legal services the firm offers, an anticipated change in regulations or the law that will affect the public. This can include press releases about specific members of the firm who might be undertaking a personal achievement such as the London Marathon.

Press releases may be sent out to remind specific groups of people about a requirement at different times in the year, for example consumer finance at Christmas time because people are spending a lot of money in the shops, or a release about a person's right to compensation if holidays do not meet standards in the summer. The idea behind these releases is to provide a public service.

It is always a good idea to have a public interest hook upon which to hang your press release.

To ensure you maintain momentum in sending out press releases, it is a good idea to sit down and pull together a 12-month calendar of planned press releases – one per month is a good starting point.

Reactionary press releases

These will be press releases reacting to:

- negative press about the firm or any of the fee earners in the firm;
- an economic situation, i.e. a press release about conveyancing if the housing market is very active;
- an unanticipated change in the law or regulations;
- negative press about solicitors in the area or about solicitors generally;
- a query raised by the press.

4. WRITING A PRESS RELEASE

Press releases are factual information sheets. They do not need to be journalistic articles in their own right. They should contain all relevant information and put forward the point of view they are meant to convey in concise and clear language.

Heading. This needs to give a clear indication of the content of the press release:

'Local solicitors' firm to provide revolutionary conveyancing service.'

First paragraph/lines. The first paragraph should set out the main facts clearly with any dates or other key information:

'From 1 December 2001, [*name of solicitors' firm*] in [*location*] will be offering clients a new streamlined conveyancing service.'

Second and third paragraphs. This should give some background detail and more information about the new service with any benefits clearly set out.

'The new service will enable clients to purchase conveyancing services at a cut price with increased information and improved client contact.' [*Further explanations should follow.*]

Fourth paragraph. This could be a quote:

'Mr. [*name*], Senior Partner at [*name of firm*], commented on the new service:

"We have been investigating new ways of offering conveyancing to clients. We had certain criteria we wanted any new service to meet, such as lower fees and greater client contact so that we can give clients more information all the way through the process. The new system means we can do this." '

Fifth paragraph. This might involve further background information or mention how this service compares to other firms' services or whether it meets any external organisation's requirements.

Sixth paragraph. It would be ideal if this paragraph included a quote from a satisfied customer, an estate agent, etc. to round off the piece.

Editors' notes. These should outline factual details of the firm. For example:

[*Name of firm*] has been established for [*number*] years.

There are five partners and the firm has 20 staff. The new conveyancing department will have six members of staff.

[*Name of firm*] offers clients the following legal services:

Private clients: Will writing
                      Conveyancing
                      Litigation

Business clients: All company and commercial work
                      Tax advice
                      Commercial property

[*Contact details*]

5. EMBARGO DATES

It is a good idea to put an embargo date on your press release. This is the earliest date the information can be announced in the press. It could be the date it should arrive or a couple of days ahead. This ensures that any announcement you wish to make will be published at the same time.

6. PICTURES AND PRESS RELEASES

It is always a good idea to send a picture with the press release, an actual photograph (though this might prove expensive) or a scan of a photograph. If you send a scan, you should include a note below it stating that a photo or high resolution scan is available on request.

Always remember to write a caption for photographs.

Evaluating your press releases

Before you can evaluate your public relations (press release) activity, you need to ensure that you are capturing any items published or broadcast about your firm. You therefore need to follow up any press releases you send out by checking the media you sent them to. It is a good idea to establish a system for this whereby every week someone goes through all the local press looking for mentions of your firm. This is often a useful exercise for the person in charge of press releases as it will help them keep up to date with what is being published in the paper and identify any opportunities for publicity.

There are three areas that you need to assess to establish how successful your firm has been at public relations (press releases).

1. Count the column inches of coverage that your firm has received in magazines and newspapers, and the air time your firm has been given on the radio and TV, that is the result of information (press releases) you have sent to the media.
2. If you sent out press releases or contacted the media in reaction to a negative story, how successful were you in limiting the damage by getting them to put your side across or bringing them round to your side? Maybe you managed to

get the media to retract (where they were incorrect) or print your defence which they may do by publishing a letter from you putting your point across. If you are given negative coverage due to a misunderstanding or misinformation, it is always a good idea to write a letter to the editor explaining the true facts. It is this letter that they will often print; sometimes they will print an apology on the front page which is even better.

3. Look at the balance between negative and positive press and which was dominant. If you received a great deal of negative press you may need to promote your firm positively both through public relations and marketing to regain lost ground and restore confidence in your clients.

Articles and radio interviews

Placing articles in the media and taking part in radio chat shows and interviews as the local legal specialist can be a good way of raising the profile of the firm and those that work for the firm. It is also a good way of building a relationship with the media.

You could try the following approaches:

- Write an article about a current subject and then try to place it with appropriate media.
- Contact different publications and discuss possible articles. Ask them what format they would like to see, i.e. an interview, a factual piece, an 'idiots' guide', etc. and ask them how many words. You can then produce the article specifically for that publication.
- Contact different publications such as local newspapers, and suggest a regular legal advice column to them.
- Contact local radio stations and offer your services, or the services of the members of your firm as legal specialist to answer listeners' phone-in queries.

Producing your article/column

The following are points to remember when producing your article:

- Articles should be as well written as possible. Depending on the subject, the publication and the re-useability of the article, it might be worth employing a freelance writer or journalist to edit your article for you, or even re-write it if necessary.
- Your article should be clear, concise and the main points explained in easy-to-understand unambiguous sentences.
- Avoid using legal jargon or long complicated words without an explanation of what they mean.
- If you are given a word count, stick to it.

- Be prepared for your work to be edited, cut down in size and re-hashed as there is a very good chance it will be.
- Read through the publication you are writing for and try to write in a style that fits and appeals to its readership.
- Be prepared with a picture to publish with the article.

Radio interviews

If you propose someone for a radio show or interview, make sure they have a clear and pleasant speaking voice, they know their subject area well and that they feel comfortable going on radio. It might be worth staging a mock-up for practice. Have someone calling on a loudspeaker phone with likely questions about the subject area and tape-record the answers given. It is surprising the number of 'umm', repeats and fades that will be heard and it is good to make an individual aware of them so that they can try to avoid them if possible. Ideally, if the interview goes well, that person or your firm will be asked back. If you plan to increase radio PR, it may be worth sending key people on a training course.

Finding subject areas

If you produce a client newsletter, articles that are included in that could be put forward to the press for publication or picked up by the radio.

It is always a good idea to send a copy of your client newsletter to the print press and local radio stations when it is produced. If they want to use any story from the newsletter, they will contact you.

Note: If you commission the article to be written for you, you should ensure that you have the appropriate rights/licence to put that article forward. Alternatively, you could change the approach and rewrite the article for those publications.

Evaluating your articles and radio interviews

This can be done simply by measuring the amount of effort that was put into producing articles, approaching radio stations and sending members of the firm along, against the number of articles published and radio interviews undertaken. If you were a success you will often be invited back or asked for further articles.

Web sites

What is a web site?

A web site is a communication and marketing tool. For some organisations, working via a web site on the Internet is their entire business, whilst for others it is simply another way of advertising services or products. Because the Internet is still in its infancy, users are still learning how to buy from the Internet and organisations are still discovering how it can generate income.

So how can having a web site help your firm?

1. A web site can help you to promote loyalty among existing clients because:

   ■ the information held on your web site can confirm their decision to choose your firm;

   ■ your web site will be a point of reference for clients and give them useful information about the law and the firm;

   ■ it will provide you with another opportunity/reason to communicate with your clients;

   ■ it provides you with an opportunity to tell clients about your areas of expertise.

2. A web site can help you to get new clients by:

   ■ providing information to clients looking on the internet for legal services or information;

   ■ directing potential new clients to a reference area.

3. A web site can help you increase work from existing clients through:

   ■ telling them more about the firm's services;

   ■ maintaining an open dialogue with clients;

   ■ creating new opportunities for delivering legal services to clients through e-commerce.

4. A web site can help you maintain or create an image of the firm through:

   ■ its design and appearance;

   ■ the way you present information about the services the firm offers, the people in the firm and the law.

It is vital that before beginning to put together your web site, you decide exactly what you want your web site to do and what you want to gain from it.

Characteristics of web sites

Web sites vary enormously but some of their general characteristics have been identified below:

■ They have a unique address – frequently with an appropriate suffix such as '.co.uk', '.com'.
■ The design should have some tie-in to the design style of the firm's brochures and logo, perhaps by incorporating elements of that style such as colour schemes.
■ They require ongoing management and updating.
■ They contain information about the firm that will be relevant to the client.
■ They should contain photographs and/or illustrations.
■ Visitors can usually visit and have access to free information.
■ They might incorporate download sections.
■ They will incorporate an e-mail response mechanism.

How do you begin?

The first thing you need to do is to register a name for your web site. There are agencies on the Internet such as **www.netbenefit.com, www.domainsnet.com**, or **netnames.co.uk** that you can use to research and register your name. Simply go to your chosen agency's site and run a search on the name and suffix you want. It will then tell you whether that name is available. It is worth checking out the prices on a couple of sites as they can vary. There are two approaches to registering a name; you might want to register your firm's name, i.e. smithandsmith.co.uk, or you might want to register a subject name – lawservices.co.uk. It is surprising what has already been registered with the different suffixes. New suffixes will be available in 2001 and '.pro' is being introduced specifically for lawyers, accountants and other professional services.

Once you have registered a name, you need to put together a plan for your web site. You need to begin by establishing:

■ why you want a web site;
■ what a web site will do for the firm;
■ what a web site will do for clients;
■ whether a web site will bring in any revenue.

If your mind goes blank at these questions, it is suggested that you go 'surfing'. Look at how other solicitors have approached their Internet sites, what the sales stories are and what services they offer.

As you surf, note down the contact details of any solicitors whose site offers particular services you could offer, or whose site you like or admire. It might be worth a quick telephone call to those solicitors to ask them:

■ how have their clients reacted;

■ what sort of response they have had from any interactive areas of their web site, i.e. forms, quotation services and enquiries;

■ what has worked well and what hasn't;

■ whether they have increased revenue.

It is probably best to telephone those that are in a different geographical location to you so that there is no conflict of interest. Whilst you are on the phone ask them:

■ about the cost of putting the site together;

■ about the budgets they have for ongoing management;

■ about the manpower that has been needed for ongoing management and responding to queries.

You may not get answers to your questions but there is no harm in asking.

In addition, you might invest in attending a seminar about web sites. The Law Society and other organisations run these regularly.

Go surfing!

A good starting point for your surfing is **www.venables.co.uk**, which links into hundreds of UK solicitors' web sites.

Throughout this section, you are encouraged to go surfing on the Internet and look at other web sites to give you ideas of what you want for your own site. As you surf, to make best use of your time on-line and collect useful information, ask yourself the following questions about each different web site you visit. Table 63 has been put together on page 266 that you can photocopy and fill in as you surf.

When asking yourself the following question, as well as giving your own opinion, try to put yourself in your clients' shoes and imagine what they might like or think.

THE LOOK OF THE SITE

■ Is your first impression positive, i.e. do you get the impression of professionalism, efficiency, trustworthiness?

■ Is the screen cluttered and is it difficult to find your area of interest quickly?

- Do the visuals look balanced on the screen and is their subject appropriate?
- Do the visuals take a long time to appear as you move through the site?
- Are the visuals consistent and logical throughout the site?
- Do the visuals add to the content or detract from it?
- What do the visuals say to you – authority, modern, established, professional, amateur, etc.?
- Is the site, in your opinion, appropriate for a solicitors' firm?

THE WORDS AND CONTENT

- Is the information easy to read?
- Is the content written in a short and concise style?
- In your view, are there too many words on each page?
- Is there a good balance between information about the law and details about the firm?
- Does the copy raise questions which the site then fails to answer?
- Does the copy invite visitors to enquire further?

NAVIGATING AROUND THE SITE

- Is the site easy to find your way around?
- Are the menus logical and helpful?
- Do the different pages download quickly and easily?
- Do you get lost in the middle of the site and find it difficult to get back to the welcome or home page?

E-COMMERCE

- Are the e-commerce services and products on offer appropriate and useful?
- Do you think your clients would find the services and products on offer useful?
- Do the e-commerce pages appear professional and trustworthy?

FORMS

- Are they easy to fill in?
- Is the information they ask for logical to their purpose?
- Are the forms attractive?

QUOTATION SYSTEMS

- Are they easy to use and fill in?
- Is the response to your request quick enough?

■ Did the solicitors follow up the quote quickly offering their services?

■ Do you think the quotes are sensible and cover all costs such as disbursements?

❑ Use Table 63 to note comments about each different web site you visit.

Table 63 Assessing web sites

Name of solicitor: _____

Web site address: _____

Element	Score 1–10 (10 being very good)	Comments	Consider for your site Yes/No
The look of the site			
The words and content			
Navigating around the site			
E-commerce			
Forms			
Quotation systems			
Other comments			

What elements might you have on your web site?

Having surfed for a while, you should have some idea of why you want a web site and what you want it to do. The next step is to establish more detail about the actual content of your site that will enable it to achieve your aims.

Again, looking through other solicitors' sites can be an enormous help. You may have already noted down elements you like about them and the services they offer. As a basic guide, a web site should include:

- information about the firm and profiles of the fee earners/partners in the firm;
- information about the different areas of law that reflect the legal services you offer;
- contact details.

Other elements that you could include are:

- newsletters and fact sheets that can be downloaded;
- a news section;
- useful e-mail addresses and contacts for other relevant organisations;
- a forum where customers can ask questions and discuss issues;
- on-line quoting systems and forms;
- an e-commerce section;
- restricted entry areas.

Take care that your web site is not simply an area to give clients access to your existing printed documents and brochures, though this could be one of the services you offer.

The elements you include in your web site will depend on your firm, your resources and the legal services you offer. Details about the different elements have been set out below.

1. Information about the firm and profiles of the fee earners and partners in the firm

You should always incorporate pages telling visitors about the firm, the legal services you offer and what they can find on your web site. It is also a good idea to include an outline of the different fee earners working in different legal services together with a direct e-mail button that visitors can use to contact each fee earner.

Make sure:

- The information is clear, concise and accurate.
- The guide to the web site is easy to understand

■ Any e-mail enquiries are answered promptly and a system is set up to ensure that this happens.

2. Information about the different areas of law that reflect the legal services you offer

This should be descriptive and useful information for your web site visitors, for example a section discussing conveyancing and taking visitors through the process. It is a good idea to make this information about the law as opposed to about your firm. The aim is to create a need for your services by educating visitors about the different areas of law.

Make sure:

■ You have a button that visitors can press if they want to register an interest in employing your firm in this area.
■ The information you give is accurate, concise and set out in easy-to-read chunks and directed at the layman.
■ The information you give does not raise more questions than it answers.

3. Ways of contacting you

You should always incorporate details of how visitors can contact the fee earners in the firm. You may have links into an e-mail response sheet for individuals or to a central enquiries address from which queries can be redirected.

As well as e-mail you should ensure that your address, telephone numbers and other contact details are included.

It is also a good idea to incorporate pictures of the different fee earners. This breaks down a barrier to communication and makes your firm more approach-able.

Make sure:

■ Someone manages any incoming e-mails appropriately or passes them on to the relevant person.
■ You have the facility to receive these messages – it is a good idea to have them come into a stand alone machine, as this ensures that if they contain viruses your network will not be affected.
■ The information you give is clear and correct.

4. A facility where visitors can download information

Visitors to your web site can easily print off the information published on it. To give this information value, it is a good idea to set it out on downloadable fact sheets. These should be branded with your firm's details including contact details.

You might also put your company brochures and newsletters into a PDF format that visitors can download.

Make sure:

■ You identify the size of the download files so that visitors have some idea of the time it will take on-line to download them.
■ You brand the download files with your logo and firm's details.
■ The information is accurate, concise, useful and set out neatly.
■ You offer visitors the option of having brochures, etc. sent to them in the post.
■ You give visitors a link to download any software they need to read any downloaded files.

5. A news section

A section where all press releases and news bites can be listed. If you send out a press release, you should list it and hold it on your web site. News bites may include scans of articles about your firm in the papers, summaries of new legislation or announcements about issues that might affect your clients. In fact, put anything of relevance to your clients that you or your firm feel appropriate onto the web site. By using your web site as a notice board, you will encourage repeat visits and position the site as a regular information source for users.

Make sure:

■ You keep this section up-to-date.
■ You list relevant information
■ You tell people about this service. You could do this by e-mailing them when a new item is posted.

6. Useful e-mail addresses and contacts for other relevant organisations

There may be areas where you give your visitors information but you also want to offer them a route to further information. In this instance you can list the appropriate organisations' web site addresses as hyperlinks (this is where a link is put into your web site which will take visitors directly to another website).

This can be risky, however, as you may lose your visitors when they do not return to your web site. One way around this is to ensure that even if they do go to another organisation's web site, your web site frame remains on their screen with the other site held within the frame.

Make sure:

- You have the other organisations' addresses correct.
- You keep your web site on screen and the new site in a frame.
- You link into the exact pages required, not simply into the home page of the other organisation's web site, as this may extend the time visitors are off your site and gives them more opportunity to leave your site.
- You check your links from time to time.

7. A forum where customers can ask questions and discuss issues

You might include a section in your web site where visitors can post queries and raise issues. When these questions or comments are posted, you will need to have someone to respond. It is suggested that a clear statement of when a reply may be expected should be given so that a response is not expected immediately, e.g. 48 hours.

Make sure:

- You have the staff available to respond to any questions or requests for information.
- You have a system in place to manage this area.
- You meet any deadlines identified.
- You have a clear protocol for the amount of information you give free.
- Any confidential information is kept confidential.

8. On-line quoting systems and forms

You can incorporate a programme that will give visitors to your web site an immediate quote for a particular transaction. This is particularly relevant with regard to conveyancing and will writing. Alternatively, if you don't want to spend on such software, you can include forms that visitors fill in their relevant details and e-mail to you and you then e-mail a quotation back to them.

Make sure:

- The figures are accurate.
- You capture contact details of anyone who requests a quote and follow it up with an e-mail or letter offering your services. If the latter you might choose to include an appropriate brochure or leaflet.

9. An e-commerce section

This is where you have an on-line facility that visitors can use to purchase products from you.

For example, you could sell will writing services over the internet, or tenancy agreements that visitors can download directly from your web site after paying a fee. Or you could sell proforma letters that cover particular situations, for example letters for landlords where their tenants have rent in arrears.

You may sell fact sheets and newsletters. You could list and sell a number of books, athough you should always be aware that you will need to have the staff in place to administer and fulfil any sales. One approach is to put in a link to an on-line site where these books are available. It might be possible to negotiate with the seller a discount for your customers and create a page that only they can access.

Make sure:

- You have the fulfilment capability.
- The information you give is accurate and well presented.
- You capture the details of those who purchase from you.

10. Restricted entry areas

You may choose to restrict entry to parts of your web site with passwords or require visitors to register before they can enter certain areas of your web site. This can be a good tool to add value to the service clients receive. For example, if you have a forum whereby your business clients can ask questions but they have to have a password, this can all be part of the service package that you offer them.

By requiring visitors to register, you also have the opportunity of building a database of potential clients, but you should be aware that any request for personal information can create a barrier to entry and might dissuade some visitors from entering your site.

Make sure:

- You have the capability to provide any passwords quickly and keep them up to date on your records.
- You have the capability to capture the details of those who register with you.

Planning your web site

Having decided what you want your web site to do and which elements you would like to incorporate, you need to put together an outline of the information you would like to include. A good way of doing this is to produce a map of the pages and information that will go on your web site. This is a fairly straightforward process. Simply create a list of subject areas and the sub-headings of information within them. Each heading could be another page, or the information could all be listed on one page with a clickable list taking the reader to the relevant area of that page.

A good way of bringing this information together is to produce a table, like the one below, that shows how the information on your web site might be broken down and what information might be included. Box 10 is only meant as an example to show how the information can be built up with layers of detail.

As you look through you will see that there is a repetition on some of the headings and this is where the same page might be linked in. Sometimes you may need to copy and change the page so that you can differ the words used such as 'When you are buying' instead of 'When you are selling' in the information about 'Our services'.

Costing your web site

Having planned the elements and information you want to include in your web site, you need to find out how much it is going to cost you to produce. If you did ring the owners of sites you particularly liked, they might have indicated how much their sites cost them.

At the moment, there is enormous variation in the amount you can spend on having a web site created, anything between hundreds of pounds and tens of thousands of pounds or hundreds of thousands for large organisations. The final cost will depend on what you want to include in your web site and how expensive the agency you use is.

Remember: As well as the initial investment in producing your site there is likely to be an ongoing management cost. The site will need to be updated, and you may need to pay for space on the server. The management and care of your site will involve some internal personnel and this will have cost implications. As with any other promotion, when deciding how much to invest, you should bear in mind the return you expect. A web site needs to pay for itself in some way.

Because of the variation in the amount of money you might be charged, it is a good idea to discuss your requirements and get quotes from two or three different site producers. Their input and ideas will also help you distil what you want to do with your site and the cost implications of including different elements. Because of the technicalities involved in creating a site it is probably a good idea to ask the web site designer to organise and quote for any programming required. They will probably expect to do this anyway.

Box 10 Planning a web site

	Level 1	Level 2	Level 3	Level 4	Level 5	Level 6	Notes
Welcome page	Intro	■ Site map ■ Legal statement					
About the firm	Intro	■ Profiles of fee earners ■ Contact details					
Con-veyancing	Intro	■ The conveyancing process (Overview)	■ Buying a property	■ Facts about buying	■ The costs involved	■ Disbursements ■ Stamp duty ■ Estate agents fees ■ Moving costs ■ Our fees ■ Link to quotation page	Hyperlinks to take visitors to appropriate parts of the web site or appropriate quotation forms or printable checklists
					■ Mortgages ■ Timings ■ Our service and solicitors involved ■ Quotations ■ Purchasing a property checklist ■ Selling a property checklist ■ Links to other web sites such as on-line estate agents in the area ■ Downloadable checklists and factsheets	(Other relevant pages for each of the headings)	
			■ Selling a property	■ Facts about selling	■ The costs involved	■ Disbursements ■ Stamp duty ■ Estate agents fees ■ Moving costs ■ Our fees ■ Link to quotation page ■ Transferring your mortgage	
					■ Transferring your mortgage ■ Timings ■ Our service and solicitors involved ■ Quotations ■ Purchasing a property checklist ■ Selling a property checklist ■ Links to other web sites such as on-line estate agents in the area ■ Downloadable checklists and factsheets	(Other relevant pages for each of the headings)	
Wills and probate	Intro	■ How to make a will (Overview)	■ Facts about wills	■ The costs involved ■ Our service and solicitors involved ■ Quotations ■ Literature/downloads		
		■ The probate process (Explain process)	■ Facts about probate	■ The costs involved ■ Our service and solicitors involved ■ Quotation ■ Literature/downloads		

The majority of designers have some Internet capability or will be able to point you in the right direction. A good start would be to approach the person who designed and produced any brochures you have. In addition, you could go to a company that produced another solicitors' web site that you like. Web site production companies frequently put their details on the sites they have produced, so it is worth noting down the details on a site that you like. If they have already produced one solicitors' site, they will be in a good position to do a second one. You may even be able to buy some of the programmes from them, i.e. an on-line quotation programme.

However, just because some other firm has spent a fortune on a special application or interactive element, does not mean that you need to, and indeed it may not be appropriate for your firm to do so.

You may even choose to produce your own web site using one of several software packages on the market. So that your site looks professional and works well, however, it is recommended that you use a graphic designer and copy writer to put your site together.

Producing your web site

1. Prepare a creative brief for your web site

The brief is the key to your web site achieving what you want it to and ensuring that the finished web site correctly reflects your firm and the image you want to give your clients and potential clients.

Your web site brief should include:

- A background to the firm.
- A background of the people working in the firm.
- An outline of the specific services that the firm provides.
- A page plan if you have produced one.
- An outline, with examples, of the firm's logo and any other advertising, or brochures produced in the past.
- Any mission statements.
- An outline of the target audience/client base.
- Technical information such as any programmes and on-line services you want.
- An indication of how eye-catching and design-led you would like the web site to be (remember, your web site should tie in with your existing marketing materials).
- A list of descriptive words indicating the image and impression you would like the web site to give, i.e. business-like, fun, professional, young, trustworthy, caring, efficient, local, international, authoritative, friendly, etc.

- Any specifications that need be taken into account, i.e. the use of a particular font, accreditation logos, etc.
- Whether you will want to use the design for posters and other marketing materials.
- An idea of the sort of budget you have in mind – you may choose not to give a figure but ask a number of firms to quote for comparison.
- Identify how you plan to update the site or manage any elements of the site, i.e. in-house, through them, etc. as this may have a bearing on the way the site is put together.

At this stage you should give the copywriter and designer as much background information as possible about the content you foresee the web site having, such as a page plan. You may decide to write the copy yourself and ask the copywriter to edit it and rewrite it in an appropriate style for the web site.

The designer and copywriter will use this information to determine how the web site will be put together, how the menus will work, how many words to a page, etc.

2. Agree the look and content

Next, the designer and copywriter should produce a design and a page plan of how the website will look and fit together.

- As with brochures, you may need to discuss the design with colleagues to gain their agreement. It is a good idea to look at the page design(s) on a computer screen as this will show you how the site will look when finished.
- The page plan will identify the contents of the web site and how the pages will flow together. This needs to be agreed before the copy is produced.

3. Agree and finalise the copy

Once you have decided on the design and page plan, the copy needs to be written and agreed by the relevant people in the firm.

WEB SITE COPY

Web sites should written in a very direct manner using 'we' or 'I', rather than repeating the firm's name, and because the copy will be read on screen it should be direct, short, sharp and concise.

Information should be set out in single pages with links through to other pages containing further information. It is like a layering process: you provide a layer of information where the visitor can then stop, go back or forward another layer to find out more.

A good way of producing copy for a web site is to write it in Microsoft Word and insert 'hyperlinks' and 'bookmarks' so that you can see how the pages and copy will flow. These links let you to move between pages and files in the same way as you would on a web site.

The information put on a web site should tie in with your other marketing materials. Once the copy is agreed, it needs to be given to the designer.

Note: At this stage, the copy should be checked to see that the facts are accurate and that it makes sense. Do not agonise for days as there will be time to change any copy once it is on the web site and can be seen in action.

4. Test drive the site

Once the copy and design have been brought together, it is suggested that the site is made available to everyone in the firm to test drive. You can do this by having the site put up but not entered into any search engines. Ask everyone to surf through the site and see how easy they find it to understand and to navigate, and whether there is any other information they would like to see. This is a good time to check that all the links and programmes work.

5. Register your site with search engines

Your web site should now to be registered with different search engines so that people will find it when searching the Internet. Key words need to be identified so that diffferent searches will find your site. Your web site producer should be able to help you register your site or you can do it yourself through agencies that you can find on the Internet such as Web Site Garage which will register you with 12 different search engines for free. They can be found at *www.register-it.com*. To find other agencies, simply go surfing to look for 'register' sites.

6. Launch your web site

When you are happy that the site works, looks good, gives the correct information and has the features you want, the time has come to launch it to your clients and the media. There are a number of activities you might want to include in your launch plan:

1. Prepare and send out a press release to the media.
2. Send out an invitation to clients asking them to visit you.
3. Send an e-mail to as many clients as possible with a link to your web site enclosed.

4. Advertise the presence of your site.

5. Encourage visitors to your site with a competition for visitors who sign in.

Managing your web site

All web sites need managing daily or updating on a regular basis after being launched, especially if you have elements such as question forums, a quotation service, a noticeboard area, etc.

It is important that this work takes place regularly and consistently, as old information or information that is no longer current will undermine the quality and trustworthiness of the information presented. Even if you have to make up a tip of the week and put it up, it shows that the web site is constantly under review.

A good way of managing your site is to appoint an editor and an editorial panel.

The editor

This is a key role in the life of the web site as their role is to make sure that the site is up to date and any changes are actioned. Their job will also be to evaluate the site (see below) and liaise with the production team (designer, copywriter, programmers, etc.) and keep the page plan up to date.

If you are looking at ways of reducing costs, it may be worthwhile sending someone in the firm (perhaps the editor) on a course so that they can amend the site inhouse without having to go to a specialist each time which will cost money. However, you should ensure that each time the site is changed or updated, the page plan is changed to reflect this. This is a busy hands-on role and therefore it needs someone who can give it time and who has the enthusiasm to do it.

The editorial panel

This should be a group of people drawn from each area of the practice whose role will be to meet, perhaps quarterly, to:

- review the site;
- discuss any issues;
- take an interest and give assistance in providing the contents of the site.

This work will have cost and time implications which should be taken into account.

How to evaluate your web site

As with all other promotional methods, you should evaluate the success of your web site. The following are methods that you can use to try to find out visitors' views of your web site and how they have used it.

Visitor numbers

You can obtain the number of hits (visitors) your web site has received over a period of time. The server holding your website will be able to provide you with this information. Check with your web site producer what reports you will be able to get as some will be able to show you the path visitors take through the information on your site.

You should keep a count of enquiries you receive, requests for information and quotations and a note of how many convert to business.

Testing the look and content of your web site

There are a number of ways you can find out what visitors think of your site. You can attach a questionnaire to the site asking relevant questions, or you could send a questionnaire to clients (by e-mail or post) asking them to visit your site and fill it in. If you choose to ask clients or visitors to your web site to respond to a questionnaire, it is a good idea to give them an incentive such as a draw. If you keep a questionnaire on your site, you could have a monthly winner and publish it (with their permission) on the site. Questionnaire 8 in Part 2 of this manual can be amended and used for this purpose.

You might choose to hold a focus group and, taking participants through your site, ask them what they think of different areas, i.e. attractive, eye-catching, useful, informative, easy to understand. You should also ask them what they would like to see and how they think you could improve the site.

Making the most of your web site

Now that you have a web site, you will want to make the best of it. There are a number of things you can do to ensure that you are getting the maximum number of target visitors to your site.

Link to other web sites

Research appropriate associated sites, contact the owners and ask them to include a link to your site from theirs. Offer to put a link from your site to theirs in return. Consider organisations such as the local authorities, local area directories, associated legal groups such as lawnet (if you are a member), local estate agents, advice centres, etc.

Remember, you need to ensure visitors come back to your site.

Follow up leads from your site

> Always follow up any leads from your site. If someone requests a quotation on-site, follow this up with an e-mail to them offering your services. If the quotation is via e-mail, provide the information as soon as possible and always offer your services.

Ensure your site is linked into as many search engines as possible

> If your web site isn't registered with different search engines, no one will find it. Make sure that your site is registered with as many search engines as possible – they are free.

Tell people about it

> Make sure that all of your headed paper, business cards, leaflets, advertisements and brochures have the web site address on them. Another idea is to have a computer in your reception area with the web site loaded onto it so that clients can browse while they wait for you.

Use your web site as an opportunity to promote your firm

> Your web site can be used as a way of building information about your clients and as an opportunity to promote your firm.

> You can build information about your clients by appending a research form to the web site. You would need to give people an incentive to fill it in such as a competition or prize draw.

> Your web site can give you an opportunity to promote your firm as each time you add information to the site (for example a new service, a new newsletter, etc.) you have an excuse to send out a press release, write to and e-mail clients to tell them.

> Overall, your web site is extremely flexible and can be used for a wide range of customer services and promotions.

Newsletters

What is a newsletter?

> A newsletter is an information sheet that you send to clients and/or non-clients on a regular basis giving them relevant information about the law and the legal services you supply.

hen do you use newsletters?

Newsletters have a broad application and can be used for a number of different purposes. They can be used:

1. To promote loyalty among clients by:

   - maintaining regular contact with them;
   - giving them useful information;
   - educating them about the law;
   - giving them something tangible for free.

2. To increase work from existing clients by:

   - reminding them of your firm's services;
   - educating them about their rights and creating a need;
   - maintaining an open dialogue with them.

3. To maintain or create an image of the firm through:

   - your newsletter's presentation;
   - the repetition of the firm's logo and the names of the solicitors;
   - reminding or informing clients of the areas of law in which the firm practices.

4. To gain new clients by:

   - showing them you have a pro-active approach to client care;
   - putting your firm's name in front of them and giving useful information.

Managing your newsletter

Before you begin to produce a newsletter, you need to set up the production and management systems for it. You will need:

- an editor;
- an editorial panel;
- a schedule;
- an annual budget;
- a production team;
- a name for the newsletter.

The editor

This is the key role in producing your newsletter. The job of the editor is to manage the contents, design and setting of the newsletter as well as its production and distribution.

It is a busy, hands-on role and therefore it needs someone who can give it time and who has the enthusiasm to do it. The senior partner should sign off the newsletter before it goes to print.

Further details of the role of editor can be found later in this section.

The editorial panel

This should be a group of people drawn from each area of the practice whose role will be to meet on a regular basis. They will:

■ review the last issue;
■ set the contents for the next issue;
■ take an interest and give assistance in providing the contents of the newsletter.

A schedule

The first editorial panel meeting of each year should decide the production schedule of the newsletter and determine the budget for it.

The editor will then need to work backwards from the publishing date to set copy deadlines, design and setting deadlines, print and distribution deadlines.

An annual budget

Before setting the budget for your newsletter, you will need to know how many copies to send out each time. You also need to take into account the nature of the recipients and the profile and image of your firm. For example, if you have large corporate clients and your firm has a smart image, your newsletter will need to reflect this.

Having set out some initial thoughts and guidelines, the editor needs to obtain quotes for producing the newsletter in different formats and using different resources. This information should then be presented to the editorial panel or senior management to decide which format is feasible and agree the budget.

Elements that will affect production costs:

■ whether the newsletter is to be one-colour, two-colour or four-colour;
■ how long it is, i.e. two pages, four pages, eight pages, etc.;
■ the number of pictures that are used and whether you commission any illustration;
■ how many you will distribute and the method of printing you use;
■ what your resources are with regard to writing and setting each issue;

- the frequency of the newsletter;
- the distribution method.

The cost of your newsletters will very much depend on the resources you need to buy in, but if money is tight, there are a number of ways that you can try to keep the costs down:

1. Negotiate a year's worth of newsletters with any writer/designer you use. They will be more willing to reduce the cost if there is regular work in the offing.

2. Ask the designer to produce the newsletter according to a standard template – this keeps the time they need to spend to a minimum.

3. Investigate whether there is anyone in-house who can use DTP software (desktop publishing). It might be worth investing in Microsoft Publisher software and training a couple of staff on it. If you do choose this route, it is also worth buying a scanner to capture photographs or illustrations. If you use images from Clipart they will be easily recognised and can look very amateurish. If you wanted to go this route and keep the production in-house, you could also ask a designer to come up with a template and header banner that can then be used for future issues.

4. If you are using an external writer, or if someone in the firm is going to write the newsletter, provide them with as much information as possible so that they can simply pull the articles together without the need for extensive research. It can be a good idea to write the articles and ask them to edit them. This will prove a useful exercise in learning how an article should be put together.

5. Have the newsletter digitally printed if you require under 500 copies. This can prove far less expensive, and though the quality is not quite as good the difference is negligible for a newsletter. In addition, you will save any reproduction costs as digital printers take the information straight from the disk without the need for films.

6. Organise the printing yourself. You will save money as there will be no markup by any third party. (However, a designer or bureau may save you time.)

Some of these points will be discussed in more detail later in this section.

A production team

This is the team that will produce the newsletter each time. Headed by the editor it should include:

- the designer, or person responsible for the layout of the newsletter;
- the writer (if one is commissioned);
- the person liaising with the printer;
- the person in charge of distribution.

The members of this team are all key to the newsletter's production, but it is unlikely that they will need to meet together. They will need to be kept in touch with the newsletter and it will normally be the editor who co-ordinates team meetings.

A name for the newsletter

The name of the newsletter is important, as is the support of the whole firm in its production. A good way of involving the whole firm is to set a competition to come up with names. The editorial panel can pick the top ten (ensure that the names are appropriate) and then have everyone in the firm vote on the name they want.

All about newsletters

Characteristics of newsletters

- Newsletters are frequently A4 in size – perhaps 4 pages long.
- They are regular – such as monthly, bi-monthly or quarterly.
- They are sent direct to clients' homes/premises.
- They contain information relevant to the client.
- They are written in a journalistic manner with articles and short information bites.
- They will often contain photographs and/or illustration.
- They are usually free to the client.

Your newsletters should always:

- be relevant to the recipient;
- be presented in an attractive and easy to read way;
- be focused on the information needs of the recipients, not solely a sales story for your firm.

Setting the tone

Your clients are unlikely to be lawyers, therefore you need to ensure that you do not use legal jargon or complicated language in your newsletter, tempting though it may be. It is also best if you avoid calling it something legal like the 'brief' – the majority of your clients might never have heard of a brief. A final point – you should not assume any level of knowledge on your readers' part.

It is worth remembering that *The Sun* is the most widely read newspaper in the UK. It stands to reason that quite a lot of your clients will be *Sun* readers – your newsletter needs to be as clear, easy to understand and use as uncomplicated language as *The Sun*.

You are writing this newsletter for your clients. Remember, you may understand it and partners in the firm might understand it; the question to ask is, will your readers understand it?

The look of your newsletter

There are a number of ways that will help make sure your newsletter looks good and the information in it interesting. These have been identified below.

THE FRONT PAGE OF THE NEWSLETTER

- A clear and recognisable name banner should be created and used on each issue so that the newsletter is recognisable to recipients.
- Give the newsletter a strap line describing what it is, for example 'A free newsletter keeping Smith & Smith clients up to date with the law'.
- Include information about the issue of the newsletter, i.e Issue No. 1, March 2000.
- Your logo should be clearly positioned in the name banner or on the front page.
- It is a good idea to have a contents or 'In this issue' list clearly set out on the front page.

PICTURES AND ILLUSTRATIONS

- It is a good idea to include photographs of members of the firm writing the article or if the article is about the area in which they work. This helps the firm appear more approachable. For example, pictures of the conveyancing practitioners with their contact details should be shown in a box alongside or at the end of an article about conveyancing, together with an invitation to contact them.
- Illustrations, photographs, tables, charts and bullet points should be used to break up text and consequently make articles look more digestible and less wordy. You can also pull out quotes and enlarge them in quotation marks to highlight points. You should never have fewer than two pictures per A4 page.
- Try not to make the pictures too small, unless the quality is very bad.
- If you run pictures behind words, they should be very faint. It can be difficult to read over backgrounds, and this will often be an area of complaint.
- Pictures ought to be a part of the article and should therefore be relevant. Sometimes a cartoon will be appropriate to lighten a weighty subject or make a point.

FONTS AND POINT SIZES

- Only one font should be used for all body copy in the newsletter and it should be a sensible point size, i.e. 11 point or 12 point. Remember, if the newsletter is going to the elderly, they may have difficulty reading small type, and if people have to strain to read your newsletter this is a barrier and they probably won't bother.
- Only one font should be used for the sub-headings. This can be different to the body copy font, but only one sub-heading font should be used in an article.

- Article title fonts can be varied to make the newsletter look more interesting, but care should be taken not to use too many on a page or double-page spread as this may look messy or confusing.

THE USE OF COLOUR

- This is your firm's newsletter and should reflect the colours of your logo.
- Do not over-use colour for headings or words.
- Try to ensure the colours you use do not clash – unless that is the point!
- If your firm's colour scheme is two colour, black does not have to be the second colour – you could use dark blue or dark green for the type which will then give you another colour to play with. Type should always be in a dark, easy to read colour.
- If you are producing a two-colour newsletter, remember to use tints and tones to give variety.
- If you are producing a four-colour newsletter, you don't have to go mad with colour. It often looks smarter to use two-colour for the majority of the newsletter with four-colour only being relevant in the pictures and photographs.
- Colour adds to cost.

APPROXIMATE GUIDELINES FOR STORY LENGTHS

- **news story** – 150 to 200 words long;
- **small article** – i.e. half page: 300 to 350 words long with picture;
- **full page article** – 650 to 800 words long with an absolute minimum of two pictures together with a bullet point box;
- **advertisement for firm** – third of page: 200 words plus picture.

OTHER CONSIDERATIONS

- Remember that your newsletter should look appropriate to its audience and to the profile of the firm. For example, it would be inappropriate to produce a glossy four-colour newsletter for cut-price conveyancing clients.
- Always try to use environmentally friendly paper or paper from sustainable forests.
- Do not send a newsletter to a client who has passed away.
- Always include details of the editorial team for comments and suggestions.
- Always include an area for clients to change their details or request not to receive the newsletter (if they do not want it, it will save you money not to send it to them).

Creating your newsletter

Step 1. Decide what you want your newsletter to do and to whom you are going to send it

Is your newsletter to be sent to private or commercial clients? Which ones, who are they and where are they? You need to have a clear idea of this before doing anything.

Step 2. Set the content of the newsletter

This should be set by the editorial panel each time, with guidance from the editor – it is always a good idea for the editor to create a list for discussion and comment. In addition, ideas that do not get included in one issue can carry over to the next. Before each editorial panel meeting it is also a good idea to send a note to everyone in the firm asking for their suggestions and feedback on the last issue, and that of their clients.

A way of finding ideas for articles is to look at the different legal services clients use, and to focus on those areas of law that are appropriate to their situation. For example, stories about the importance of having a will would be appropriate in a newsletter sent to clients who have employed your firm for a conveyancing transaction.

Always remember that your newsletter will be competing for reading time with information that has been requested by your clients or directly affects them. The most you can do is to ensure that the information you provide is, or could at some stage, be relevant to the recipients, so that even if it is not read immediately it may be kept until needed.

ARTICLE IDEAS FOR PRIVATE CLIENTS

Legal service	Description of article
Property	The conveyancing process – an outline of what is involved in a conveyancing transaction
	What mortgages – an outline of different types of mortgage and what they mean to the client
	Sub-letting – a guide for landlords and tenants
	Subsidence – what to do if it happens to you
	Noisy neighbours – how do you cope and how can the law help you?
	Leases – What your client's responsibilities are and how they can check them out
	Buying with a friend – what you need to know

Consumers	How can the law help?
	A guide to safety marks
	A guide to compensation
	Buying on the Internet – a guide to pitfalls and practices
Relationships	What status do you have in your relationship?
	Divorce and children
	A father's rights and a mother's rights
Personal injury	How do you know if you have a claim?
	What do conditional fees mean to you?
	An explanation of the claim process
Employment	Your contract – what it means
	Health and safety at work
	What is industrial espionage?
	What does your employer owe you?
General	Human rights – what do your new rights mean to you?

ARTICLE IDEAS FOR BUSINESS/COMMERCIAL CLIENTS

Legal service	*Description of article*
Employees	Contracts – what should you include in your employment contracts
	Maternity/paternity leave – the facts
	Part-time workers – a guide for employers
	Disciplinary action – a guide
	Tribunals – a guide
	Sexual harrassment – what you need to be aware of
	The Disability Act – a guide
	Redundancy – the facts
Property	Renting offices – what you need to be aware of
	A guide to the law with regard to Health and Safety At Work
	Working conditions – a guide
	Business rates – how to keep your rating accurate
Insurance	Insuring your employees
	Professional indemnity insurance
	Industrial injury – are you covered?
Computers	The legal requirements
	Safeguarding against hackers
	The Internet – legal implications

Intellectual property	Copyright – who owns what
	Applying for a patent – the pitfalls
	Confidentiality – how to keep a secret
	Trademarks – the process and what to do
General	Limited companies – how to set them up and what they are
	The corporate veil – keeping on the right side of the veil
	Bad debts – what action can you take?
	Consumer complaints – how to cope with them
	Directors' liability

REGULAR FEATURES

It is a good idea to have regular columns that contain either very short 'bites' of information or perhaps 'lighter' items. The aim is to attract readers' attention, but care should be taken not to include too much trivia and 'dumb down' the newsletter.

General regular sections:

- Letters' section: if necessary, you can create your own letters and responses, like an agony aunt column.
- 'In the news' column: you could publish brief news about interest rates, ground-breaking cases, changes in the legal profession, etc.

Private clients' regular sections:

- A regular competition section.
- A 'fascinating facts' section: you could put legal trivia in small boxes throughout the newsletter or in one area.
- You could put a regular cartoon strip in each issue.

Business/commercial clients regular sections

- Tax update – a regular column looking at current tax legislation.
- IT – a look at the legal implications of IT in business and data protection.
- Health and safety update section.
- 'About discrimination' section.

Step 3. Gather the relevant information for the stories

You could ask members of the firm to write an article about their area of practice or someone in the firm who has some writing ability may interview others in the firm and write up the article. Alternatively, you may choose to employ a freelance writer. This can prove expensive; to save costs, however, you can cut down on the writer's research time by providing them with relevant background information, or ask appropriate members of the firm to write a very rough article which the writer can edit and re-write if required.

With this last option, you should remember that you need to take into account the hourly cost of the firm member's time which might be far more than a writer's hourly charge.

ARTICLE FORMAT HINTS

- If an article is quite complex in nature, it is a good idea to simplify it by creating questions and writing the answers – a little like an agony column or FAQ (frequently asked questions).
- It is always a good idea to put an information box containing the main points as a bulleted list.
- Where possible, it is a good idea to interview clients about what they want as this can result in a far more interesting and relevant story and quotes will give the information more credibility.
- You can explain a point by creating a case history or using a real case but changing the names. Remember to ask your client's permission or inform them of what you are doing, as they may recognise the scenario even if their names are not used.

Anyone who writes an article should always sleep on it and then review it before submitting it.

Step 4. Set a copy deadline

Set yourself a date when all the copy should be finished. Any quotes from interviewees should be approved by all parties concerned. Keep to your deadlines so that producing the newsletter does not drag on.

It is important to have a schedule for sending out your newsletter so that recipients get used to receiving it and even expect it.

Step 5. Editing the newsletter

This is one of the most important aspects of the production process. When editing the newsletter you should do the following:

- Check that the stories are relevant.
- Check that they are grammatically correct.
- Check that the language is easy to understand and there is no jargon or that complicated words are properly explained.

- Check that articles, where appropriate, are short, sharp and interesting to read.
- Ensure headlines are correct and eye-catching.
- Check whether articles look too wordy and boring. Make sure that long articles have lots of sub-headings and incorporate charts or bullet point boxes, where appropriate.
- Check that there are enough illustrations or photographs to make the newsletter look interesting.
- Make sure that there is enough white space and that the newsletter does not look cluttered. If it does, go through stories and cut out bits. You will be surprised how a ruthless editing session will result in a far better newsletter.
- Check that articles are factually correct.

While editing your newsletter, always keep in mind the readers. There is no point publishing a newsletter that is boring, irrelevant or difficult to read.

Production and distribution

A newsletter is not a brochure, it is an information sheet or newspaper. The look of the finished product needs to reflect this. The following are points to be aware of when producing your newsletter. Remember:

- Your newsletter may be the only contact some of your less active clients have with your firm.
- Your newsletter will often have a wider audience that those targeted, i.e. it may be seen lying around or may be passed on.
- Your newsletter needs to reflect the firm's profile and image.
- You may choose to send your newsletter to attract new clients. If this is the first contact they are likely to have with your firm, it is important that the newsletter looks sufficiently professional.

Distributing your newsletter

One of the most important issues to resolve when deciding how to produce your newsletter is how you plan to distribute it. You might choose to distribute your newsletter through the post as a printed item, have it available to pick up at your office or via e-mail or on-line through your web site.

Your choice depends on how many clients you have, where they are and whether they have access to a computer, e-mail or the Internet. If you are planning to have quite sophisticated targeted newsletters, you will need to hold quite a lot of information about your clients to understand what they might find interesting. You will also need facilities to record marketing information on their file and you will need the staff to send the newsletters out to these different groups.

Remember, not everyone has access to a computer, e-mail and/or the Internet, especially private clients. Therefore, you may have to print the newsletter for private clients.

Via e-mail or your web site

If you plan to distribute your newsletter via e-mail or your web site, you will still need to go through the steps to creating your newsletter, but instead of printing your newsletter, the designer can convert it to PDF and put it on your web site for users to download. It is then a good idea to e-mail your clients about the newsletter and include a link to the web page in your e-mail.

You might choose simply to e-mail the newsletter to clients, but you need to be wary of its size. You could just send either the whole text or particular bits of information in the body copy of an e-mail.

If you are e-mailing information to clients, you can save time by setting up e-mail groups (remember to put them all in the blind copies box so that they don't see each others' details).

Remember: Whatever distribution method you choose, you need to ensure that the information you send is written in a style that is clear and easy to understand. It should look good and reflect well on your firm.

Printing your newsletter

Points to note:

- Print on paper appropriate to the colours and look, i.e. it might look strange to print two-colour on very glossy thick paper but in the same vein, it would look cheap to photocopy black and white.
- Remember to keep the weight of the newsletter under 60 grammes to keep the postage down (including envelope).
- It is a good idea to print on environmentally friendly paper and state this in the newsletter.

The most economical way to print your newsletter depends on the number you print. The main pros and cons of different print methods have been set out below.

FROM AN IN-HOUSE PC

If you choose this route, it is worthwhile investing in a colour printer.

For   Can be inexpensive
            Can be produced on demand

Can be altered on demand
Can be sent electronically without extra expense

Against   Only appropriate where very few are being produced and sent
Limited as to format, i.e. usually only A4 possible
Limited with regard to use of design
Limited with regard to type of paper that can be used
Can look amateurish

DIGITALLY PRINTED

This is where images are taken direct from a disk or CD and run out on a printer.

For   Less expensive than other printing methods for small quantities such as up to 500 or so
Good quality
Different paper stocks can be used
Can have same design input as other printing methods

Against   Only economical up to 500
Quality not as good as litho printing but sufficient for a newsletter

LITHO PRINTING

This can be done in one, two or four-colour by the printers who will usually print brochures for you.

For   Can be less expensive than other methods where you need over 500
Good quality
Very flexible on design and finishing

Against   Only economical over a certain number
Will cost more as films need to be produced
A designer will be needed unless you have sophisticated in-house capability

It is always worthwhile having quotes from both digital and litho printers. Let them know that this is a regular job and negotiate a price per issue if possible.

How to evaluate your newsletter

Because a newsletter is a one-way means of communication, it will not always be easy to establish its value. The following are methods that you can use to try to find out how your newsletter has been received and used:

■ You can include a response mechanism or competition in the newsletter. People are generally not very good at responding to competitions, so you will need to encourage them with a prize draw for a big prize or a number of prizes such as bottles of champagne. In addition, it is a good idea not to make the competition too difficult.

■ You can send out a questionnaire, either with the newsletter or just after the newsletter has been received. A suggested questionnaire and a guide to client research can be found in Part 2 of this manual. Again, to encourage response, it is a good idea to offer small prizes such as bottles of champagne for all those who respond.

■ You can also invite a number of clients to give you regular feedback (on forms you provide) on each newsletter issue. This will help you get a feel for the most popular types of article and how good your writing and production is. You should then use this information to fine-tune your newsletters.

Making the most of your newsletter

A few marketing approaches and ideas have been listed here to help you to maximise the benefits of your newsletter.

1. Give a file, branded with your logo, to clients to hold their newsletters. This would be particularly appropriate for commercial clients. It could be done fairly inexpensively by purchasing files with sleeves on the front and spine and producing pages to insert in the sleeves, branded with your firm's logo.

2. Contact local restaurants, theatres, cinemas, etc. and ask them to give your clients a discount. You could then include discount vouchers in your newsletter for clients to use. This would give added value and encourage clients to keep your newsletter, and therefore increase the likelihood of it being read. You could also ask local businesses if they would like to advertise in the newsletter for a small fee – for example, removal firms in a newsletter for conveyancing clients. This will help with your production and distribution costs. If you do this you should always include a disclaimer about the advertisers and their products.

3. Have a classified section for local associated businesses which will provide an extra service to your clients and add value for them. This could also be a service you could offer 'connector clients' to build value into your relationships.

4. Send it regularly to potential new clients to make them aware of your firm.

5. Give your 'connector' clients copies to distribute.

Direct mail

What is direct mail?

Direct mail is when you write to clients and non-clients to encourage them to use the legal services your firm offers. It is most often used:

1. To gain new clients by:

   ■ introducing the firm to non-clients;
   ■ encouraging potential clients to try the firm's services, perhaps at a discount or for a test period;
   ■ encouraging referrals for potential new clients from existing clients.

2. To increase work from existing clients by:

   ■ informing clients of a new service;
   ■ reminding them of an old service;
   ■ educating them about the possibility that they may require a particular service;
   ■ giving them an incentive to use a particular service.

3. To promote loyalty amongst existing clients by:

   ■ offering loyal clients a bonus in the form of a discount on another service or similar promotion;
   ■ keeping clients informed;
   ■ expanding the range of services a client uses.

Characteristics of direct mail

   ■ It is usually used as a method of offering a specific promotion or service.
   ■ It frequently includes an incentive to recipients to respond.
   ■ It is often in a letter format.
   ■ It is usually personalised to a named individual.
   ■ It often includes a leaflet about the promotion, the service on offer or your firm.

Planning your direct mail shot

The first thing you need to do is to identify what you want to offer and to whom you want to make the offer.

The offer

You begin by deciding what you intend to offer the recipients. This might be a new service, an enhancement to an old service, the opportunity to try your firm, an introduction to your firm, or a quotation.

The recipients

You now decide to whom you wish to send this offer. This may be existing clients, clients who have used you in the past but no longer do so, or a completely new target audience.

If the mail shot is to existing clients or old clients and you have their details on computer, it is often possible to mail-merge their details quickly onto the direct mail letter.

If you are buying a list of potential clients through a mailing house, they will often be able to supply the details on disk in software compatible with your system so that you can then mail-merge the details with the mailshot. You may also require labels with their names and addresses on if you are not using window envelopes.

The more personalised the direct mail letter, the more likely it is to achieve a response.

Using an incentive

You may decide to encourage recipients to respond to your direct mail shot by offering them an incentive. Depending on the purpose of the mail shot, this may take various forms. If you are trying to gain new clients, you might offer a free initial meeting, a regular newsletter, or a free on-line question forum. If you want to encourage clients to refer others to your firm you could offer a bottle of champagne for every referral received.

Whatever the reason, it is essential that the incentive used has the following characteristics:

1. It is likely to be attractive to the recipients and their way of life.
2. It is fitting to the direct mail shot.
3. If taken up by all those who are sent the mail shot, it will not break the bank.

Listed below are a number of different incentive approaches that you might wish to use:

- **A prize draw.** This sort of incentive is frequently used to encourage recipients to verify details, request further information or perhaps attend a free surgery or seminar.
- **A free gift.** This type of incentive is more appropriate where you are asking the recipient to spend money. It might be used as an encouragement to purchase, i.e. 'All those first-time buyers who use this firm for their conveyancing transaction will receive £30 in Ikea vouchers on completion', etc.
- **A discount voucher.** You may simply state that all those who register now and subsequently use your firm, e.g. for their conveyance, will receive a 10 per cent discount off the fixed price of £375, etc.

■ **The offer of free services.** You could offer the first consultation free, or a free analysis of the client's situation, etc. This may be offered to encourage recipients to attend your offices to discuss their case or to research further information.

One important thing to remember is that whatever the offer, you must be able to fulfil it should the maximum expected response occur.

Creating your direct mail shot

Having identified who is to receive your letter, what you want to offer them and whether you want to include any incentive, you now need to decide how you will present these in the mail shot and how you will ask recipients to respond.

The letter

A direct mail letter will usually include the following elements:

■ an outline of the purpose of the mail shot;
■ an incentive;
■ a call to action;
■ a response method.

The body of the letter can generally be set out in the following way.

Address and salutation. The letter should have the recipient's name and address on the top left-hand side and then open with their name.

First paragraph. Introduce the firm and the offer.

Second paragraph. Give further details about the firm including credibility 'hooks' and the reason behind the offer.

Third paragraph. Give further details about the offer and the incentive.

Fourth paragraph. Call to action and identify response method.

Final paragraph. Close and sign off.

Ideally the letter should only be one page long and should be upbeat, positive and easy to read.

Producing the letter

Depending on the number being sent in the direct mail promotion, it may be possible to produce the letter in a number of different ways and personalised to different degrees:

■ Print the letter onto headed paper from the computer and mail-merge the recipients' name and address at the same time. (Each will need to be signed separately unless you are able to scan your signature into the computer.)

■ Print a master letter (with a Sir/Madam salutation) onto plain paper (sign the original), photocopy onto headed paper (either in-house or through a print bureau) and mail-merge the name and address onto each. (*Note*: it is important that the photocopying quality is high and is not obviously a copy.)

■ Have the letters printed by a printer with a Sir/Madam salutation and signature and mail-merge the name and address via your own computer. For this, you may either provide your own paper, which will help keep the costs down if you have a two or four-colour logo, or have the whole letter created, including the logo.

The method which proves to be most economical for you to use will depend on the resources you have available and how many mail shots you intend to send.

The response mechanism

Your direct mail shot should always include a way for recipients to respond and take up any offer. This might take the form of words in the letter or it might involve enclosing a response card or envelope.

Different postal response mechanisms include:

■ freepost or postage paid postcard;
■ form on the letter or stand alone and freepost envelope;
■ voucher or letter to be presented on attendance;
■ freephone telephone number, i.e. 0800, 0700, etc.

The first three mechanisms should be personalised where possible. Where a postal response is an option, the recipient's name and address label might be stuck on the response side. This might also be done with a form or voucher. Apart from lessening the respondent's work, it also gives you an audit trail for each response.

It is perfectly acceptable to offer recipients access to a number of these different response mechanisms, i.e. a postcard and telephone number. Ease of use and simplicity is the key.

The response mechanism may differ according to your resources such as manpower to answer telephone responses.

Enclosing a leaflet

You may choose to include a leaflet about the firm and the offer with the letter. This can help establish your credibility and gives the recipient a much broader view of you and the offer.

The format and type of leaflet used will depend upon the contents of the mail shot. Listed below are a number of different approaches that may be used – for further information about producing printed materials, please see pp. 247–50.

- The leaflet is a general one about the firm and the services it is able to offer clients.
- The leaflet is a specific one about the service being promoted through the direct mail shot.
- The leaflet is a specific one to the offer.

Again, the method you use will be dictated by the resources you have available and whether you already have any marketing materials that you could use.

The cost implications of direct mail

Any direct mail promotion will have the following cost elements:

1. Postage.
2. Materials, i.e. envelopes, printed letters, brochures, etc.
3. Offer cost.
4. Staff time.
5. Cost of list, if purchased.

Direct mail promotions are frequently costed per 1,000 addresses. Obviously, where you are using lower numbers then you might cost it by the tens or hundreds. However, any reduction in numbers will not necessarily show a pro-rata reduction in cost, this is because of the set-up charges, etc. which will not reduce whatever the numbers.

Below is an example of the cost of a direct mail shot and how that is broken down.

Mail shot 1

Quantity	1,000		
Target audience	Non-clients		
Elements	Personalised letter, leaflet and response form		

Postage		1,000 × £0.26	= £260.00
Materials: envelopes		1,000	= £17.00
printed letters (externally)		1,000	= £299.00
leaflets		1,000 × £0.75	= £750.00
response form		1,000	= £50.00
Reply-paid postage for an estimated response of 10%		100 × £0.24	= £ 24.00
Offer – 12 bottles of champagne			= £135.00
List		1,000	= £135.00
Total cost			£1,670.00

Total cost per mailshot is £1.67

Mail shot 2

Quantity	200		
Target audience	ST clients		
Elements	Personalised letter, brochure and response form		

Postage		200 × £0.26	= £52.00
Materials: letter (produced internally)		200 × £0.12	= £24.00
envelopes		200	= £3.40
leaflets		200 × £0.75	= £150.00
Reply-paid postage for an estimated response of 10%		20 × £0.24	= £4.80
Offer – 12 bottles of champagne			= £135.00
Total cost			= £399.20

Total cost per mailshot is £1.99

As can be seen from the above, although the mailing to 200 is much simpler with the letters being printed on the computer, the list not having to be purchased, no pre-printed response form, etc., the cost per mail shot is actually higher.

If time was factored into these costs it would produce an even greater disparity, as the time writing and creating the mailshot is fixed. A large mail shot to many thousands might be costed as low as £450 per thousand as economies of scale come into play.

The response

The response you receive will vary according to the list of recipients who receive the direct mail and the nature of the offer. The British Direct Mail Association suggests a response rate of between one and five per cent may be expected.

You should ensure that you have the resources to handle a five per cent response rate at any one time, although it is unlikely you will achieve this rate.

If a mail shot asks for some sort of response and you have a large number to send, it makes sense to send them in batches, i.e. if you are sending 1,000 distribute them at a rate of 200 per week over 5 weeks. This helps spread the workload required to send the promotion out and also helps to break up the response into easily manageable numbers.

Evaluating your direct mail promotions

In order to evaluate whether a direct mail exercise is a feasible and cost-efficient method of gaining clients for your firm, you need to look at the response you receive and the income generated together.

Example

If you are trying to create demand for your conveyancing services, you need forecast what sort of response you need to receive to pay for the promotion. If you forecast a 1% response, which, based on a mail shot of 200 is two responses, would two new clients pay for the promotion?

i.e.	1% of 200 mailshots	=	2
	Revenue per conveyancing client	=	£375.00
	Cost per conveyancing client	=	£120.00
	Profit per conveyancing client	=	£255.00

Therefore if 1% of those mailed converts to a sale, the revenue raised is £510.00. If the cost of the mailshot is approximately £375.00, the promotion has covered its costs and made a profit of £135.00 for the firm.

The hidden response

It should be noted that a promotion such as the one described above might have an easily measured response in the short term but also a second stage effect over a longer period of time. By keeping a close record of conveyancing figures and comparing this year with last year, you can check whether the trend is up, level or down. Any promotions you have undertaken should be taken into account when analysing why the trend is a particular way.

It should be noted that the above is a general example only. Though the promotion has made a profit, sending 200 mail shots may not be the most efficient way of gaining two new clients in the short term.

It is extremely important that you keep a close check on the response you receive from any direct mail promotion you undertake.

Seminars

What is a seminar?

A meeting set up for the dissemination of knowledge in which a 'leader' discusses a subject with his audience rather than expounding it. Frequently a small and informal grouping in UK but can be organised on a large scale of conference proportions.

This is one description of a seminar, given in the Institute of Marketing's 'Glossary of Marketing Terms'.

How can seminars help?

Seminars promote your firm as a central point of information, particularly where you can identify a subject area that might be of interest or concern to an identifiable group of clients and non-clients. As well as staging your own seminars, members of your firm may be invited to speak at a seminar organised by another organisation. This can also prove to be a very good opportunity to promote your firm through members of your firm promoting themselves. This section identifies the steps to staging a seminar, though a lot of the information will be useful and relevant if a member of your firm is invited to speak at someone else's seminar.

Running a seminar can help you:

1. To promote loyalty amongst existing clients by:
   - providing an extra service to clients and increasing contact opportunities;
   - educating your clients and giving them useful information about an area of the law that is specifically applicable to themselves or their situation;
   - giving something tangible to clients for free;
   - establishing that you have an understanding of their business and appreciation of their legal needs.
2. To increase work from existing clients by:
   - reminding clients of your firm's services;

- educating clients about their rights and creating a need;
- maintaining an open dialogue with clients.

3. To maintain or create an image of the firm through:

- the presentation of seminars;
- establishing the firm as having specialist knowledge and expertise in this area of law;
- reminding/informing clients of the areas of law in which the firm practices.

4. To promote to potential new clients by:

- inviting those who are not clients of your firm, as well as existing clients, with whom create the opportunity to meet and establish a personal connection;
- inviting non-clients to whom you are promoting the fact that your firm has specialist knowledge/expertise in this area;
- inviting them alongside existing clients to show that you have a credible client base who use your services.

Characteristics of seminars

- They have a specific subject matter.
- They have a small number of participants.
- They can be free though if successful you might wish to charge for them.
- They are frequently held in the evening, lunchtime or even breakfast.
- They include a presentation and discussion section.
- They have a social element attached, i.e. refreshments and an opportunity for attendees to chat as part of the event.

Organising your seminar

There are several aspects that should be noted about seminars:

- They should always be relevant to the attendees.
- The presentation should be professional and easy to follow and understand. Suitable visual aids should be used.
- The presenter should be clear, concise and, ideally, have had some training.
- The main focus should be on a specific issue
- There should be a real benefit to those attending, i.e. the subject matter must be of an operational and applicable nature.

Steps to organising your seminar

There are a number of steps to go through in setting up your seminar.

IDENTIFY A SUBJECT AREA THAT WOULD LEND ITSELF TO A SEMINAR

This could be:

- a change in the law that will affect certain of your clients, i.e. the new Disability Act;
- an area of the law or regulations that commonly cause your clients problems, i.e. dismissal;
- an area of the law or regulations that could cause your clients problems if they are not fully aware of them, i.e. health and safety;
- a system that your clients need be aware of, i.e. tribunals.

IDENTIFY THE TARGET AUDIENCE AND NUMBER AMONGST YOUR CLIENTS

If they are private clients, how will you qualify them as appropriate? For example, those on your list who have purchased a property with two surnames, i.e. co-habitees, might be interested in the law with regards to wills, mortgages, etc.

If they are business clients, identify the size of the business or type of business affected by particular changes or able to make use of the information.

IDENTIFY WHO WOULD GIVE THE TALK

It is very important that the person giving the presentation at the seminar is a competent public speaker, knows the subject and presents himself or herself in a friendly, authoritative and believable manner.

OUTLINE THE SUBJECT AREA COVERED BY THE PRESENTATION

Identify the relevant information that the audience would actually find useful. Do not go through detailed legal explanations – your audience is not made up of lawyers. Using scenarios is a good way of putting a point across.

IDENTIFY WHERE TO HOLD THE SEMINAR

The location would ideally be at your premises as this gives you an opportunity to show off your offices and facilities. However, if they are not to a high enough standard then a local hotel might be more appropriate, though this will increase the expense considerably.

IDENTIFY OTHER ORGANISATIONS THAT MIGHT LIKE TO JOIN FORCES WITH YOU

This might be appropriate where an area of law needs explanation and there is a body that will be responsible for enforcing that area of regulation or for ensuring the organisation does not fall foul of a rule. Or, it might be where the law needs explaining and a workshop could be included to bring home the ethical or moral aspects, i.e. a disability discrimination workshop where a representative from an advisory body could attend.

If there are other organisations that it would make sense to invite to take part, contact them to see if they do want to take part. Identify with them what they would like to discuss, the running order of the presentation and what presentation tools would help them.

It is also a good idea to establish that the person giving the presentation is good at doing so. You do not want your part to be well done and theirs to be boring, switching off your audience.

ESTIMATE THE NUMBERS YOU WOULD LIKE TO ATTEND

You should ensure that attendees will be able to see, are comfortable and will not feel cowed by the number of attendees asking questions. 'Small, intimate and very relevant' is a good phrase to bear in mind.

IDENTIFY ANY NEGATIVES THAT MIGHT ARISE

Ensure that you are not presenting a subject that will create negatives, for example a subject that solicitors have been slow in sorting out for clients, or an area in which some clients have outstanding issues with your firm. Remember, clients may, unknown to you, meet together, attend the same church, be members of the same chamber of commerce, etc. You do not want to expose happy clients to unhappy ones or spend the seminar making excuses.

IDENTIFY APPROPRIATE DATES

This might be dependent on the time of year, when a new regulation is due to come into effect, where an area has been in the press, or where the economy makes that area of particular relevance at any time.

Whatever the timing is, you should ensure that the seminar is presented at a time that enables attendees to make use of the information you impart before the 'horse has bolted', i.e. ensure that attendees will have the correct amount of time, after the seminar, to meet any legal requirements you are explaining to them.

DECIDE WHO SHOULD INVITE THE ATTENDEES AND BE IN CHARGE OF THE INVITATIONS AND RESPONSES

This involves client contact and therefore needs to be undertaken competently and efficiently.

Depending on the subject being discussed and the target audience it may be appropriate for the solicitor who deals with the clients to invite them, or the senior partner or the appropriate department could issue the invitation.

EVALUATE POSSIBLE ATTENDEES

If you are in any doubt about who might attend or whether enough people will wish to attend, it is a very good idea to send a letter to the target audience prior to inviting them. The letter should say that you are thinking of holding a seminar on a certain date and include a response form asking the relevant questions below.

If the invitation is being sent to a business client:

- Who would be the most appropriate member of staff to invite? Even if you deal with the managing director on a regular basis, you may hold a seminar where the person in charge of human resources would be the most appropriate to attend.
- Ask whether your contact and/or their colleagues might be interested in attending.
- Identify a number of dates on which you might hold the seminar and ask whether any or all of them would be convenient.
- Ask whether there are any particular areas of this subject that would be of interest, and if there are any questions they would like answered or problems solved.

If the invitation is being sent to a private client:

- Who would be the most appropriate person to invite?
- Are there any others who would be interested in attending?
- Identify a number of dates on which you might hold the seminar and ask whether any or all of them would be convenient.
- Ask whether there are any particular areas of this subject that would be of interest, and if there any questions the client would like answered or problems solved.

The letter should have a response form, with a return stamped addressed envelope.

The level of response to this letter will enable you to gauge whether you will have enough attendees to invite and will also enable you to gain some insight into what the attendees would like to talk about.

Sending out the invitations

The following should be confirmed before sending out the invitations:

- the date;
- the venue;
- the speaker(s);
- the members of staff who will attend;
- the time.

INVITE POTENTIAL ATTENDEES

Where you have sent out a pre-invitation letter, an invitation should be sent to those who responded that they would be interested.

However, if a person indicated an interest but identified a date other than the one the majority requested and on which the seminar is to be held, a covering letter should be sent with the invitation. It should state:

■ This was the majority date choice.

■ If they are unable to attend, you would be happy to send them any information handed out during the seminar and/or you will ensure they will be invited to any future seminar.

■ If they are unable to attend, would they like to send a representative to the seminar to pose any questions on their behalf?

In addition, it is a good idea to send an invitation to those who did not respond to the pre-invitation letter.

Where you have not sent a pre-invitation letter, simply send an invitation to all those who you think would be interested in the seminar.

WHAT SHOULD THE INVITATION COMPRISE?

The invitation should comprise a covering letter with a card invitation (this could be an off-the-shelf card with the details written in ink, or an invitation designed on Word or Powerpoint and printed on good quality paper). Alternatively, the invitation might simply be a letter with the details of the seminar.

It is a good idea to include a response form in the invitation covering letter or invitation letter with questions about parking, number attending and special needs, i.e. wheelchair access. You should also include:

■ a map of the area and location of your office;

■ an itinerary of the evening;

■ a contact telephone number for queries;

■ a date by which you would appreciate the form returned.

Managing the responses

If you do not receive responses to your invitation by the date you asked them to respond, it would be a worthwhile exercise to telephone those invited to confirm whether they would be able to attend.

What happens if you are oversubscribed?

Depending on the numbers, it may be possible to stage two seminars instead of one. It is a better idea to stage two small seminars than one large one, as this ensures that members of the firm are able to talk to all attendees and there will be time to answer all of the attendees' queries in full.

If you do decide to split the seminar, it is probably a good idea to contact respondents by telephone to organise for half of them to attend the second date.

What do you do if you do not have a good response?

It is possible that after telephoning to prompt a response, you do not gain enough attendees to hold a reasonable seminar, i.e. only four respond in the affirmative. Rather than go ahead and hold a seminar where the number of attendees might give your firm a negative image, it would be a good idea to shelve the idea of a seminar on this subject.

If you decide to do this, you might like to approach the different groups of potential attendees in the following ways.

To confirmed attendees: you could send them a letter to apologise that the seminar has been cancelled because 'though the seminar appeared to attract a great deal of interest, very few were able to attend on the set dates, therefore we have decided instead to send an information pack explaining the subject area'. In addition, you should include a form for the recipients to pose any questions about the subject that they may have.

If you sent a pre-invitation letter: you could write to all those who expressed an interest with an information pack covering the subject area that was to be discussed at the seminar. In addition, you might like to include a form that the recipients can use to pose any questions about the subject they may have.

Staging the seminar

Having invited attendees you need to ensure that the seminar is staged in a professional manner. There are a number of things that will need to be prepared before the seminar takes place:

- any presentation visual aids that are to be used;
- hand-out materials;
- follow-up materials.

Presentation visual aids

There are a number of different visual aids that you could use in your presentation. These are:

    (a) computer-generated slides;
    (b) overhead projector;
    (c) writing boards;
    (d) video;
    (e) Internet.

(a) SLIDES

These are the most commonly used as they can be pre-prepared, are very flexible and can be made to look professional and attractive using in-house software.

The most commonly used software is Microsoft Powerpoint. This software enables you to produce slide shows with builds, fades and visuals.

The visual image

There are a number of points that should be borne in mind when preparing a slide show:

- The background design or colour scheme should match the firm's logo.
- The background should not be too busy or interfere with any words or images on the slides.
- The firm's logo should be in evidence on all slides.
- Slide headers should be of a consistent font and point size on all slides.
- Body text or bullets should be set out in the same font or point size on all slides.
- Continuity in the bullet point styles should be used, i.e. arrows, dots, stars.
- There shouldn't be too much information on each slide, i.e. only four bullet points per slide – however, this might depend on the style used.
- If slide transitions are being used, they should be consistent throughout the presentation.
- If bullet point builds are being used, they should be consistent within each slide.
- The slides should be attractive, interesting to look at and aid the presentation. They should not make points not discussed.

To show the slides, you could either use a projector or an LCD screen (with an overhead projector), both of which can be plugged into a desktop or laptop computer. These can be hired on a daily basis. This might be the best option as they can be expensive to buy.

Preparing your slide show

Before beginning to prepare slides, the speaker needs to write the narrative of the presentation. This can be done fairly roughly or in full, depending on the skills of the speaker. It is often a good idea to prepare the talk in some detail as it not only helps in producing the slides, but also ensures that there is a comprehensive guide for the speaker to refer to should it all go 'horribly wrong', or stage fright set in. In addition, this text can be used to prepare any handouts for the audience.

Having written the notes or narrative, the speaker needs to identify the key points or messages in the narrative and summarise them in a logical manner for the slides. It is a good idea to have bullet points that are built up on a slide as a point is explained. These help the audience keep pace with the explanation and remember what the speaker is talking about as they identify the key issues being discussed.

Having identified the bullet points, text, or visual identifiers for the slides, someone, i.e. the speaker or another member of the firm, needs to pull the presentation together.

Once this has been done, it is a good idea for the speaker to run through the presentation and identify on the script when the slide changes need to occur. This will either be as the speaker uses a word where they are following a script, or simply when they come to a point. It is useful to do this to remind the speaker when to change the slides, as it is very easy to forget to bring in another bullet point or slide when the speaker is in full flow. Indeed, it is often a good idea to have someone else operating the slide show with the speaker's script in front of them.

Having created a slide show for the presentation, it is a very good idea for the speaker (or the speaker and slide operator) to go through the talk a couple of times to ensure that the slide changes come in the right places. It is also a good idea for them to do this in front of other members of the firm to ensure that the slides make sense and give the correct information at the correct time.

(b) OVERHEAD PROJECTOR

If the transparencies are well prepared, using an overhead projector can give a professional image. They will also tend to give a more interactive and intimate perception of the presentation, i.e. more of a classroom feel.

You can prepare the overheads in the same way as the slides, except that you will not be able to put builds into the bullet points or fade them in or out.

Once the presentation is finished, you can print them off onto transparency sheets if you have a colour printer, or you can send the disk to an agency to print off for you.

If you are thinking of undertaking a number of presentations, it will probably save you money to invest in an inkjet colour printer. You can buy one for between £100 and £150.

(c) WRITING BOARDS

If you want to take notes or suggestions during the presentation or any discussions, it is useful to have a flip chart on which to write them.

This should really be used in conjunction with either slides or overheads and is more suited to training sessions.

(d) VIDEO

To make your own specific video is a very costly business if you do it professionally.

However, you might like to use a video of a television programme or news clips, to introduce your seminar or make a point. In this instance you need to video the programme or news clips you would like to use and then take the video(s) into a video editing shop for them to edit for the presentation. You can also fade sound and voice-overs on the video.

This is relatively inexpensive and can create an extremely professional impression.

You can often play videos on PCs and it may therefore be worth having your video saved onto a CD so that you can play it through the same system as the one for slide projection. Alternatively, you will probably be able to hook a video player directly into the PC or projector. Care should be taken to avoid a great deal of stopping and starting in changing plugs, etc. during the seminar.

However, remember that it is better to have no video rather than a bad video; you may feel that the time and money that need to be invested in the video is not worthwhile for a one-off or small seminar.

(e) INTERNET

You might like to include information on web sites during your presentation. If you do, take care to download the web pages you want onto your cache before the presentation to avoid interruptions while waiting for the information to download.

Hand-out materials

There are two occasions where you might like to give attendees a handout:

1. **At the beginning.** This handout might include an agenda for the seminar with an outline of the subjects to be discussed and the presenters.
2. **At the end.** As the final rounding off point, it is a good idea to give attendees to the seminar an information pack.

   - Include notes about the subject covered in the seminar. This could take the form of a paper copy of the slides printed three to a page with notes next to them or the script next to them. *Hint*: It looks nice if the slide show is copied to a new file and every other slide is the notes for that slide; you can then print out six slides to a page. The slides can be viewed on the left and the notes on the right.

- Include a brochure about the firm.
- You could include an evaluation questionnaire about the seminar, asking attendees how useful and interesting they found it. You could also send this in the week following the seminar. However, the best way to ensure a response is to hand the evaluation questionnaires to attendees at the seminar whilst they are seated, with pens/pencils, and ask them to fill the questionnaires in before they leave.

In addition, it is a good client care exercise to send out this pack to those who were unable to attend, but expressed an interest when invited.

Follow-up materials

There are a number of different follow-up materials that you might wish to send to attendees or those who could not attend:

- a letter outlining the answer to questions that were not answered at the seminar;
- a questionnaire asking attendees' views of the seminar if this was not included in the information pack.

Evaluating your seminar

As mentioned above, you can distribute evaluation questionnaires to attendees either at the seminar or immediately following the seminar. A suggested questionnaire can be found in Part 2 of this manual.

Making the most of your seminar

1. **Include refreshments.** One incentive for people to attend your seminar may be the opportunity to network, especially those from small businesses. You should therefore try to ensure that there is sufficient networking time built into your agenda. This could be over refreshments, which, depending on the time and length of your seminar, may be a buffet lunch, wine and nibbles, or only coffee or tea and biscuits. Whatever is provided, try to allow enough time for attendees to chat and be on hand to introduce them to each other. Badges identifying attendees' names and organisations (if it is a business seminar) are often a good way of helping the flow of conversation.
2. **Have staff attending to chat with attendees.** This is not only a golden opportunity for attendees to chat and for you to position your firm as a central source of information. It is also an ideal opportunity to strengthen ties with attendees and for them to meet members of the firm. Therefore, ensure that members of your firm attend, and it is even a good idea to require them to attend.

3. **Set up boards in the refreshment area outlining the services the firm offers.** As mentioned above, it is a good idea to provide time for your attendees and colleagues to mix and get to know each other. To gain maximum benefit from having your clients on site and a 'captive' audience, it is a good idea to set up boards, such as exhibition stand boards, promoting the services your firm offers. This is an opportunity to show attendees the full range of work your firm carries out from business to private work. It could result in them putting different work your way, i.e. business clients may employ your firm for their personal legal requirements or private clients may remember your firm for their work requirements.

4. **Distribute brochures to attendees.** It is a good idea to send your firm's brochures to attendees either when they are on site or afterwards. This will help consolidate information about your firm that they were shown or told at the seminar, and gives them a reference document for their files. Obviously, it does not make sense to send brochures or leaflets to clients who already have them or you know would not appreciate or need them. New clients should always be sent or given information about your firm they can refer to.

5. **Invite attendees to subscribe to your newsletter (if you produce one).** Again, to make sure you take advantage of all opportunities it is a good idea to offer attendees an opportunity to request to receive your newsletter (if you produce one).

Sponsorship and supporting charities

Sponsorship involves supporting a sports event or other community event by giving either money or time, and supporting charities involves your firm raising or donating money to a charity.

Sponsoring a sports event or other community event can help your firm:

1. To promote loyalty among existing clients by:

   ■ putting your firm's name in front of clients allied to a community cause;
   ■ promoting your firm as being in touch with the local community;
   ■ promoting your firm as being not totally profit-oriented;
   ■ giving something tangible back to the community.

2. To maintain or create an image of the firm through:

   ■ the nature of the event sponsored;
   ■ the repetition of the firm's logo and the names of the solicitors.

Supporting a charity can help your firm:

3. To promote loyalty among existing clients by:

- promoting your firm as being not totally profit-oriented;
- giving something tangible back to the community and society.

How to research sponsorship and charity support opportunities

To be honest, the majority of them will find you – local events, sports clubs and charities will be in touch requesting your support.

To avoid being plagued and put in the embarrassing position of saying no, it is worthwhile spending a short time discussing, among partners, the sort of organisations or events your firm might consider sponsoring or donating money to. This could be a number of different organisations.

It is also a good idea to ask all the staff for their thoughts or suggestions for causes or organisations. Make a list of them and have the members of the firm vote on who they would like to support and then contact them and organise your support.

This approach will ensure that members of the firm will feel included and will be more likely to take part and help out with any sponsored events. It will also enable you to state that you sponsor or support a particular charity when you have unsolicited telephone calls requesting money.

Evaluating your sponsorship or charitable activities

Though some may feel that looking for a return from such activities is against the spirit of supporting them, these activities do create good opportunities to build your firm's profile in your market place. But how can you measure this?

One of the main benefits to your firm of undertaking sponsorship or adopting charitable causes as cited above is that they can help raise the firm's profile and present your firm as having an interest and involvement in the local community. These activities also create public relations opportunities for your firm.

Therefore, in terms of evaluating the success of these activities, the objective of raising your profile and presenting your firm as caring about the local community can be measured by the positive press coverage you receive.

You can assess this in two ways. The first is simply to measure the number of column centimetres of coverage for these activities that you have received in the press. This is coverage you would not have received ordinarily.

You could also conduct research into the perception of your firm by the local community. Because of the costs involved, it is unlikely to be cost-efficient to conduct research purely to establish the effect of sponsorship (unless that sponsorship is for a lot of money) or of charitable contributions – this money is probably best donated to charity.

However, it is worth conducting regular research to understand how your firm is viewed, perhaps every year or two years (see Questionnaire No. 4 in the Research Section). Sponsorship and charitable donations may only form a small part of other work you are undertaking to position the firm and therefore as a whole you may not be able to identify their effect. What you can do is look at the descriptive phrases applied to your firm (see Q19 on the questionnaire referred to above) and find out whether your firm is perceived to be more, or less, involved in the local community, and whether it is viewed as having a caring culture or as merely concerned with profit.

The effect of your sponsorship or charitable donations on your firm's profile is extremely difficult to measure with any certainty apart from monitoring press coverage.

So far we have only looked at the value of sponsorship or supporting a charity with regard to the reaction of those outside the firm. What should also be taken into account is the positive effect on the internal culture of the firm – especially with regard to charitable donations. Everyone would prefer to work for a caring organisation and being involved in the local community also means being involved in the outside lives of your staff, who are also part of your local community.

Making the most of your sponsorship activities

1. **Take advantage of any public relations opportunities.** It is a good idea to bear in mind the public relations opportunity afforded to you by the organisations you sponsor or charities you support. For example, when you begin to support a charity or sponsor an event or organisation, send a press release to the local press announcing this – preferably with a picture of you handing over an oversized cheque (obtainable from most banks) to a member of the sponsored organisation or charity. If staff undertake any money-raising activities, ensure someone is allocated the role of photographer (if appropriate) and send any pictures with a press release to the local papers.

2. **Tell your clients about them.** Inform clients of any sponsorship you do or charity you support. For example, if you sponsor a local event, write to your clients to tell them about the event and that you are a sponsor. If you choose to sponsor a local charity you could position yourself as a conduit for money that your clients might like to donate (remember to point out the tax aspect of this). In addition, if your firm supports a charity and holds events to raise money for those events, you can feature this in your newsletter and web site and you can also list such organisations in your brochure.

3. **Provide materials to advertise your firm at events.** This may involve having a banner or logo boards made that can be displayed at events to advertise your firm's involvement. It may also be worthwhile having a couple of small advertisements put together that can be used for programmes or local papers. You can create a template into which you can simply drop different words. This will cut the on-oing cost and time you need to fulfil requests for such advertisements. It is always a good idea to have a colour and a black and white version produced as local event programmes vary enormously in their sophistication and method of production.

4. **Review your sponsorship or adopted charities.** This might be every one, two or more years. Reviewing and possibly changing your firm's chosen organisations or events gives other causes a chance to benefit from your patronage and changing charities creates 'launch' public relations opportunities. It is also a fair way to take into account your staff's wishes for different causes and will regenerate interest among them to raise money for charity or attend events.

Advertising

There are a number of different ways that advertising can be used, depending on what you are trying to achieve. You might use advertising to:

- generate enquiries from potential clients;
- create an image of your firm;
- raise awareness of your firm, a particular service you offer or a legal issue;
- back up another promotional exercise.

Advertising is an extremely flexible promotional tool but can prove expensive. Because of this, it is important that you use the correct form of advertising to achieve your desired result. There are a number of different types of advertisement, such as:

- classified advertisements;
- directory advertisements;
- display advertisements;
- inserts;
- radio advertisements.

These different types of advertising might be placed in:

- national newspapers;
- regional newspapers;
- trade press/magazines;
- directories;
- posters at bus stops or bill boards;

- local or national radio;
- programmes for events.

Before undertaking any advertising you should ensure that you check that you are advertising according to the rules set out in the Solicitors' Publicity Code. These rules identify acceptable and unacceptable advertising.

Planning your advertising campaign

Before launching into any advertising campaign you need to identify clearly what you want to achieve from that campaign. Do you want to generate a response, raise the profile of your firm or simply back up another exercise? The type and number of advertisements and media in which you advertise depends on what you want to achieve.

The first thing you have to do is to identify your target audience. Who do you want to reach with your advertisement? Your target audience is of enormous importance and will help you identify the correct media for your advertisement.

Identifying your target audience is a narrowing down process. You break down your target audience according to where they are, what type of person or profession they are. Once you know this, you are in a good position to start researching and creating a short list of the media that will reach the target audience you have identified.

There are two vital things you need establish from the start. First, where are those you want to reach located geographically? If they are limited to one geographic area, it would make sense to approach local papers and perhaps to use bill boards or bus stop posters. If your firm is national and you want to reach a wider geographical area you could then consider using the national press or other national media.

The second thing you need establish is the type of person you want your advertisement to attract and reach. The media tend to have identified reader profiles. They will often have age breakdowns of their circulation, perhaps figures on the demographics (i.e. A, B, C, D or E), figures about income, profession, job titles, etc. The amount of information held by different media about their readers or listeners ranges from highly sophisticated to simple circulation numbers.

When looking for publications or radio stations with a suitable reader or listener profile, you should first telephone all the media that could be relevant to your target audience and request a media pack. In the case of local papers, this will usually include an outline of distribution together with a guide to the costs involved. Magazines and radio stations usually have slightly more sophisticated media packs with detailed reader or listener information and research.

Indeed, media packs are a very good source of research information and it is a worthwhile exercise getting hold of copies from a broad range. They frequently contain useful market information that can help you gain an insight into how you might approach your desired audience.

British Rates and Data (BRAD) is one of several directories produced that list all of the publications and other media in which you can advertise. Updated each month, you can purchase a copy from EMAP Business Communications, telephone 020 7505 8000 for approximately £265. You could also go to their web site at www.brad.co.uk; they will give you a password to enter the site on a one-day trial, after which you may decide to take out a subscription.

BRAD will also prove useful for your public relations. However, because of the expense, it would probably make sense to try to track down a copy of BRAD through your local library or ask around to see if anyone would lend you a copy. Alternatively, you can undertake local searches as below.

LOCAL NEWSPAPERS AND MAGAZINES

Details can be found in the Yellow Pages for your local area under 'Newspapers and Magazines'. In addition, any local papers you or any of your fee earners receive may be appropriate.

LOCAL RADIO STATIONS

Details can be found in the Yellow Pages under 'Broadcasting Services', or if you visit the Radio Authority's web site at www.radioauthority.org.uk you can see a list of all independent radio stations and their coverage areas. For local BBC radio stations, simply telephone the local BBC offices or the London offices to establish their details.

TRADE PUBLICATIONS

Unless you know the different trade publications produced for different areas such as construction, it might be a good idea to get hold of a copy of BRAD to look them up. You could also search for the publications on the Internet. A number of them will have their own web sites.

What do you want your advertisement to achieve?

Once you know who you want to reach, where they are and which publications might serve them, the next question is, what do you want your advertisement to achieve? Do you want to generate enquiries, attract new clients from a new market place, reposition your firm or simply tell people you are there? Are you seeking to recruit new staff, advertise a specific service or back up another promotion by repeating the message through a different channel?

How much do you want to spend?

The answer to this will often be 'as little as possible'. This is not a bad start as advertising, especially display advertising, can prove to be expensive and can sometimes be difficult to evaluate in terms of your bottom line.

To get advice on any advertising you plan to undertake and understand the sums involved, it is useful to arrange a visit from the media sales people to discuss their publication(s), or telephone them to tell them your plans and ask them to put together a campaign. They will be keen to sell space, but it will also be possible to pick up some good ideas and tips on how to approach your advertising. In addition, a publisher will often publish a number of titles in the same locality or subject area, with slightly different audiences or different distribution methods. If you choose to place your advertisements with one publisher in a range of titles, it gives you a good basis to negotiate low rates for each advertisement.

The main questions to ask the media sales people for local radio, newspapers and magazines is about the distribution method (circulation or listenership) and how it is controlled and/or measured:

- *Newspapers* will be sold through newsagents, etc., distributed free to certain local areas or may have an element of subscription.
- *Magazines* can be distributed in the same way as newspapers, and also through controlled circulation and requested readers. Controlled circulation is where a trade publication is sent to a specific mailing list, i.e. *Plumbing Weekly* will be sent to a list of plumbers that is held by the magazine. Many controlled circulation magazines have a further qualifier called requested readers, those who have filled in a form to request to receive the publication each issue. Often controlled circulations publications will rotate their circulations, especially where there is a large potential audience, as the cost of sending the magazine to all of them might prove prohibitive.
- *Radio stations* talk in terms of listener profiles which are identified through research by official radio bodies and by the radio stations themselves. They will often have demographics about who listens, for how long and when. For example, the morning and evening rush hour are frequently peak times and will be priced accordingly.
- *Directory* publishers will be able to identify who they are sent to.
- *Posters at bus stops or bill boards* are arranged through agencies who will usually discuss the local area and may have research on the results of such exposure for different advertisers.
- *Information on programmes for events* will focus on the past figures of visitors to the events and, if available, who they were.

You could also ask whether they have any reader research on the buying habits of their readers and who they are, on the type of advertising available, i.e. display, classified, inserts, etc. and any research on the response to each type. Finally, ask if they give any series discounts. If you run a series of advertisements (if appropriate), the price will reduce the more advertisements you run.

This will all initially take time, but is worthwhile as you will begin to build a good knowledge base from which to work.

Once you have investigated ways of putting your advertisement in front of your chosen audience and you have some idea of the type of advertising that will achieve the response you want and that you can afford, it is time to sit down and plan your campaign or single advertisement.

Single advertisement vs. a series of advertisements

You may want to run only one advertisement, and for many media this is sufficient, i.e. classified, directories, recruitment or inserts. However, with some campaigns it is recommended that you run a series of advertisements. This is because your advertisement may need to be repeated several times before it is effective in achieving your aim, i.e. in display or radio advertising where you want to raise or change the profile of your firm.

The different forms of advertising have been listed in Box 11 with an indication of whether they should be run in a series rather than as a one-off.

Box 11 Advertising as a one-off or in a series

Type of advertisement	Used to back up other promotional work	Used as a one-off exercise	Should be run as a campaign or series
Classified advertisements	✗	✓	✓
Directory advertisements	✗	✓	✗
Display advertisements	✓	✗	✓
Inserts	✓	✓	✗
Radio advertisements	✓	✗	✓
Programme adverts	✗	✓	✗
Posters – bus stops/bill boards	✓	✓	✓

✓ denotes where this form of advertising can be used.
✗ denotes where this form of advertising would be inappropriate.

Evaluating an advertisement or advertising campaign

The cost of your advertisement or advertising campaign will vary according to the type of advertisements you use and the number you insert. Whatever you spend on buying space or producing your advertisements should be set against any results from the advertisement or campaign.

Whenever a new client contacts your firm, they should be asked where they heard of your firm or saw it advertised (if you do any advertising). This information should be fed into your database, if possible, or a central record should be maintained. This will help you evaluate the response to an advertisement.

Classified advertisements

These are used to:

- advertise a service or a job vacancy;
- generate a response, i.e. purchasers of a service or applicants for a job.

They have the following characteristics:

- They are placed in a particular classified section of the media used.
- They appear in national newspapers, regional newspapers and trade magazines.
- They can include some design elements such as a border, a logo or simple graphic but the message is primarily carried in the text.
- Contact details will always be included.
- They are frequently one-colour – black.
- If they are for a service, they will tend to appear on a regular basis.
- They are usually purchased by the column centimetre.
- Frequently they are a one-off, i.e. a job advertisement.
- A service can be placed in a classified section over a period of time, to be reviewed regularly in light of response rates.

Producing your classified advertisement

A classified advertisement should always contain the following elements. If it is a job advertisement:

- heading;
- firm's logo (if possible), otherwise the firm's name could simply be mentioned in the copy;
- brief outline of the firm;
- job description with salary details or indication;

- response deadline and method of response required;
- contact details.

If it is a classified advertisement for a service:

- heading;
- firm's logo (if possible), a mention of the firm's name in the copy;
- brief outline of the service being offered;
- brief outline of the firm;
- response and contact details.

Often, newspapers or magazines will offer an in-house design service, which may be free. If they do, simply send them the copy and your logo, if it is to be used. They will set your advertisement for you and send you a proof.

Evaluating your classified advertisement

On one level this will usually be fairly straightforward as the level of response will give an immediate count. However, it is also a good idea to try to reach some sort of evaluation of the actual quality of those responses.

If it is a job advertisement:

- What was the reponse rate?
- What was the level of candidates who applied?

If it is a classified advertisement for a service your firm offers:

- How many enquiries actually convert to business?
- Are those responding primarily looking for quotes only?
- What is the income from that business?

After gathering this information at the end of the lifespan of the advertisement, you will be in a position to evaluate whether the advertisement produced an adequate number of the right type of job candidates. You can then judge whether to advertise in that media again.

Directory advertisements

Thomsons Local, Yellow Pages and Business Pages are three very well known directories. Some directories will automatically list your firm while others will only list those who pay.

They are used to:

- ensure your firm has a presence for those to whom the directory is aimed;
- advertise a service relevant to the audience of that directory;
- generate a response, i.e. enquiries.

They have the following characteristics:

- They are placed in a particular directory relevant to the business being advertised or users of that business.
- They will appear under specific headings for businesses supplying the same or similar services.
- They can appear in buyers' guides in specialist/trade magazines.
- They can simply be alphabetical lists of suppliers or could have the option to include design elements such as a border, a logo or simple graphic, but the message is primarily carried in the text and positioning of the advertisement.
- Contact details will always be included.
- They are frequently one-colour – black.
- Weekly, monthly, bi-monthly or quarterly publications may have directories for services and it may make sense to place an advertisement regularly. However, on the whole they will usually be one-off advertisements.
- They frequently have a long lifespan, i.e. one year with annual directories.

Producing your directory advertisement

It will depend whether you are simply paying to have your firm listed under certain headings or whether you opt to have a small display advertisement. A listing will normally have a word limit and would simply list your services and contact details. A small display advertisement might include:

- heading;
- firm's logo (if possible), or a mention of your firm's name in the copy;
- brief outline of the service being offered;
- brief outline of the firm;
- response and contact details;
- border.

Directory publishers often offer an in-house design service – frequently free. Simply send them the copy and your logo, and they will set your advertisement for you and send you a proof.

Evaluating your directory advertisement

As with classified advertisements, this will usually be fairly straightforward as the level of response will give an immediate count. As with classified advertisements it is also a good idea to try to reach some sort of evaluation of the actual quality of any responses.

To do this you should keep a record of:

■ How many responses actually convert to business?
■ Are those responding primarily looking for quotes only?
■ What is the income from that business?
■ When does that business come in, i.e. in the first month of the directory being published or throughout the year?

Whenever a new client contacts your firm, they should be asked where they heard of your firm or saw it advertised. This information should be fed in to your database, if possible, or a central record should be maintained. This will help you evaluate the response from that advertisement.

Having collated this information at the end of the lifespan of any advertisement you will be able to evaluate whether the advertisement has paid for itself and from there make a judgement as to whether you want to advertise in that directory again.

Display advertisements

They are used to:

■ raise awareness and position an organisation, or product (here a legal service);
■ create an image of your firm;
■ generate confidence in your firm;
■ back up another promotion.

They have the following characteristics:

■ They are placed among the articles and main body of a publication, frequently alongside an article of relevance to the service you are offering.
■ They appear in national newspapers, regional newspapers and trade magazines.
■ Their lifespan depends on the lifespan of the document in which they appear, i.e. a weekly magazine would indicate a short lifespan whereas a display advertisement in a directory published annually would last a year.
■ They are frequently design-led and their visual impact is as strong as the copy.

Usage

- A series of advertisements over a period of time and in a number of relevant publications will enable any message to have the greatest chance of being seen.
- Display advertisements might have a design and theme of their own. However, they will have greater effect if the visual and copy approach is reflected in brochures about the firm. In particular, where a response form or request for further information is sent in, any materials sent out should reflect the style of the advertisement.
- They can be used to support another promotion, such as an advertisement telling people to look out for a mail shot, or to promote the launch of a new service where other promotional approaches are also being used.

Producing your display advertisement

The visual impact of a display advertisement is of enormous importance. The visuals need to match the firm's image and appeal to the target audience. There are two different approaches:

- The graphics are based around the firm itself.
- The graphics provide a visual interpretation of the message being put across.

When producing display advertisements, it is recommended that you use a graphic designer. They will often work with a copywriter to put the words with the design to match a brief given to them.

The brief is the key to achieving a good display advertisement. Creating a brief is fairly straightforward. The factual information you need to include is as follows:

- a background to the firm;
- a background of the service being promoted;
- an outline, with examples, of the firm's logo and any past advertising;
- examples of the firm's brochures and any mission statements.

Information specific to the advertisement you wish to place may include:

- an outline of the different media to be used and an outline of the target audience;
- an outline of the required result, i.e. to generate enquiries, to raise the firm's image. etc.
- an indication of how bold or bright you would like the advertisement to be;
- a list of descriptive words indicating the image and impression you would like the advertisement to give, i.e. business-like, fun, professional, local, etc.;
- any specifications that need be taken into account, i.e. the use of a particular font, regulatory logos, etc.;

- an outline of the specific services that are being sold, or the firm in general;
- whether the advertisement is one in a series of advertisements or simply a one-off;
- whether you will want to use the design for posters, brochures, etc.

All of this information will give the designer and copywriter enough to come up with some ideas which can then be discussed.

Remember, you know your firm and target audience better than the designer, so your views are very important. An attractive design may fail to present the right image, elicit the response you want of it or attract any enquiries.

Having decided on your design and approach, the designer will need information about the specifications required by the media. These can all be found in media packs or by asking the advertising sales teams at the different media.

Evaluating your display advertisement

Display advertisements placed merely to create an impression or raise awareness of your firm can be difficult to evaluate. You may need to undertake research before and after the advertising to determine if perceptions of your firm have changed because of it.

If the advertisement has a response mechanism, such as a cut-out form, a telephone number, an e-mail address or a reader response number, you can evaluate whether it is successful by the response it generates.

Before undertaking any advertising you should ensure that you check that you are advertising according to the rules set out in the Solicitors' Publicity Code. These rules identify acceptable and unacceptable advertising.

Inserts

These are used to:

- generate a response – they will usually have a response form attached;
- advertise to a particular audience in a particular area.

They have the following characteristics:

- They take the form of brochures or leaflets inserted into national papers, local papers and magazines.
- They are usually design-led, though there will be more space for copy to give greater detail about the firm or service the firm is promoting.

- They will often include a specific sales hook, maybe an offer.
- They may have a lifespan longer than the publication in which they are placed, i.e. 'keep this and present it when you require our conveyancing services to receive a 10 per cent discount, valid for one year'.
- It is possible to insert them in copies of a publication that are distributed in a specific area.

Usage

- Inserts can be used on their own as a method of generating enquiries.
- They can also be used alongside other promotional materials as part of a campaign. For example, an invitation to attend an open day might be run as an insert alongside bus stop posters or bill boards, or even display advertising in the events section of the local papers.

Producing your inserts

The visual quality of the insert is very important, especially the front page as this is what must catch the recipient's eye to entice them into picking up and opening the insert. As with display advertisements, the visuals throughout need to match the firm's image and appeal to the target audience.

There are two different approaches.

- The graphics and copy are based around the firm itself.
- The graphics provide a visual interpretation of the message being put across, with the copy reflecting the graphic theme.

When producing inserts, as with display advertisements, it is recommended that you use a graphic designer. They will often work with a copywriter to put the words with the design to match a brief given to them. It is a good idea to write the copy yourself and then give this to the designer and copywriter to edit.

Again, an important part of producing an insert is the brief that is given to the designer and copywriter. Creating a brief for inserts is practically the same as for a display advertisement (see pp. 324–5) but in addition to the design brief, a detailed copy brief will be required.

A copy brief might include:

- a draft of the copy;
- a list of the different sections and facts that need to be covered;
- the sales messages and sales hooks to encourage a response;
- any exceptions or restrictions that are to apply to the offer.

All of this information will give the copywriter a good basis to come up with some ideas that can then be discussed.

Evaluating your inserts

Inserts are normally placed with the aim of generating a response. If the advertisement has a response mechanism such as a cut-out form, a telephone number, an e-mail address or a reader response number, you can evaluate whether it is successful by the response it generates:

■ How many responses did you receive?
■ How many of those responses actually converted to business?
■ What income did the new business generate?

Radio advertising

This can be used to:

■ raise awareness and position an organisation or product (here a legal service);
■ create an image of your firm;
■ generate confidence in your firm;
■ generate enquiries for a service your firm is offering.

They have the following characteristics:

■ They are placed with radio stations that have a relevant audience for the advertisement.
■ They will be repeated at frequent intervals and form part of a campaign over a period of time.
■ They are normally produced using professional voice actors and a production house.

Usage

■ Radio advertising depends upon 'opportunities to hear' and advertising space is sold on this basis. This is similar to a display advertisement campaign where a series of adverts are run in order for the target audience to have the opportunity to see them and absorb the message. In the same way, radio advertisements need to be run over a period of time. They could be run as 30-second, 20-second and 10-second advertisements at particular times of the day over a week or longer period.
■ Radio advertisements need to be professionally written and performed, as this is a specialist area. However, the spoken approach should reflect the written

approach taken in any other advertisement materials or brochures about the firm.

- It could be used to support another promotion, such as an advertisement telling people to look out for a mail shot, or to promote the launch of a new service where other promotional approaches are also being used.

Producing your radio advertisements

Radio advertising is a specialist area. It is recommended that you contact the radio stations you are considering and find out about their audience figures and whether they have production facilities. If they do, it might prove cost-effective to work with them to produce your advertisement. Alternatively, you can contact an agency to produce the advertisements and book the radio time for you, though this can prove expensive.

The best way to begin is to ring up local radio stations and discuss your needs with their space sales people who will create a campaign for you and give you an estimate of its cost.

Evaluating your radio advertisements

The radio stations can provide you with the number of opportunities your target audience have had to hear your advertisement. However, to understand whether your advertisement has achieved its aim, i.e. raised your firm's profile or encouraged people to use your service, you will need to analyse whether you have seen an increase in business. Alternatively you could undertake research to see whether your advertisement has worked and your firm has achieved greater recognition among the target audience. See Part 2 for further information on this.

Advertising in the programmes of local events

These should be approached as one-offs. You should be guided by the organisation producing the programme and the methods they intend to use.

It is worth remembering that if you appear in an event programme, you are likely to be invited to take part in others. It may be worthwhile having a couple of small advertisements put together that can be used for programmes (and/or local papers). You can create a template into which you can simply drop different words. This will cut the on-going cost and time you would need to fulfil requests for such advertisements. It is always a good idea to have a four-colour and a single colour (black) version produced, as local event programmes vary enormously in their sophistication and the way in which they are produced.

Further details about how you can evaluate this type of advertising can be found in the section on sponsorship on pp. 313–14.

Posters

Posters at bus stops or bill boards (outdoor)

Putting posters at bus stops and bill boards in your local area can be a good way of advertising that your firm is there and letting people know about the services you offer.

They can be used to:

- raise awareness of your firm in the local area;
- tell people about the services you offer;
- create an image of your firm;
- generate enquiries for the service being advertised;
- back up another promotion such as the launch of a new service or advertise your support for a local event.

Posters at bus stops or bill boards have the following characteristics:

- They are placed at sites relevant to the target audience for your firm's services.
- They are placed for a specific period of time.
- They are design-led and their visual impact strong.
- They will usually be in four-colour
- Their message will be stated in short concise sentences and should be immediately understood at a glance.

PRODUCING OUTDOOR POSTERS

The approach to producing these posters is similar to the approach for producing display advertisements. However, your posters may also have the following:

- a map of where your firm can be found;
- a far simpler approach and message than a display advertisement;
- a more local and welcoming feel to the way in which they are designed.

The visual impact is important and the visuals need to match the firm's image. The message needs to be very direct in its approach to the target audience as the posters will often be seen in passing.

When producing posters for bus stops or bill boards it is recommended that you use a graphic designer. They will often work with a copywriter to put the words with the design to match a brief given to them. For further information, see the section on display advertisements on pp. 324–5.

EVALUATING THE EFFECT OF YOUR POSTERS

Posters placed to raise awareness of your firm can be difficult to evaluate. You may need to undertake research before and after the advertising to determine if perceptions of your firm have changed because of them.

If the poster invites passers-by to drop into the firm or visit the firm for a quote, you can evaluate whether it is successful by the response it generates.

Remember: Whenever a new client contacts your firm, they should be asked where they heard of your firm or saw it advertised (if you do any advertising).

Posters to be displayed in relevant local organisations where potential clients visit (indoor)

CHARACTERISTICS

- They are frequently A4 or A3 in size.
- They are usually sent to the relevant organisations with a letter request that they be displayed on notice boards or walls, or you may approach organisations direct.

USAGE

- They could be used as a vehicle to promote different legal services to specific market sectors i.e. posters about personal injury claims in doctors' surgeries or hospitals.
- They could be used as part of a promotion campaign surrounding an event or the launch of a new service.

PRODUCING INDOOR POSTERS

The approach to producing these posters is similar to the approach for producing bill board or bus stop posters in that they will frequently include a map, or address of where your firm can be found.

As with bus stop posters and bill boards, the visual impact is important and the visuals need to match the firm's image. However, because your posters may be placed where people have longer to read them, you can include more information. You can treat them as simplified leaflets to a certain extent.

Again, when producing these it is recommended that you use a graphic designer. They will often work with a copywriter to put the words with the design to match a brief given to them. For further information see the section on display advertisements' on pp. 324–5, or 'Brochures, leaflets and other printed materials' on pp. 247–50.

EVALUATING THE EFFECT OF YOUR POSTERS

You will usually be able to measure the success of these posters by the number of enquiries they generate, which could come immediately or some time after the poster appeared when clients remember your offering a service they now require.

Posters are not usually very expensive to produce and can be a good way of telling people your firm is there, though this is less easy to measure. In addition, they can be a good way of keeping your name in front of those who might refer clients to you, your connector clients. And, by your poster being on display, you may be preventing a competing firm from having their details on display.

How to make the most of your posters

- If you are running an insert in the local press, it is a good idea to have posters produced along the same lines and ask appropriate organisations (connector clients) to display your leaflets and poster together. By advertising your firm, they are offering their clients an extra information service.
- Always include a small map of the local area pinpointing where your firm can be found.

Open days

These are a good way of raising awareness of your firm in the community and building new clients.

They can help:

1. To promote to potential new clients:
   - by raising awareness of your firm in the local area;
   - by offering people a no-pressure way of asking questions about their legal needs and the opportunity to meet members of the firm;
   - by allowing you to present your firm in the way that you want it to be viewed;
   - by giving you the opportunity to be in contact with prospective clients.

2. To promote loyalty amongst existing clients:
   - by increasing contact opportunities;
   - by getting to know your clients better and on a more personal basis to help promote loyalty to your firm.

3. To increase work from existing clients (if they come to the open day):

- by reminding clients of your firm's services;
- by educating clients about their rights and creating a need;
- by maintaining an open dialogue with clients.

Some hints and tips to organising open days

- Ensure you advertise far enough in advance.
- As well as information about the work of solicitors, it is a good idea to invite other relevant organisations to attend.
- It is a good idea to offer visitors the opportunity to talk about a legal problem for free on the day. It may be a good idea to advertise this and take bookings for 15-minute slots before the actual day. This way you are guaranteed some visitors, at least.
- A face-painting artist is always a good idea for small children, as are balloons.
- Ensure you have enough staff on-hand.
- Ensure you have adequate sign-posting and lock the doors of rooms you do not want anyone to enter.
- Make sure you have sufficient leaflets and/or brochures to give out to visitors.

Evaluating your open days

You can judge them quite simply by the number of people who come. Always bear in mind that the first open day will be most difficult to attract people to. If you do a good job, however, the subsequent ones will become easier.

Client entertaining

The point of entertaining your clients is to provide an opportunity to build a closer relationship with them. There are a number of aspects that should be borne in mind:

- What is the value or potential value of the clients – does it warrant the entertainment spend on them?
- The appropriate staff should attend to make use of this opportunity to interact with clients.
- Your firm's part should be very well organised – a badly organised event can damage your firm's reputation and lose you clients.
- They should have a purpose and this should be communicated to the guests. For example, it may be to say 'thank you' or to introduce satisfied clients to

potential clients or get to know clients better. Clients will feel more comfortable if they know why they are there.

■ Appropriate mixes of clients should be invited. If you have a very disgruntled client, it may be unwise to mix them with satisfied clients. They may turn positive to negative rather than the other way around.

Client entertaining can take any of the following forms:

■ a box or seats at a special (frequently sporting) event such as horse racing or tennis;
■ lunches at the firm or in a hotel or restaurant;
■ parties at set times in the year, i.e. the summer and Christmas.

Seats or a box at special events

These can help you:

1. To promote loyalty among existing clients by:

    ■ increasing contact opportunities and enabling members of the firm to build a relationship with clients;
    ■ giving clients something tangible as thanks for their business and to say 'we value you';
    ■ giving members of your firm the opportunity of getting to know clients better and on a more personal basis, which may help promote loyalty to your firm;
    ■ maintaining an open dialogue with clients.

2. To promote to potential new clients by:

    ■ providing you with an opportunity to invite and meet potential new clients in a relaxed atmosphere.

The following are useful points and tips to note about any special event:

■ Give attendees an itinerary of the day.
■ Give attendees a list of those attending, together with a list of firm members with their picture and a short biography.
■ If it is a large event, provide name badges for firm members and attendees.
■ Always check to see if attendees have any special requirements, i.e. wheelchair access, vegetarian food, etc.
■ Allocate a central administrator. If the numbers warrant it, they should attend the event. It is worth the cost of a seat to have a well organised event, especially as the point of the event is to impress and treat your clients.
■ Special events can be expensive to organise, therefore a careful decision of who should be asked, and why, should be taken. The current value of the invitees should be looked at, as well as their potential.
■ Try not to impinge on a work day, unless the invitees are very senior, as

otherwise this may cause problems at their work place. It also raises the cost of the event as firm member's time must also be taken into account.

Evaluating your events

As with other promotional work, special events need to be analysed for the return they yield. In all probability, this will simply be that clients are happy and you have forged stronger links. You will also have gained a better understanding of your clients so that you can anticipate their needs.

Lunches at the firm or in a hotel or restaurant

This can provide you with the opportunity to discuss business and get to know clients better. These are often very good opportunities to introduce clients to those in the firm who work in different legal services, so that should they need those services, they will already know a lawyer who can help them.

Lunches are generally a good opportunity of building business and expanding your contacts.

Parties

You may choose to have parties for non-business or business clients, or mix them all up together. Parties can help you in the following ways:

1. To promote loyalty among existing clients by:

   ■ increasing contact opportunities;
   ■ as a way of linking your firm more strongly into the community by giving them opportunities to network and meet each other;
   ■ giving something tangible to clients for free;
   ■ as a way of getting to know your clients better, and on a more personal basis to help promote loyalty to your firm;
   ■ maintaining an open dialogue with clients.

2. To promote to potential new clients by:

   ■ providing you with an opportunity to meet potential new clients in a relaxed atmosphere.

There are no set formats for holding parties. They will depend upon your resources and set-up. However, the following are a few things to remember about them:

■ Make sure you have enough staff on-hand to ensure everyone is entertained.
■ Ask everyone to sign a visitors book so that you know who was there.
■ Invite some non-customers whom you want to woo.
■ Make sure they are well organised.

Index

Administration staff 101, 115–16
Administrative skills 112
Advertising 241, 315–31
    classified advertisements 320–1
    costs 318–19
    directory advertisements 318, 321–3
    display advertisements 323–5
    inserts 325–7
    newspapers and magazines 317, 318
    planning the campaign 316–20
    posters 318, 329–31
    programmes of local events 328–9
    radio 317, 318, 327–8

Brochures 239, 242–3, 246–51
Business cards 242

Charity support 312–15
Client care
    skills 112
    systems 102, 119–20
Client groups 11–12
    number of 15–16
    profiling 39–43
    sub–dividing 39
    value of 16–36
Clients
    activity levels 12–14, 37
    characteristics 37–43
    commercial and business clients 12
    connector clients 12, 80–6, 117
    contact with 111
    database system 111
    entertaining 241, 332–4
    estimating value of 15–36
    grouping *see* Client groups
    identifying 11–14
    large clients 17
    legal aid clients 12
    loyalty 235
    number of 15–16
    priorities of 44–56
    private clients 12
    profiles 36–56
    targeting 39
    value requirements 44–79
Competitors

active 128
aggressive 128
assessing services 131–3
contacting 126
gauging activity of 128–9
matching or improving on 134, 236
passive 128
pigeonholing 130
researching 125–7
Complaints systems 120
Computer literacy 101, 113, 115
Computers 111
Connector clients 12, 80–6, 117
Cross–selling 116, 234–5

Direct mail 240, 293–301
    cost implications 298–300
    creating 296–8
    evaluating 300
    hidden response 300–1
    planning 294–6

Fee earners' skills 100–1, 112–13
Focus groups 162–3, 168–9

Image of firm 39, 225–6
Information telephone lines 120
Internet 111, 240, 310
    see also Web sites

Leaflets 239, 242–3, 246, 251–2
Legal services offered
    classifying 5–7
    client requirements 44–79
    estimating profitability 8–10
    evaluation of 7–10
Logo 245–6

Management skills 112
Management time and systems 101,
    113–14
Market knowledge 113
Market research *see* Research
Marketing report
    collating 145
    example 146–52
Marketing systems 102, 116–18